DOWN-TO-EARTH
Vegetable Gardening
KNOW~HOW

featuring Dick Raymond

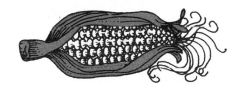

Editor and Designer
CHARLES COOK

Associate Editors
STU CAMPBELL
LINDA GRAY

Garden Way Publishing
Charlotte, Vermont 05445

The contributors of the many gardening tips which appear on the following pages are identified only by initials. Their names are listed below. We are grateful for the help of these and all the other gardeners we interviewed.

Rich Alther, Stu Campbell, Earl Cook, Walter A. Fair, James Gary, John L. Gilliam, Charlie E. Hunt, Mable Lauhall, Herb Linthicum, David Martin, R. A. Moore, Howard Pumphrey, S. W. Richardson, Donald Roberts, Mamie Roberts, S. W. Robinson, Ralph Ruppenthal, Charles Smith, Eli Stoltzfus, James E. Speight, Sky Thurber, Fred Tucker, and John Zircke.

Development of this book, especially photos and information on the Troy-Bilt Roto Tiller–Power Composter, was made possible by Garden Way Manufacturing Co., Troy, N.Y. The Troy-Bilt Roto Tiller–Power Composter is an integral part of the techniques described in this book, and so it is frankly cited and recommended.

Library of Congress Catalog Card Number: 74-12664

ISBN: 0-88266-079-9 paperback

ISBN: 0-88266-080-2 casebound

COPYRIGHT © 1975 BY GARDEN WAY PUBLISHING
CHARLOTTE, VERMONT 05445

Printed by Capital City Press,
Montpelier, Vermont 05602

Twelfth Printing, March 1979

The garden way to a happy life

There are plenty of gardening books crowding library and bookstore shelves nowadays, each one claiming to be the definitive work on its particular subject. So why publish another one? How can this book be significantly different or better than all the others? Because this book is a distillation of years of collective gardening experience—of experience handed down from generation to generation and shared among neighbors and friends. Most of the facts in this book were not researched in a lab by disinterested scientists, but in back-yard gardens, on family farms, and at the Garden Way Research Center, by gardeners vitally interested in the results of their efforts. The editor traveled through many states photographing and interviewing successful gardeners; the results of these efforts are contained in this book. The main text centers around the wisdom of Dick Raymond, Garden Way's resident gardening expert. His credentials are impressive—forty years of successful gardening experience.

In addition to Dick Raymond's text and the personal advice of other successful gardeners, this book includes plenty of relevant charts, tables, and maps. Their purpose is to make this a valuable reference book for years to come. Be sure to read the individual-vegetable section, in which Dick provides a wealth of general cultural information. In fact, we've included so much gardening information that you'll probably never use it all. But you never know what questions or problems will crop up, and when they do, we want you to be able to find the solutions within these pages.

At the very heart of this book is an abiding reverence for the soil. It is expressed in Dick Raymond's emphasis on building up the soil, feeding the earthworms, co-operating with nature, and concentrating on the fundamentals. This is not a book of fads and tricks; it's basic gardening at its best.

This book is published by Garden Way Publishing Company. This company is one of several organizations and people who are working to develop a greener, happier world. They can best explain their philosophy themselves.

We see that the earth is facing a population, pollution, and resources crisis, but we do not believe that has to be bad news. On the contrary, we believe that may well be the best news the human race has ever had, if it brings us to our senses and teaches us how spaceship earth can be operated as a pleasant, long-term home for man.

We believe a greener, happier world for all of us can follow the crisis, as more and more people turn toward the garden way of living. This does not mean going all the way back to primitive peasantry. It does mean applying science and technology intelligently and beneficially. It does mean matching population levels and lifestyles to earth's resources and to the carrying capacities of its various environments. Each of us as an individual can do something about his or her future —the garden way.

The more families who have large fruit and vegetable gardens, the better able they, their communities, their nation, and their world will be to solve the environmental, economic, and social problems of our time.

The Editors

The Dick Raymond success story

A garden, lush and green, orderly, and productive, is a good set of credentials for the author of a gardening book.

Dick Raymond has earned the right to give gardening advice, and it shows—both in his writing and in his garden. When one is fortunate enough to visit Dick's garden, his first impressions are of precision, order, and neatness. The rows are arrow-straight, and the areas in between are smoothly cultivated and weed-free. Vegetables like lettuce, greens, peas, and beans grow lush and thick in wide rows. It's easy to tell by the wide variety of vegetables Dick grows that he is an experimenter, and a creative one, at that. In one wide row, his many different varieties of lettuce form a patchwork of varying colors and textures. One area is devoted to experimental rotation of vegetable crops and green manures; recently he has been alternating corn and soybeans. From the looks of his corn, the experiment is working. At one side of his garden, he planted a crop of buckwheat which will be tilled under to improve the soil and provide an area into which Dick can expand his already large garden.

It is Dick's inventiveness which makes him an invaluable member of the Garden Way organization. This is the one real secret of his gardening success. As soon as he picks up a new idea, he studies it, tests it, and modifies it until he determines whether the idea is sufficiently workable to add to his collection of tried-and-true garden techniques and tools. Wide-row planting, which makes old-fashioned single rows seem anemic and downright wasteful, is but one example of the results of this sort of creative thinking and effort.

Dick didn't come by his gardening skills easily or quickly. He was the youngest of nine children in a very poor family. With them, gardening wasn't a hobby; it was a necessity. As Dick says, "If we didn't garden, we didn't have enough to eat." But the whole family gardened together and they all had plenty to eat, summer and winter. Dick remembers his mother canning as many as 1,400 quarts of vegetables and fruits. It's no wonder that Dick says his family, though poor, was healthier than most. Obviously, such a background makes him well suited for his complex job, for which he must possess the abilities of a troubleshooter, a researcher, an inventor, a gardening consultant, and a lecturer.

Dick does not, however, claim to be a writer. But then, this is not a book about Dick Raymond; it's a book meant to spread his ideas for successful gardening. To accomplish this purpose, Dick expressed his ideas and experience to Stu Campbell, a gardening writer, who put them in the order in which they appear in the text. Dick, of course, appreciates Stu's great help on this project.

After completing the writing of the text, he said, "I could have written twice as much on some areas." And he could have. Since that time, he's come up with so many new ideas that he's already talking about his next book.

Dick and his grandson are reaping the bountiful rewards of their labors.

A gardening book for all seasons

This book is dedicated to the philosophy that gardening is a way of life; an enjoyable experience that never ceases to be profitable, to provide lots of fun, and to create wonder throughout every month of the year.

Anyone can garden. All you need is access to a small piece of land, a few simple tools, a minimum of knowledge, a little spare time, and some ambition. Don't forget the ambition. No one has ever said that gardening does not involve a little work! In fact, a green thumb means a busy thumb.

Even if you don't own one square inch of land, you can have a garden. Maybe you have friends or relatives with some idle land that you could put to good use. You might think about renting a plot somewhere. There are many community gardening projects around the country which make land available to people who want to garden, but don't have access to land themselves. Gardens for All, which has its national headquarters in Connecticut, is a national, non-profit organization that knows a lot about helping people find gardening space. If you drop them a note at 299 Westport Ave., Norwalk, Connecticut 06852, I am sure they will be glad to help you.

You can have a productive garden that will save you hundreds of dollars in food bills the very first year. It is not as complicated as you might think. This book is meant to give you a little confidence and a little understanding of vegetable plants.

A plant's main purpose is to reproduce and propagate its species. When you plant a seed, it germinates, grows, and produces seeds, thus fulfilling its purpose. Once the plant gets big enough to support its seed pods, it sort of hesitates, as if to catch its breath, and then blossoms. From this point on, much of the plant's strength goes into the production of blossoms and fruit. Until a plant figures that it has produced enough seed to carry on its species, it will continue to blossom and bear fruit.

This book will answer basic questions like what to plant and when to harvest, which plants like "sour" soil, how to get rid of troublesome bugs, and many, many others. It is designed for everybody—beginners and experts alike. I will try to keep things as simple as possible. I will also tell you about many of the special gardening tricks that have helped me in my past forty years of growing vegetables and fruits. I will share my own personal gardening theories and methods with you. I hope they work as well for you as they have for me.

Dick Raymond
North Ferrisburg, Vermont

CONTENTS

Getting off to a good start

Few gardeners have a wide selection of garden spots. Gardens will grow most anywhere — but if you have a choice, keep the following fundamental advice in mind.

Some of us have very little choice about where our gardens are going to be because we don't have lots of land. Others of us will have to spend some time weighing the advantages and disadvantages of a number of different spots. We all know, for example, that full sunshine is ideal for a garden. But this doesn't mean that you can't have a successful garden where there is some shade. I have a friend who, I swear, can catch trout anywhere—even in a mud puddle. The same sort of thing is true with certain gardeners. If you know a little about what you are doing, you can grow food almost anywhere.

Say, just for openers, that you have a big lawn. You know that growing and caring for grass just to have it look nice is a serious waste of resources and energy, so you have decided to plant some vegetables in part of the area. There are a number of things to consider. First, the garden should be located as close to the house as possible. It would be especially nice if it were handy to the kitchen door. This way, you could run out, pick a few vegetables and maybe some salad greens, and prepare them at the peak of freshness. Second, you have to give some thought to water. Obviously, the garden must be somewhere near a source of water. Third, there is the question of sunshine and shade.

If you have a spot where there is particularly lush growth, this is the part of the lawn that you should sacrifice, painful as it may be. If grass grows well there, so will vegetables. Maybe you have a place that just seems to grow weeds. This might not be bad either. If the soil there will grow good, healthy weeds, there is every reason to believe that it will grow good, healthy food crops.

Drainage is an imporant question too. Soil has to breathe, and earth that is drowned does not do so because oxygen cannot penetrate between the soil particles. This is why plants growing in very wet ground sometimes look yellow. The soil organisms which release nutrients to the plants have been deprived of adequate air. If you have a choice, it is best not to have a garden on an extremely wet site. If you have no choice, the site should be drained as much as possible. Try digging a ditch around the perimeter of the garden and putting in some drainage tile and gravel.

GOOD GRADES FOR GARDENING

Slope has a lot to do with the success or failure of a garden. Just a couple of degrees of pitch to the south or west exposes the soil to more direct rays from the sun, allows the garden to warm up earlier in the year, and lets you start planting sooner. The ideal garden spot, I would say, should have a three-degree tilt toward the south.

Too much slope will cause problems with erosion. If your potential garden plot is on a steep hillside—anything more than a ten-percent grade—some kind of terracing may be necessary. This may involve more work than you care to do—especially if you have to do it by hand. You might want to reconsider using this place for a garden.

TURNING PROBLEMS INTO ASSETS

The garden site you choose is likely to be varied. There may be sunny spots, wet spots, hilly spots, and shady places, but with a little planning, you can use each area to best advantage. We know, for instance, that early in the spring, the hilly sections are going to dry out first, so these areas would be particularly good for early plantings. What should be planted early? You could try carrots, beets, lettuce, radishes, dill, spinach, kale, onion seeds, onion sets, and early peas.

Different crops do well in different environments. "Hardy" crops like cabbage and broccoli can take some cold weather.

CLIFFTOP GARDENING

Some sites look completely unsuitable for gardening. Stu and Jill Campbell own just such a site atop a bluff overlooking picturesque Lake Champlain. The rocky, rough, untamed soil had never been gardened before.

After rolling the largest boulders over the cliff, the Campbells broke up the soil with a powerful rear-end tiller. They built up the soil by putting on all the organic matter that could be begged, bought, and hauled. Much material was composted first. After two years, the result of their labor is evident — a scenic, productive kitchen garden.

With no room to expand, Stu and Jill grow as much produce up in the air as possible. Along the fence, which they use as a trellis, they grow pole beans and cucumbers. Winter squash is planted along the edge of the garden and allowed to climb up the rocks and into the woods.

Because their garden is so compact, the Campbells prefer to mulch the entire plot. Cultivation is impractical because they put their rows close together and plant intensively to get maximum returns from minimum space.

Jill froze lots of vegetables and canned many pickles and relishes.

Ideally, your garden should slope 3 to 10 degrees to the south.

In fact, they do poorly when it gets very hot. Because their large leaves are able to absorb a lot of sun, they will grow in partial shade and in fairly damp soil. An area with as little as forty to fifty percent sunshine is fine for most leaf crops. Some shade, then, is all right, but don't plant vegetables within the drip line of trees or the trees' roots will rob moisture and nutrients from your crops.

Cucumbers, tomatoes, squash, corn, eggplant, melons, pumpkins, and beans like warmer, drier soil. They cannot be planted until after the last frost and should be placed where there is maximum sunshine— on a slight slope with a southern exposure, if possible.

GET TO KNOW YOUR SOIL

If you have a choice of soils, sandy loam is best. It is light, crumbly, and rich with the decayed organic matter that gardeners call "humus." You can improve almost any soil of poor quality in fairly short order by working in generous helpings of leaves, manure, compost, old hay, or similar material.

Depth of soil can be a factor in the selection of a garden spot. If the site is on a ledge and you can dig only about five or six inches without hitting bedrock, you'd better look for another place. A garden with such a shallow layer of soil would dry out very quickly in the heat of summer and would probably grow poor vegetables.

It is wise to take a soil sample and send it either to your state university or to some private testing laboratory to find out exactly what condition your soil is in. The laboratory will furnish a container for the soil if you ask. Testing services are busy in the spring, so it will speed things up if you submit your sample early. If you are a first-year gardener, don't sit idle waiting for the test results to come back. There is plenty you can be doing to get ready.

Once you have figured out where your garden is to be, you must give some thought to how much land you need and can conveniently work. If you're planning your first garden, start small. Don't be afraid to experiment, but don't let your enthusiasm cause you to overestimate your time and abilities. Remember that a small, well-tended garden is more productive than a large, neglected one.

RAISING VEGETABLES WITHOUT A GARDEN

Even if you have very little land available for gardening, you can grow enough fresh vegetables to brighten up your spring and summer menus.

You can grow enough snow peas in a wash tub or in half a barrel to supply all you need for most recipes. Run strings up to a center pole, and let the vines form a tepee.

Cucumbers and cherry tomatoes make attractive hanging-basket plants.

A strawberry jar is a fine place to grow a portable assortment of herbs. Thyme, parsley, chives, oregano, and basil would be good choices.

You can use railroad ties or 2 x 12's and stakes to make attractive raised beds. Brick or stone beds take more work. Make each bed deep enough for the plants you will grow.

PLANTING IN CONTAINERS

John Zircke uses a lot of cut-off drums for planting crops needed in small amounts, like parsley, peppers, lettuce, and patio tomatoes. This practice allows him to use special soil mixtures that are not practical in a larger garden area. Each container becomes a small compost pile, getting richer year by year. It's easy to cover these containers when frost strikes.

CROPS TO GROW IN THE SHADE

You can grow vegetables under a tree if you know what to plant. Mr. Farley has discovered cabbage, green beans, and sweet potatoes will grow fine. Corn and tomatoes won't do any good.

BUYING LAND FOR GARDENING

"The time to look at land for gardening is when the weather is hot and dry. If you want water, you want it running when the season is dry. A bubbling stream in spring may be a dry stream bed in August.

"Look at the weeds. In the fall of the year look for cockleburs. If they're big and healthy, don't say anything, just buy the land. If they're short and scrawny, get in your car and leave.

"The best vegetable-growing land in this country is fast disappearing. If you can find good, productive land, it's worth whatever you have to pay for it.

"One acre of rich, fine-textured land is worth more than fifty acres of rocky, infertile land. Twenty acres of good land would provide an independent living for a family growing vegetables." JLG

INSECT-DETERRENT PLANTS

Asters	Most insects
Basil	Repels flies and mosquitoes
Borage	Deters tomato worm—improves growth and flavor of tomatoes
Calendula	Most insects
Catnip	Deters flea beetle
Celery	White cabbage butterfly
Chrysanthemum	Deters most insects
Dead Nettle	Deters potato bug—improves growth and flavor of potatoes
Eggplant	Deters Colorado potato beetle
Flax	Deters potato bug
Garlic	Deters Japanese beetle, other insectss & blight
Geranium	Most insects
Horseradish	Plant at corners of potato patch to deter potato bug
Henbit	General insect repellent
Hyssop	Deters cabbage moth
Marigold	The workhorse of the pest deterrents. Plant throughout garden to discourage Mexican bean beetles, nematodes & other insects
Mint	Deters white cabbage moth and ants
Mole Plant	Deters moles and mice if planted here & there
Nasturtium	Deters aphids, squash bugs, striped pumpkin beetles
Onion family	Deters most pests
Petunia	Protects beans
Pot Marigold	Deters asparagus beetles, tomato worms & general garden pests
Peppermint	Planted among cabbages, it repels the white cabbage butterfly
Radish	Especially deters cucumber bettle
Rosemary	Deters cabbage moth, bean beetle & carrot fly
Rue	Deters Japanese beetle
Sage	Deters cabbage moth, carrot fly
Salsify	Repels carrot fly
Southernwood	Deters cabbage moth
Summer Savory	Deters bean beetles
Tansy	Deters flying insects, Japanese beetles, striped cucumber beetles, squash bugs, ants
Tomato	Asparagus beetle
Thyme	Deters cabbage worm
Wormwood	Carrot fly, white cabbage butterfly, black flea beetle

THE IMPOSSIBLE DREAM

Many of us are talking a lot these days about living "self-sufficiently." Complete self-sufficiency, as you know, is an impossible dream. But trying to live as independently as possible is a good thing—one of the things gardening is all about.

As a gardener, there will be times when you will be confronted with a simple but difficult choice: either spray the crop to save it, or lose it and risk going hungry. Don't spray just because some gardening book says it is time to do it; but if you have a problem that needs attention, take care of it! The conscientious home gardener who cares about his land and his family will only use strong chemicals when he feels it is absolutely necessary. When you grow things out there, you become the responsible steward for your own land, and you have to make the choices.

"Organic" gardening has become very popular in the last few years. Because the world is quickly running short of fertilizer, and because many of the chemicals used in commercial fertilizers, herbicides, and insecticides are poisonous to us, much of the thinking behind what is often called organic gardening, makes a lot of sense.

One of the best things to come out of this new gardening interest is an awareness of the value of recycling. If you are a good conscientious gardener, you try to use any and all organic matter you have on hand or can get—manures, garbage, compost that you have made, and all sorts of vegetable matter that you can gather up around your property.

I have seen people bag up their leaves and put them beside the road for the trash man to cart away. I'm sure you see this all the time. They are throwing away one of nature's most valuable organic fertilizers. Rather than getting rid of their leaves, they should be collecting them! They are a natural food for earthworms and are loaded with nutrients. Any gardener should know that it is almost sinful to send once-living material off to the dump. Organic matter is much too valuable to be wasted. It is wrong to ship out anything that contains so many precious nutrients.

Gather up all the available organic matter you can, regardless of the kind of garden you are planning. Work this matter into your soil. Your garden needs to be fed just as you do.

If you choose to garden without using poisons, you have to learn to accept some failures in your garden. There are diseases and insect infestations which occur each and every year, depending on the weather and on what part of the country you live in. These conditions are painful, but they are facts of life. There are various companion-plant combinations and natural, nonchemical remedies which can ease the insect and disease problems somewhat.

I would have to say that organic gardening on a small scale is a whole lot easier than trying to do it on a large scale. If you have a very small plot, picking insects off your plants with your fingers is not much of a job, but there is no way you can do this in a big garden. There are certain sprays, like rotenone and pyrethrum, which have been okayed by strict natural gardeners. I like to use hydrated lime, which is another acceptable alternative to chemical insecticides. The main trouble with it is that you have to use it every morning, and I can't always get to it each day. Generally, I am afraid that pure organic gardening takes a lot more time than gardening the conventional way. There is no way that a natural gardener can plant his garden, spray it once a week or so, weed it once in a while, and not worry about it until harvest time. You have to look after everything constantly.

Poisonless methods seem to work better in some parts of the country than in others. Certain plants which require very little attention here in Vermont, for example, do not do so well down south. Southern gardeners have a lot more trouble with bugs, diseases and nematodes—tiny worms that attack the roots of plants. So they need more strong chemical insecticides.

Of course, you should choose the gardening methods that you feel most comfortable with. But you should know that there is a big difference between the "orthodox" organic gardener, who refuses to use any kind of chemical fertilizer or spray, and the person who believes in the principles of organic gardening but is not a purist. I guess I am a member of the second group. I use some chemical fertilizer when I think it is needed, but I try to avoid any kind of really toxic herbicide or insecticide.

You don't have to use a lot of toxic dusts and sprays to grow vegetable plants as beautifully healthy as this one.

13

Planting your garden on paper

Take advantage of snowy, winter evenings to carefully plan what, how much, where, and when to plant in your garden. You'll avoid future disappointments and problems.

Whichever garden type you choose, start by sketching out exactly where you are going to put each vegetable and herb. Be very careful about the things you select for a summer garden. Don't choose more than two varieties of each vegetable. As you get more experienced, you can experiment with different varieties, but try the old standbys first. Check the Garden Way Sure Crop Chart to see the ones I specifically recommend. Ask a neighbor who gardens to help you choose the varieties that grow best where you are. Try to decide just how much of each vegetable you will need, and allow adequate space on your plan. A plot twenty-five feet by thirty feet is just about the right size for a summer garden to feed a family of four. If it is cared for properly, it should provide more than enough vegetables all summer long.

As you lay out your garden, remember that taller plants will shade shorter ones. This means that corn, pole beans, staked tomatoes, and other tall plants should be on the north or northeast side of the garden.

CHOOSE A SIZE TO SUIT YOUR NEEDS

There are three basic types of gardens. First, there is what I call the salad garden, which is very small. It might be right beside the house and might measure only three feet wide and ten feet long. In fact, it might contain only two or three vegetable plants. Perhaps a few chives, a little lettuce, some radishes, some tomatoes, onions, parsley, or herbs could be planted in among the flowers and other ornamentals which border your lawn.

The summer garden is one that keeps a family eating fresh produce during the growing season, but provides very little surplus that can be stored or preserved. Then there is the winter-storage garden, in which the gardener plants enough for his family to eat during the summer as well as enough to can, freeze, and store for the winter.

If you are thinking about a salad garden or a "mini-garden," you might want to investigate some of the mini-vegetable varieties. You can get miniature corn, spinach, Butter Crunch lettuce, and tomato plants. These plants, though dwarf in size, produce a great deal of food in very little space. You can find these space-saving varieties in the catalogs of most major seed companies.

Mini-gardens can be planted in containers too. There is no reason why you can't grow at least a little food for yourself, even if you live in a city apartment. You can plant vegetables and herbs in large pots, in urns, in window boxes, or in large cans that you can decorate yourself. Use your imagination. It's lots of fun to see how much you can produce in practically no space at all.

CHILD'S PLAY

Encourage your children to have gardens of their own if you can afford the space. Gardening is one of the most valuable skills a child can learn. Not only will he always know how to grow himself something to eat; he will also come to understand more about the meaning of life and about the importance of the soil to all the creatures on earth.

Help your child select vegetables that are sure to do well with just a minimum of care. Success should be his most important crop —especially the first year! Kids like things that grow fast. Onion sets grow very quickly, and radishes are ready in just a couple of weeks. He will be able to see noticeable progress in a bean plant each day. Don't let him get bored. He will enjoy seeing a pepper take shape and seeing a tomato turn from green to red. And believe me, he will be thrilled when he eats that first radish he grew himself.

Even if there is no room for a separate child's garden, set aside a row or two in the family garden where your child can experiment a little. Let him share some of the

Combination planting is based on mutually beneficial plant relationships. For example, as this healthy corn stalk grows it will provide a support for a companion pole bean planted in the same hill.

IMPORTANT
Be sure to consult the charts and maps on pages 146 through 153. We feel certain that they will help you plan, plant, and tend a successful garden.

Plan your succession crops long before planting time. Lettuce likes cool weather and can be followed by warm weather crops in the same space. Also be sure you're planning to plant enough to can and freeze to meet your winter-storage needs. And don't forget to order some fun vegetables for your children.

responsibility. Let him tend—or neglect—a few short rows. Either way, he will learn a valuable lesson. He might have fun with some unusual vegetables, such as the "yard-long" bean or the "silly" bean, which is purple until it is cooked. Keep kids interested, keep the work to a minimum, and they will become expert gardeners at a very young age.

SOME SUCCESSFUL SUCCESSIONS

Some vegetables take up garden space all summer because it takes them so long to ripen. But there are others that mature much faster, and once these have been harvested or have passed their peak, the space they occupied will stand idle unless you make use of it. It is wasteful, as far as I am concerned, to have a single unproductive spot in your garden. Get something growing there! Plant succession crops—crops that can be planted after a previous fast-matur-

ing crop has been harvested.

Crops that mature early include radishes, beans, peas, beets, cauliflower, cabbage, kohlrabi, onions (from sets), mustard, spinach, turnips, and early corn. As soon as these have been harvested, either pull them up and put the plant residues in the compost pile, or till them directly back into the garden soil. Have a succession crop ready to go in right away. It is not a good idea to plant the same crop that was there before. If there were beans in an area, replace them with some carrots or beets. Some crops can be planted more than once in the same season, but there are some that don't do well during really hot weather—peas, for example, and lettuce, spinach, and turnips. Wait at least until late July before replanting these vegetables so that they will mature during the cool days of fall.

As you plan your succession crops, remember to use early-maturing varieties of

A plot twenty-five feet by thirty feet is just about the right size for a summer garden to feed a family of four. If well cared for, it should provide more than enough vegetables all summer long.

When deciding how large to make your garden, remember that a small, well-tended plot is more productive and satisfying than a sprawling, neglected one.

the various vegetables. The later varieties take too long to mature, and there is likely to be frost before the last plantings have a chance to make it. It pays to experiment a little with different types of vegetables and to gamble that the first fall frost will be late rather than early. I usually take this chance. Sometimes I win and sometimes I lose. But if frost kills some of my later plantings, I don't feel that I have lost much.

GOOD COMPANIONS

There are many combinations of crops that do well side-by-side in the same row. Some plants will actually help each other by shading one another or by acting as insect repellents. Beans seem to go well with corn; radishes with just about anything. Parsley does well with both onions and carrots. And it is always a good idea to plant something else in with parsnips.

If you plant a vegetable that matures before another in the same row, just harvest whatever is ripe and allow the other plants to take over the space that has just been vacated. This way, you can get more vegetables out of a restricted amount of space. There are a number of combinations that you can try: tomatoes with pepper plants, onions with cabbages, pole beans with corn.

After the plan is drawn up, your next task is selecting the seeds and plants that you will use. The directions on the back of some seed packages will tell you how many seeds the packet contains and how many feet of row they will plant. Remember that these lengths refer to single rows. If you are going to use wide rows, you will need five times as many seeds to reach the same distance. In other words, if the pack says there is enough seed for a hundred-foot row, there is enough for only twenty feet of a wide row.

Picking the right varieties

The varieties you select will, in large measure, determine the quality and quantity of your harvest.

Always buy seed from reputable seed companies. Most of us get only one whack at the gardening season, so good seeds are a must. Plant seed from packets that have this year's date printed on them, and, if you can, from packs that have a guaranteed germination percentage. There is nothing more discouraging than planting old seeds and having them not come up. You can lose as much as two weeks of the gardening year this way.

Because there is so much emphasis on organic gardening these days, most seeds are no longer treated with fungicides. In the past, these chemicals prevented the fungus which causes damping off from getting to the seeds and destroying them before they had a chance to germinate. In years when spring is particularly wet, you may have a problem with damping off. Captan, an effective fungus killer, is still available at most gardening centers. Treating a package of seed with it doesn't take much effort. Take a paper match, and dip about one-fourth of it in the Captan. The amount of fungicide that sticks to the match is just about the right amount for a small package of seed. Put this bit of Captan into the packet along with the seed and shake the package vigorously. Once this is done, you can be pretty sure that your seeds will be safe from damping off and similar problems.

BE SURE OF YOUR SEEDS

There will be times in your gardening career when you will get very poor seed

18

germination. Sometimes it will be the fault of the seed; sometimes it will result from damping off caused by cold, wet weather; and sometimes it will be caused by a mistake made in planting. The wet-towel technique is a good way to check seed germination. Count out ten seeds and put them on a wet paper towel. Wrap the paper towel in a soaked, terry-cloth face towel, and put in a plastic bag. When the seeds have had time to sprout in four to ten days, unwrap the towels and count the number of seeds that have germinated. If eight out of the 10 seeds have tiny sprouts growing out of them, you have an eighty-percent germination rate. You might want to repeat the test a couple of more times if you doubt your first results. If you still come up with an eighty-percent germination rate, you know that you should plant twenty-percent more than you ordinarily would.

SOME NEIGHBORLY ADVICE

It is also possible to grow and save your own seeds, keep them over the winter, and plant them again in the spring. Let me remind you again to select seed varieties which are sure to do well in your area. Don't be afraid to contact your local Agricultural Extension Service Agency or ask your neighbors for advice. Growing conditions can change drastically in as short a distance as 100 miles. Find out what is best for you. What has always worked well for Uncle George in the next county may not work at home!

GROWING AND SAVING YOUR OWN SEEDS

There are already signs that vegetable seeds are going to be in short supply. Saving and growing seeds is something that more and more gardeners may have to start doing in the years to come. There is nothing to it, really, if you know a little about what to watch out for and if you realize that different plants produce seeds in different ways.

One of the main things to remember is that you cannot save seeds from hybrid plants—plants that are a cross between two different varieties. These seeds will not grow successfully. You have to grow seed from plants that are "open pollinators."

If you are just getting into the seed-

TESTING SEED GERMINATION

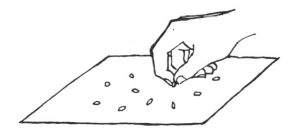

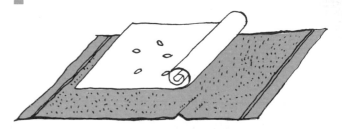

1 Spread ten seeds on a wet paper towel.

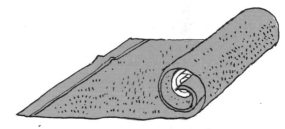

2 Roll up the seeds in the paper towel.

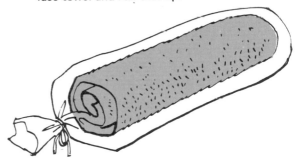

3 Place the rolled paper towel on a soaked terry-cloth face towel and roll that up.

4 Put both rolled towels in a plastic bag and seal it.

5 In four to ten days, when the seeds have had time to sprout, carefully unwrap the towels and count the number of seeds that have germinated. If, for example, eight of the ten seeds have sprouted, the germination rate is eighty percent.

saving business, you should not rely completely on seeds that you have grown yourself. The best plan is to experiment with them over a several-year period to see which ones you can do well with. Plant some of your garden with the seeds you have saved, but continue to buy quality seeds from a dependable seed company. This is good insurance against garden failure.

Some of the easiest seeds to grow at home are beans, squash, lettuce, tomatoes, spinach, and dill. Make some plantings that are specially earmarked for seed growing. It is best if these can be placed in a separate part of the garden. Your seed garden doesn't have to take up much space because each plant will produce lots of seeds. You might be able to plant a few beans, one or two tomatoes, and some spinach in the same row, for instance.

SAVE THE BEST FOR SEED

Plants that are raised for seed should be grown in the most ideal conditions possible. Treat them with extra "tender loving care" so that they will grow healthy and strong, because strong plants produce good, rugged seeds. Once the seeds have formed, select the plants that are the best-looking specimens. Take tomatoes, for example; it is a mistake to save seeds from the largest tomato you can find if it is growing on a spindly plant. Choose seeds from the plant that grows the most, best-shaped, disease-free fruit. Select squash for seed the same way.

Beans and peas are not much of a problem. All you have to do is grow a few special plants and harvest them when they are dry. Take those that have nice, large pods filled almost to bursting with uniform seeds. These are the ones that will start the best crop for you next year.

It is a little more difficult to save seeds from plants like beets, carrots, and chard. These vegetables are slow to bolt, so they must be planted very early in the spring if they are to produce seeds. Seed-growing beets and chard can be started indoors and later transplanted outside to stay in place for the entire growing season. The easiest way to get carrot seed is to plant a carrot that you have stored over the winter. Three

SAVING YOUR OWN SEED

TOMATO-SEED FERMENTATION

Allowing your home-grown seed tomatoes to ferment is probably the best method for destroying seed-borne diseases. This treatment destroys disease-causing organisms within the seeds, such as bacterial canker. Allow fresh fruit pulp to ferment for seventy-two hours at room temperature before extracting the seed. Remove the seeds and allow them to dry.

To keep ripe seed from falling on the ground, cut the whole plant and put it, upside-down, in a paper bag.

RECOMMENDED SEED-PROTECTANT FUNGICIDES

FUNGICIDE	CROP
Captan	Beans, cantaloupes, corn, cowpeas, cucumbers, muskmelons, peas, seed-potato pieces, watermelons
Thiram	Beans, cabbage, cantaloupes, carrots, cauliflower, corn, cowpeas, cucumbers, okra, peas, spinach, tomatoes, turnips
Polyram	Seed-potato pieces
Zinc-Coord. Maneb	Seed-potato pieces

STORING SEEDS

If you're a photographer as well as a gardener, you can make good use of the airtight containers in which 35-mm rolls of film are sold. A film processing lab might give you all you need.

When you have leftover seed, take them out of the original package on a day when the humidity is low and seal in the 35-mm film cans. You don't want to get moisture in the cans, as it might cause the seeds to mold. Write the variety of seeds and the date on the can.

Small plastic bags are good for storing seeds, too. Paper bags tend to collect moisture. Put all the individual plastic bags in a coffee can or similar container and store on a closet shelf or in a cool, dry, storage area. It's not cold but heat that destroys germination. In the spring, use the paper-towel test to determine the rate of germination.

or four carrots will give you more than enough seed. You can do the same thing with beets.

I have never had much luck growing onion seeds. The seed pods seem to break off in the wind, and the seeds usually get dumped on the ground before I have a chance to get them. Potatoes are another story, though. All you have to do is save medium-size potatoes which have five or six eyes in them. Corn grown for seed has to be left on the stalk until it is very ripe. The seeds will not germinate the next year unless the corn has been exposed to frost or is completely dead before it is harvested. Take seed from the fullest, most uniform ears.

Squash and pumpkins are even easier than potatoes and corn. Take seed from a nicely shaped, medium-size squash or pumpkin that grew on a healthy vine. Pick the fruit in the fall as you normally would, store it in the root cellar, and collect the seeds whenever you eat it during the winter. When you cut open a squash or pumpkin, take out the seeds and remove the thin, outer membrane from each one. To do this, you will have to wash them in lukewarm water, rub the tissue off them, and then rinse them several times. Once you are satisfied that they are completely clean, spread them out on a screen or cookie sheet. Be careful not to pile them on top of one another; just lay them out in one thin layer. It may take quite a while for these seeds to dry out. They will snap in half between your fingers when they are dry enough for storage. Put them in moisture-proof jars or plastic packages. Film containers, by the way, are excellent for storing small quantities of seed.

Trying to grow radish seeds is a waste of time, as far as I can see. Cauliflower is also very difficult. But getting seeds from broccoli is quite easy! Asparagus is another easy one. Choose seeds from the largest stalks.

How do you know when to harvest seeds that you have grown yourself? Lettuce, chard, spinach, beet, Brussels sprout, and carrot plants do not all ripen at the same time, unfortunately. One carrot might be ready today, but the one right next to it might not be ready for another week or so. Different seed pods on the same plant may not mature at the same time. If you wait

MAIL ORDER SEED COMPANIES

Seed catalogs are great shopping fun, but they make comparison buying impossible. Each company likes to give newly developed varieties its own unique brand names. Another company may have a very similar variety — or even the same variety — but call it by a different name. Some nationally known varieties, which are usually available at local seed stores, are sold under different names by mail-order companies.

But seed shopping by mail does have a lot of advantages. The catalogs almost always offer a better, larger selection than local stores. And they give a description of the advantages — seldom any disadvantages — of each variety. Plus it's so exciting to get a boxfull of seeds in the mail when the last snow is still on the ground.

We give you a list of mail-order seed companies from which to make your selections. All are reputable, and you'll get good service.

W. F. Allen Company
Salisbury, Maryland 21801
(Strawberries)

Brittingham Plant Farms
Salisbury, Maryland 21801
(Strawberries)

Burgess Seed and Plant Company
Galesburg, Michigan 49053

W. Atlee Burpee Company
Philadelphia, Pennsylvania 19132

Burrell Seed Company
Rocky Ford, Colorado 81067

Conner Company
Augusta, Arkansas 72006
(Strawberries)

De Giorgi Company
Council Bluffs, Iowa 51501

Desert Seed Company, Inc.
El Centro, California 92243

Evans Plant Company
Ty Ty, Georgia 31795
(Vegetable plants)

Farmer Seed & Nursery Company
Faribault, Minnesota 55021

Gurney Seed & Nursery Company
Yankton, South Dakota 57078

Joseph Harris Company, Inc.
Rochester, New York 14624

Herbst Brothers Seedsmen, Inc.
Brewster, New York 10509

Le Jardin du Gourmet
Ramsey, New Jersey 07446

J. W. Jung Seed Company
Randolph, Wisconsin 53956

Keystone Seed Company
Hollister, California 95023

Kilgore Seed Company, Inc.
Sanford, Florida 32771
(Florida varieties)

Earl May Seed & Nursery Co.,
Shenandoah, Iowa 51601

J. E. Miller Nurseries, Inc.
Canandaigua, New York 14424
(Strawberries, asparagus,
rhubarb, horseradish)

The Natural Development Company
Bainbridge, Pennsylvania 17502
(Organic supplies)

L. L. Olds Seed Company
Madison, Wisconsin 53701

George W. Park Seed Company
Greenwood,
South Carolina 29646

Peto Seed Company, Inc.
Saticoy, California 93303
(Warm-season crops)

Piedmont Plants
Albany, Georgia 31702
(Vegetable plants)

Rayner Brothers, Inc.
Salisbury, Maryland 21801
(Strawberries, asparagus,
rhubarb)

Reuter Seed Company, Inc.
New Orleans, Louisiana 70119
(Southern varieties)

Robson Quality Seeds, Inc.
Hall, New York 14463

R. H. Shumway Seedsman
Rockford, Illinois 61101

Seedway, Inc.
Hall, New York 14463

Spring Hill Nurseries
Tipp City, Ohio 45371
(Strawberries, asparagus,
rhubarb)

Stark Brothers
Louisiana, Missouri 63353
(Rhubarb, strawberries,
asparagus)

Steele Plant Company
Gleason, Tennessee 38229
(Sweet potatoes)

Stokes Seeds, Inc.
Buffalo, New York 14240

Sunsweet Plant Farms
Chula, Georgia 31733
(Vegetable plants)

Otis S. Twilley
Salisbury, Maryland 21801

Vaughan's Seed Company
Downers Grove, Illinois 60515

Vita Green Farms
Vista, California 92803

Wetsel Seed Company
Harrisonburg, Virginia 22801

Willhite Melon Seed Farms
Poolville, Texas 76076
(Melons, Southern peas)

Specialties are indicated under name of company. If nothing is stated the seed or nursery company is likely to carry a general variety of vegetable seeds. Some companies may supply primarily fruit, flowers, berries, or general nursery stock.

too long, the seeds will form, then drop off onto the ground and be lost. A plant might have a number of seed pods on it—some ripe and some still green. When some of the seed pods seem to be ripe and the seeds are beginning to fall to the ground, it is time to act.

Cut off the stem of the plant somewhere below the seed pods and put the whole thing into a paper bag with ventilation holes poked in it. Hang the bag in some airy place, such as a breezeway or garage, where it will be in the shade. Be sure you remember which plants are inside which bag. Labeling the bags will help avoid confusion. The seeds should be left in the bags until they are totally dry. This is extremely important. Once they are dry, they should be quite hard and brittle.

I usually start harvesting seeds sometime in August and continue to harvest them un-

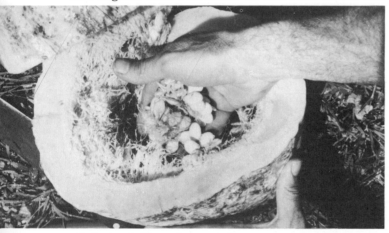

Squash and melon seeds are very easy to save.

til late fall. I leave the paper bags alone until some long winter evening in January or February when I have nothing important to do. Then I remove the seeds from the stalks and pods and store them for the coming spring. Seeds should be kept in clean, dry containers and placed where it is not too warm. Freezing will not hurt them, but it tends to create excess moisture. I put mine in a kitchen cabinet where they will stay at a more or less even temperature.

In the spring, you should give all of your seeds a germination test. Wrap a sampling in a wet paper towel, and count the number of seeds that grow tiny roots and sprouts. It is a good idea to test more than ten seeds of each home-grown variety. If you sample as many as fifty seeds of each variety, you will get a truer picture of the germination percentage.

I usually leave bean seeds on the plant until after the frost has hit them or until the plants are all dead. I do this with both string and yellow wax varieties. Once most of the plants have been killed, I pull them up and either put them in mesh bags or stack them around a stake. I take an old piece of pipe, drive it into the ground, pull up several bean plants, and stack them, placing the roots next to the pipe, until I have a pile that is three or four feet high. Rain water will run through the stack easily, and the beans will get good air circulation and begin to dry out. So I can just forget about them for a while.

Sometime before the first snowfall, I collect the dried bean plants from the garden and spread them out on a dry floor in a spare room or garage. I leave them there until the middle of winter. When I shell them, I do it the easy way. I put the plants in a burlap bag, tie it closed, and then roll it around, walk on it, or beat it with a stick. This shakes the beans out of the pods, and they sink to the bottom of the bag. To get the beans perfectly clean, you can take them outside on a windy day and "winnow" them by pouring them from one container to another and letting the breeze blow away all but the seeds themselves.

Storing bean and corn seed is a little different from storing other kinds of seed; you have to protect them from worms once they are completely dry. It is a good idea to put them in a jar, screw the cover on tight, and put an identifying label and date on the outside. Don't forget the germination check in the spring. You may get poor germination, especially if you did not allow the beans or kernels to ripen quite enough in the fall. Cover all your bets by supplementing your home-grown seed with some reliable purchased seed.

A number of good books dealing with growing and saving seeds are available. Your local Extension Service can tell you which vegetable varieties are open-pollinated and therefore good for raising seed. Check seed packages and catalogs to be sure that you are not trying to raise seed from a hybrid plant.

Saving seed can be a big money saver, and it is a very satisfying thing to do. Just be sure to do a little homework before you get started.

Serpent Cucumber

Vegetable Spaghetti

Ground Cherry
Garden Huckleberry
White Wonder Cucumber

TRY SOME "NOVELTY" VEGETABLES

You probably do a little experimenting in your garden already. Maybe you try out a few new varieties each year, or perhaps you occasionally plant a vegetable you've never grown before. But have you ever planted anything really different — as different as a radish that grows as large as a watermelon? If not, you're missing out on some good gardening fun.

Most major seed companies include at least a few novelty vegetables in their catalogs; some specialize in little-known, unusual vegetables and herbs.

The watermelon-size radish is called the Sakurajima radish. These giants may weigh fifteen pounds or more and are said to have excellent flavor.

For a little variety in the cucumber patch, you could try the White Wonder variety. The name is accurate; these cukes are solid white. They're fine for pickling or for eating fresh. Even more unusual is the Serpent cucumber; its slender, green fruits grow in coiled, snake-like shapes. Because this plant is not a member of the cucumber family, folks who can't eat real cucumbers often find that they can eat these strange, serpentine vegetables.

There are a lot of unusual members of the squash family. One is known as vegetable spaghetti because its flesh, when cooked, can be forked out in long, spaghetti-like strands. It can be served hot with your favorite spaghetti sauce, or cold with a salad dressing. For "spaghetti," harvest the yellow fruits when they are eight to ten inches long. If you prefer, you can harvest the squash at an earlier stage, slice them, and fry them like eggplant. Don't expect vegetable spaghetti to taste exactly like the real thing; it has a bland flavor and is less substantial.

The only thing the banana squash has in common with its namesake is its shape. The cylindrical fruits grow much larger than bananas — up to three feet long. They have pink skin, and their pale orange flesh is fine textured and sweet. Banana squash will thrive and produce abundantly where other winter squash will not.

The Dyuga early black winter squash has been grown and enjoyed in China for countless centuries, but few American gardeners have ever tried it.

More should. The warty, odd-looking squash have full-flavored, sweet flesh.

The Guatemalan blue squash was being grown by South American Indians over a thousand years before Columbus discovered the New World. The vines produce abundant crops of three-foot-long squash. Their smooth, hard shells make them good keepers. Both the protein-rich seeds and the sweet, fiber-free pulp are delicious.

As you browse through your catalogs, you'll find many other unusual squash. But you don't have to buy seeds to get novelty squash; you can save your own hybrid seed if you grow two or more varieties in adjoining areas. The results of your accidental cross-breeding will be totally unpredictable and unique. You probably won't get the same results two years in a row. But you'll have a lot of fun.

If your family is fond of preserves, marmalade, pies, and other sweet, fruity treats, you might like to plant some unusual annual fruits in your garden. The vine peach or mango melon is about the same size and color as a peach, and it can be used in the same ways, except that it is not usually eaten raw. Garden huckleberries aren't good for eating fresh either, but they're fine for making pies and preserves and for canning and freezing. The ground cherry produces small, yellow fruits inside Japanese-lantern-shaped husks. The sweet fruits can be eaten raw, dried, or used for making jam, jelly, or preserves.

There are, of course, many other novelty vegetables from which you can choose. There are blue and yellow potatoes; purple-podded beans; yard-long beans; lemon-flavored cucumbers; twenty-foot-tall corn plants; tampala, a climbing, spinach-like green; luffa gourds which can be made into sponges; and many, many more. If none of these examples arouse your curiosity, send for some of the catalogs listed below. You'll certainly find something to suit your fancy.

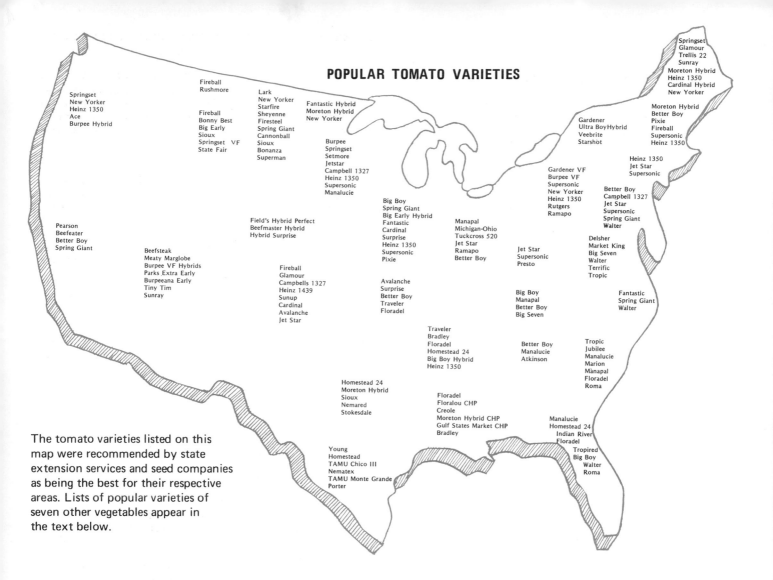

POPULAR TOMATO VARIETIES

The tomato varieties listed on this map were recommended by state extension services and seed companies as being the best for their respective areas. Lists of popular varieties of seven other vegetables appear in the text below.

WHICH VARIETIES ARE RIGHT FOR YOU?

We wanted to find out which vegetable varieties were most successful in various parts of the country, so we sent letters to a sampling of state extension services and seed companies. In each letter, we included a list of eight vegetables — tomatoes, snap beans, corn, lima beans, cucumbers, peas, cantaloupes, and squash. We asked the recipients to name the three best varieties of each of these vegetables for their area and to list any miscellaneous favorites.

Because our sample was small, our results were not conclusive. But they were interesting. To give you an example of the complexity of our results, on the accompanying map, we listed tomato-variety recommendations for many areas of the country. The varieties with the most "votes" were Better Boy, Supersonic, Jet Star, Heinz 1350, New Yorker, Spring Giant, Moreton Hybrid, and Floradel. As you can see, many other varieties were cited — so many that choosing among them is difficult and confusing. Some of the regional selections may be at least partially a reflection of the buying habits of the population or of the availability of certain varieties. The situation is made even more complex by the fact that the same variety is sometimes offered by two different companies — under two different names.

If your own favorite tomato variety is not recommended for your area, don't abandon it if it has done well for you. You might, however, like to experiment with some of the recommended varieties too. Maybe you'll find a new favorite.

Below are the varieties most frequently cited in the seven other categories (excluding tomatoes) that we listed. Asterisked varieties are outstanding favorites in their respective categories.

Snap Beans: Tendercrop*, Contender, Provider, Bush Blue Lake, Harvester.
Cucumbers: Marketmore, Pioneer, Poinsett*, Victory Hybrid.
Peas: Little Marvel*, Freezonian, Wando, Frosty.
Corn: Silver Queen*, Gold Cup, Spring Gold.
Lima Beans: Fordhook 242*, Henderson, Thaxter.
Cantaloupes: Burpee Hybrid*, Gold Star, Harper Hybrid.
Squash: Elite Zucchini, Summer Straightneck, Butternut, Buttercup.

For further help in choosing varieties, ask the advice of a neighbor with gardening experience or of your local extension service agent. Either should be able to help you pick varieties best adapted to the particular conditions of your area. R. R. Rothenberg, the home environment specialist at the University of Missouri Extension Service, listed varieties best for his state, then added, "It is difficult to be so limiting as there are many other varieties that have performed well. Some of the responses are influenced more by local soil types and conditions than the general climatic conditions." So local advice may be the best.

SOME ADVICE FROM FELLOW GARDENERS

VARIETIES BEST FOR LOCAL CONDITIONS

In every area of the country, there are distinctive cultural techniques and old favorite crops that have been developed over hundreds of years. Ask some of the veteran farmers and gardeners in your community about the methods and varieties that have proved successful in your particular climate and soil conditions.

SILVER QUEEN CORN

"Silver Queen is the best eatin' corn I know. But besides that, it's the only corn to plant for roadside selling, because it will last longer on the stalk than any other corn. I used to like to grow some Golden Bantam, but when it gets ripe, you have to pull it or it will get hard and tough. You can leave Silver Queen on for two weeks after it's ripe, and it's good the entire time. It just holds up better than any corn I know of." HL

CANTALOUPES

Burpee Hybrid cantaloupe is popular all over the country and is a highly planted and recommended variety by many experienced growers. Gold Star, sold by Harris Seed Company, is also of excellent quality and is a very similar melon. It's hard to tell the difference between the two.

MANAPAL TOMATOES

"Manapal is a fine all-around tomato. It is smooth all over without any cracks; they're firm and will ripen good if picked at any stage. It will keep for two weeks in the refrigerator even when picked dead ripe. Pick it at a solid white stage, put it in the window to ripen, and it will have good flavor. Manapal is medium in size." JLG

HYBRID VARIETIES

There is disagreement among experienced farmers over the comparative advantages of hybrid varieties and standard varieties. Some will plant nothing but hybrids; others believe the only difference is the price — hybrids usually cost twice as much. HP

VALIENT TOMATOES

It's an extra-early tomato, too. Valients have been around for a long time. Some Maryland farmers don't like hybrid tomatoes; they prefer the Valient, a "straight" or open-pollinated tomato. You can easily save the seed from this variety. HL

For a selection of all-time favorite varieties that will produce a good crop in most areas of the country and in practically any soil type, see the Garden Way Sure Crop List on page 146.

MINI-VEGETABLES

Quite a few vegetables are now available in miniature varieties. You might like to plant a sampling in containers, indoors, or in limited garden space. Most major seed-company catalogs offer at least a few mini-vegetables. Burgess Seed Company has a good selection.

Following is a list of some of the varieties you can choose from.

CABBAGE — "Dwarf Morden," a very early variety, produces heads four inches in diameter. This midget can be planted eight inches apart in rows twelve to fourteen inches apart. "Little Leaguer" produces baseball-size heads which can be cooked whole.

CARROT — "Tiny Sweet" is a delicious mini-carrot that grows only three inches long. "Short 'n Sweet" is another good choice. Both should be thinned to 1½ to 2 inches apart.

CUCUMBER — Within sixty days, "Cherokee" will cover its three-foot vines with fruit measuring up to seven inches. Heavy fertilization and watering will insure good yields. Two or three plants will do nicely in a five-gallon container.

SWEET CORN — "Golden Midget" bears four-inch ears on thirty-inch stalks in less than sixty days. "Midget Hybrid" matures just a few days later, and its ears measure five inches. Both varieties are sweet and delicious. If you prefer white corn, choose "White Midget," with ears four to six inches long on 2½- to 3-feet-tall stalks.

Plant mini-corn six to eight inches apart in rows two feet apart. Be sure to plant more than two rows for even pollination.

EGGPLANT — "Modern Midget" makes an attractive, sturdy, small plant which bears medium-sized purple fruits. Set the plants 1½ feet apart in rows two feet apart, or place one plant in a three- to five-gallon container.

HEAD LETTUCE — "Tom Thumb," a butterhead-type lettuce, produces a head the size of a tennis ball. The quality is excellent, and one head is just the right size for an individual salad.

MUSKMELON — "Minnesota Midget" will produce high-quality, four-inch melons in sixty days. The vines grow only five feet long but bear heavily. Space them three feet away from each other in all directions, or plant one or two in a five-gallon container.

PEAS — The six-inch vines of "Mighty Midget" peas produce an abundance of 3½-inch pods, filled with tender, sweet peas. Plant them one inch apart in rows 1½ feet apart. Or grow some in a window box.

SQUASH — Bush types of squash take only about four to six feet per plant. For summer squash, plant "Baby Crookneck," which will bear heavily in fifty-three days. "Chefine" is a green, zucchini-type squash. "St. Pat Scallop Hybrid" is a new, bush-type, patty-pan squash. For winter squash, plant "Golden Nugget," which bears 1½- to 2-pound fruits; they are delicious baked whole at 250° F.

TOMATO — "Tiny Tim" is the best-known miniature tomato. It grows only six inches tall, but produces abundant clusters of cherry-size fruit in forty-five days. Small-fruited pear tomatoes are available in yellow and red varieties. "Patio" and "Pixie" tomatoes bear larger fruits than "Tiny Tim," but they too are fine for container growing.

WATERMELON — "Early Midget" produces six-pound melons in eighty days. "New Hampshire Midget" matures in seventy days; its fruits are seven inches long and six inches across and weigh about six pounds. Plant both varieties in four- to six-foot squares; neither does well in containers.

For more information on mini-vegetables, write for the USDA Home and Garden Bulletin No. 163, available from the Superintendent of Documents, U.S. Government Printing Office, Washington, D.C. 20402, for fifteen cents.

Starting plants early

Get a big jump on Mother Nature — and your neighbors — by using an experienced gardener's techniques and tricks for bringing in the season's first pickings.

Many experienced gardeners like to start some of their garden plants inside the house. A first-year gardener might want to experiment with growing a few plants indoors, but he should probably not rely completely on home-grown plants. There is nothing wrong with buying a few things from the local nursery.

For starting plants inside, it is important to have either a good, sunny window with a southern exposure or some electric "grow lights" which emit rays similar to those given off by the sun. Keep heaters and heating ducts in mind as you select a place to start your plants. For example, if there is a heater directly under your seed-starting window, you can be sure that your seedlings are going to dry out very quickly, and that you will have to water them quite often.

There are all kinds of seed-starting containers for sale: peat pots; jiffy sevens, little cubes complete with soil; and "flats." You can also use tin cans, milk cartons, and egg boxes. A lot of people use cardboard egg boxes, but I find that they absorb a lot of water, which causes plants to dry out too quickly in them. The egg boxes that work best are the ones made of styrofoam or "dyefoam." Try cutting the cover off and setting the bottom part of the box inside the cover. This double reinforcement will make the box more solid.

Any container used for starting seeds must have holes in the bottom to allow excess water to escape. Most purchased pots and flats already have them. Peat pots, being very absorbent, drain readily, even without holes. Poke a dozen holes in an egg container with something sharp, like a nail. If you're using a large container, like a two-quart milk carton, make some holes in the bottom, then put in about half an inch of gravel or crushed stone before you add soil.

BUILDING YOUR INDOOR NURSERY

Fill your first containers, whatever they may be, with potting soil. You can buy packaged potting soil at a garden center, or you can make a batch of starter mixture from your own soil, some sand, vermiculite, peat, or compost. If you do decide to use a homemade mixture, be sure to treat it against damping off. Sterilizing it is easy enough. Put some soil in a cake pan or on a cookie sheet, moisten it, place in the oven, and bake at 300 or 350 degrees for about an hour or until the soil is dry. This will kill most of the microorganisms in the soil, including the fungus that causes damping off. The young seedlings will not require the nutrients required by microbial activity at this stage.

Level off the soil before you sprinkle any seeds on it. If you are using seed flats, a little piece of shingle works fine for leveling. Scrape over the top to make sure the soil mixture is completely even and smooth, then plant the seed.

If you are going to plant the seeds in rows, use the edge of the shingle to make ¼-inch-deep troughs in the soil. Otherwise, spread the seed over the soil, evenly and not too thickly, then press them in with the flat side of the shingle. Cover them with a little more soil, remembering that they should be buried at a depth about three to four times their own diameter. Obviously, very fine seeds will require very shallow covering. Try to make sure that you spread an equal amount of soil over the whole area. Use the shingle to firm the soil a second time.

Newly planted seeds should be watered liberally but gently—preferably with a fine spray that will not disturb them. Next, the flats or pots should be put in plastic bags or covered with plastic or Saran wrap to seal in moisture. You should not have to do any more watering until the seedlings come up. Put them in a warm place—somewhere where the temperature remains in the

1 Soils

Seeds can be started in any of several soil mixtures or in soil substitutes, such as vermiculite or sifted sphagnum. Seeds started in these sterile soilless mediums are protected from damping off; just be sure to transplant the seedlings to a soil mixture which will provide adequate nutrients as soon as the first true leaves appear. Some good commercial soil mixes (based on the excellent Cornell Mix): Redi-Earth, Jiffy Mix, Pro-Mix.

PEAT SAND PERLITE

HOMEMADE SOIL MIXES

You can use good garden soil in your mix, but you may have to "lighten" it with sand or peat moss.

To make a batch of Cornell Mix at home, blend together 4 quarts of vermicultie or perlite, 4 quarts of shredded peat moss or sphagnum, 2 level tablespoons of ground limestone, and 4 level tablespoons of 5-10-10 fertilizer.

STARTING SEEDS INDOORS

MORE SOIL RECIPES

For a large batch of soil, you might mix 2 bales of peat moss, 3 4-cubic-foot bags of vermiculite, 6 pounds 5-10-10 fertilizer, 2 pounds superphosphate, and 5 pounds agricultural lime. To mix large batches, shovel roughly mixed ingredients from one cone-shaped pile to another, adding each shovelful to top of pile and allowing soil to tumble down sides of cone.

Here's a simple mix: 1 part loam, 1 part clean sand or perlite, and 1 part leaf mold or moist peat.

STERILIZING SOIL

Sterilizing soil kills off weed seeds and potentially harmful disease organisms, but it is a messy job. Large quantities of soil can be fumigated with methyl bromide, chloropicrin, and other similar chemicals. Follow manufacturer's instructions exactly.

Smaller amounts can be sterilized in the oven. Put soil in a shallow tray and bake at 350 degrees for 1½ hours. Shallow containers take less time. To test, place potato in soil; when it is done, soil is ready. Do not overcook.

Alternate methods: Thoroughly soak soil and bake at 275 degrees until the surface begins to cake (about 1 hour). Or place soil in fine-mesh sieve and pour boiling water through it. When water running through soil gets very hot, soil is sterile.

2 Containers

There are two types of containers — individual pots in which a single plant is grown and flats or other containers large enough for starting many seeds. Some plants (tomatoes, peppers, etc.) are started in flats and transplanted to individual pots; other large-seeded plants (melons, squash, etc.) must be started in individual pots. They don't tolerate transplanting because of their large root systems. (See chart on page 29).

FLATS

You can buy flats or build your own. Or you can recycle some common household items and end up with ideal seed-starting containers.

INDIVIDUAL POTS

There are plenty of individual pots on the market, some complete with soil and nutrients, but you can save money and resources by improvising. Make sure all pots have adequate drainage.

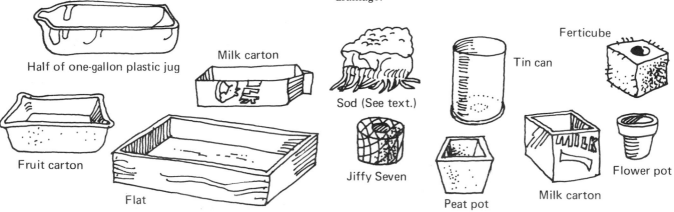

Half of one-gallon plastic jug

Milk carton

Fruit carton

Flat

Sod (See text.)

Jiffy Seven

Tin can

Ferticube

Peat pot

Milk carton

Flower pot

3 Sowing Seeds

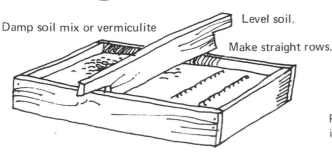

Damp soil mix or vermiculite

Level soil.

Make straight rows.

Cover seed with a fine layer of vermiculite, soil mix, or sand.

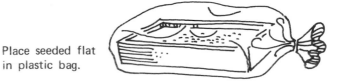

Place seeded flat in plastic bag.

SOWING SEEDS IN INDIVIDUAL CONTAINERS

Plant 3 or 4 seeds in each individual pot or container. Later remove all but one plant in each pot.

If you have a cold frame, one of the best and least expensive containers for starting all melons, squash and cucumbers is the common tin can. Save your cans. Cut off the top smoothly and punch holes in the bottom for drainage. All cans should be the same height.

Fit them tightly against each other in the cold frame or hotbed. Shovel cans full of potting mixture and smooth off with a board. Make an indentation in the soil in each can. Drop 3 or 4 seeds in each can and cover with soil. Later remove all but one plant. Don't plant as early as tomatoes and cole crops. (See chart.)

When transplanting to garden soak can thoroughly, turn can upside down holding the soil in with one hand, (plant stem will be between your fingers) while tapping the sides and bottom of the can with your trowel. Shake can a little and the entire root ball and soil will slip out together ready for planting.

VEGETABLES SUITABLE FOR TRANSPLANTING AND METHODS OF SOWING SEED

Easy to transplant. Can be sown in flats in rows and transplanted bare root.	Must be started in individual containers and transplanted without disturbing roots.
Broccoli (5-7)	Cantaloupe (3-4)
Brussels Sprouts (5-7)	(All Muskmelons) (3-4)
Cabbage (5-7)	Cucumbers (3-4)
Cauliflower (5-7)	Squash (3-4)
Celeriac (7-12)	(summer & winter)
Celery (7-12)	Watermelon (5-7)
Chinese Cabbage (5-7)	+
Collards (5-7)	
*Eggplant (6-8)	
Lettuce (5-7)	
Onion (8-10)	
Parsley (8-10)	
*Peppers (6-8)	
Sweet Potato (3-4) (start from tuber and not seed)	
*Tomato (6-8)	

* Sometimes sown in flats and then transplanted into individual containers before transplanting to garden.

+ Many vegetables like corn, beans and beets can be started early in pots and flats, but seldom are because the large number of pots needed is impractical.

( )Number in parentheses is approximate time (weeks) from sowing seed to transplanting to garden.

4 Transplanting Seedlings

When the first true leaves appear, lift the plant out of the growing medium, holding it by the leaves, not the stem to avoid crushing the stem. Seedlings may be left to grow 3 to 4 inches tall before transplanting.

Transplant seedlings to a larger, deeper flat, to an individual pot, or into a cold frame.

Don't try to transplant extra seedlings of melons, squash and cucumber growing in individual pots; remove all but one plant. Pinch them off or carefully pull them out so as not to disturb the other plant's root system.

Heating cables (sold by many gardening centers and listed in seed-company catalogs) provide the extra heat necessary to give your plants a boost.

SWEET POTATOES

When sprouting sweet potatoes for slips to set out, slice the potato in half lengthwise. Place the side with the eyes facing up in your planting bed. This prevents shoots from sprouting beneath the potato. JZ

SETTING OUT PEAT POTS

When planting peat pots, be sure they're thoroughly soaked. A hot, dry spell will prevent the roots from penetrating the pot.

neighborhood of seventy to seventy-five degrees.

Germinating seeds do not require any light. In fact, if the flats are left in a very bright place, you might want to shade them with a piece of newspaper. Once the seeds begin to come up, remove the plastic immediately and place the flat in a sunny window or under grow lights. From this point on, you will have to water your plants regularly, as often as once a day if they are near a heater.

GIVE YOUR SEEDLINGS ROOM TO GROW

The first leaves to push through the soil are not true leaves. As soon as the first true leaves do appear, the tiny plants should be moved to larger, deeper containers. They will be anywhere from one to three inches tall at this point and will probably be growing too close together. The seedlings should be transplanted a little deeper than they were before. This is especially true with tomatoes. The part of the stem below ground will grow roots, making the plant much stronger. Don't replant peppers or cabbages more than an inch deeper than they were in the flat or you will risk smothering them. Transplanting sets a plant back a bit, stopping its upward growth and encouraging it to grow outward as it establishes a stronger root system. Every time you transplant, the seedling's root system will increase in size, sometimes even doubling. This enables the plant to pick up more nutrients from the soil and to better support itself as it grows.

It is a good idea, by the way, to transplant whenever a plant starts to get "leggy," or too elongated. Transplanting will set it back a bit and make the plant grow out instead of up. If I start early enough, I sometimes transplant three or four times to keep the plants from getting too long and spindly looking.

Now is the time to add some sort of fertilizer—compost, manure, or a complete chemical fertilizer containing all three major nutrients, nitrogen, phosphorous, and potassium. Store-bought potting soil does not always have fertilizer in it. In fact, many potting compounds are just a neutral medium, so it is up to you to feed the plants. Check the instructions on the potting-soil

bag to see if additional fertilizer is needed. If you have used your own soil, it can probably use a little shot of fertilizer even if it is naturally rich.

Seeds of non-hardy plants, such as tomatoes, peppers, and eggplant, should be started six to eight weeks before they will be set out in the garden. Less delicate plants, such as cabbages, Brussels sprouts, broccoli, and cauliflower, should be planted four to five weeks before they are to be transplanted to the garden. Starting cabbage and tomato plants at the same time is not a good idea. The cabbage will be much too big after eight weeks.

HOME-GROWN ONIONS FROM SEED

You might try growing some of your own onion plants from seed. Get a 4- or 5-inch-deep container with holes in the bottom, and put in some gravel or crushed stone. Fill it to within one inch of the top with a rich potting mixture and add a little fertilizer. Onion seeds need to be planted very early—twelve or more weeks before you plan to set them out. I do this each year with Bermuda onions, and I have had great success.

The thing to remember about onions is that the tops may grow quite leggy looking because they have no leaves to absorb the sun. When the tops get to be somewhere between three and four inches tall, they need to be cut back to a height of about an inch and a half. Every other week or so—whenever they get three or four inches tall again—cut them back. You will have to do this continuously until it is time to set the plants outside to harden off. With onions, we are naturally interested in the bottoms. Every time the tops are cut off, the plant's energy goes into growing a larger root. Don't bother to transplant onions inside. Plant them once, keep them cut, and when the time is right, harden them off and transplant outside.

SAVE MONEY WITH SOD

Here is a good trick that you can use with hard-to-transplant vegetables like cucumbers and melons. Cut a good, thick piece of sod out of a field, turn it bottom-side-up with the grassy side down, and cut it into pieces about two inches square. Plant a seed or two in each of these pieces. After

When transplanting tomatoes, remove all but the topmost leaves and set the seedling deeper than it was growing before.

You can see from this photograph that roots will form all along a buried tomato-plant stem. This is not true of other vegetables.

Lettuce, cabbage, and other cole crops (like broccoli and cauliflower) can be moved from their original flats directly to the garden as soon as the plants are large enough.

the seed has germinated and the plant has grown a bit, transplant it, sod and all, into a pot or into the garden. This way, the plant's tender roots will not be disturbed at all. The soil in sod is apt to be quite rich, and as the grass decomposes in the pot or in the ground, nutrients for the plant will be released. This is a good way, incidentally, to avoid buying expensive peat pots.

Cucumbers and melons can be started in pots or sod, but they should not be planted until two or three weeks before the last frost. Otherwise, they will get too tall and may not survive the transplant.

PREPARE YOUR SHELTERED SEEDLINGS FOR A SHOCK

Have you ever noticed how easy it is to get a sunburn or a windburn in the early spring? Because you have spent most of the winter inside, your skin is not as accustomed to the weather as it would be, say, in August. Plants can be just as tender as you are in this respect. They have been sitting on your window sill or in a cold frame for weeks. If you suddenly change their environment by taking them out into the bright sun, wind, and colder air, they can really suffer. You can spare them this shock if you allow them to make the adjustment gradually, or to "harden off." You can do this by moving your seed flats or potted plants outdoors for a few hours each day. As time goes on, and as the weather gets warmer, they can be left out for longer and longer periods of time. Even if you buy your plants from a garden market, they should be hardened off. The process of hardening off takes a week or two.

I think it helps to stop watering your plants a day or two before they are to be hardened off. Once you place them outside, they won't need to be watered quite so often because there is normally a lot more humidity outside the house than inside.

If the sun is particularly bright as you begin hardening off your plants, leave them in partial shade for a while the first day, and bring them back inside at night. It may take several days to adjust to full sun.

Try to leave your plants in a spot that is sheltered from the wind. Strong winds can burn them; more important, if the tender plants bend too much in the breeze, they may snap off.

THE POOR MAN'S GREENHOUSE

Cold frames are sometimes called the "poor man's greenhouse" because they are so cheap and simple to build. Most people make them out of boards of some kind. A cold frame does not have to be any specific size, but most of the ones I have ever seen measured about three feet by six feet. Don't make the frame too wide or you'll have trouble reaching all your plants.

All you have to do is nail the ends of four fairly wide boards together to make a square or rectangle. This simple frame can then be covered with glass—an old window sash, maybe—or some sort of plastic which will let light through. It is best if this bottomless cold frame can sit on a slope that slants slightly to the south. This will provide maximum exposure to the sun's rays and will keep the box warmer.

The reason for building cold frames or hotbeds in the first place is to allow yourself time, either in the early spring or late fall, to grow plants in a place protected from frost. (Most people use cold frames more in the spring when they are starting new plants, but they can be used to extend the growing season into the fall, too.) You can either plant seeds in the ground under the box, or you can put starter flats inside it. Personally, I like to start seeds in the house, and then either transplant the seedlings into the cold frame or put the flats out there.

A cold frame will hold its own heat quite well, but it needs some extra protection on very cold nights. If you hear that the temperature is going to drop far below freezing, cover the box with a canvas or an old blanket just to be on the safe side. Bright sun can be something of a problem. Cheesecloth spread over the cold frame cover will prevent sunburn.

During the day, you have to be careful not to let it overheat. On a bright, sunny afternoon, you may have to encourage air circulation by opening the window a little or by leaving the top ajar. I think you will be pleased to discover how early you can grow vegetables like lettuce and radishes in your cold frame. I can start seeds in early March and have fine lettuce by the first of April. A cold frame is also a very good place to harden off young seedlings. Set flats inside and let them get accustomed to the out-

APPLE BOX COLD FRAME

You can make a small temporary cold frame from a sturdy wooden box and a pane of glass or old window frame. After removing the bottom of the box, sink the frame about 2 or 3 inches into the ground. The top of the box should slant toward the south. Drive two nails into the top, one in each of the lower corners. Prop the glass on the nails.

MANURE-HEATED BEDS

Now that electricity is both scarce and expensive, heating hotbeds with manure again seems practical. Horse or mule stable manure with no more than 1/3 bedding material is ideal. Seven to ten days before planting, fill 18- to 24-inch-deep pit to within 6 inches of ground level. Pack firmly and wet down. After 3 or 4 days, turn manure, pack, and wet if dry. If manure is heating evenly after 3 or 4 more days, add soil — 6 inches for direct planting, 2 inches if you will plant in containers.

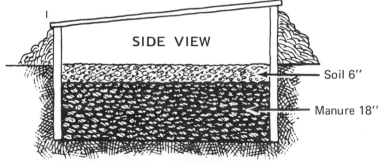

ELECTRIC-HEATED BEDS

You can use either 25-watt frosted light bulbs or lead- or plastic-coated heating cables. Fasten light bulbs to strips of lumber or suspend from non-electric wire 10 to 12 inches above soil. Use one 25-watt bulb per 2 square feet.

A standard 60-foot cable will heat a 6 x 6 or 6 x 8-foot bed. Lay cable loops (about 8 inches apart) directly on floor of bed unless drainage material is necessary. If so, cover with old sacks, add a 2-inch layer of sand, and place cable on sand. Cover cable with 2 inches of sand or soil and a layer of chicken wire or hardware cloth to protect it from rakes, hoes, etc. For direct sowing, spread 4 inches of soil on top of wire.

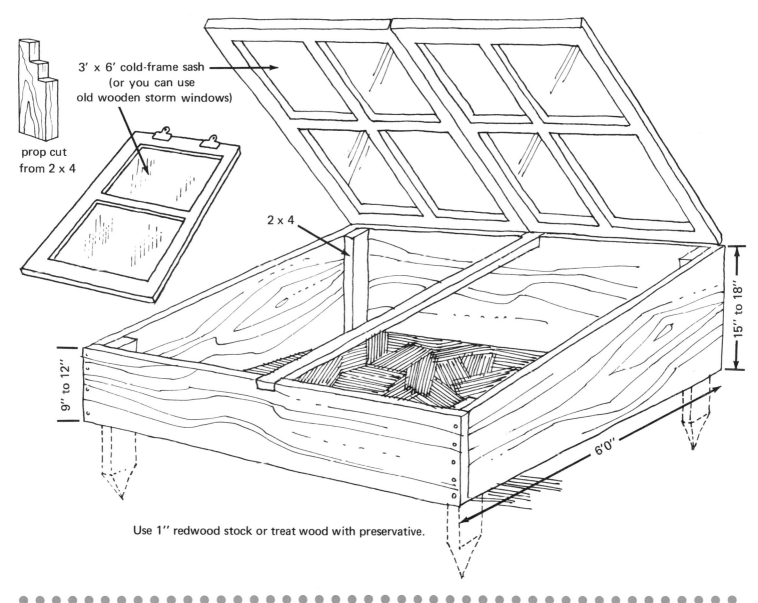

3' x 6' cold-frame sash
(or you can use
old wooden storm windows)

prop cut
from 2 x 4

2 x 4

15" to 18"

9" to 12"

6'0"

Use 1" redwood stock or treat wood with preservative.

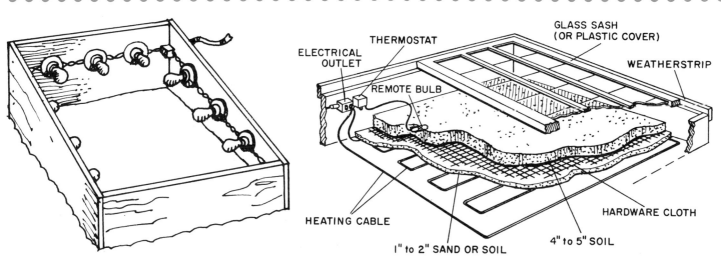

You can use ordinary electric light bulbs
wired in a series to heat a hotbed.

THERMOSTAT

ELECTRICAL
OUTLET

REMOTE BULB

GLASS SASH
(OR PLASTIC COVER)

WEATHERSTRIP

HARDWARE CLOTH

4" to 5" SOIL

HEATING CABLE

1" to 2" SAND OR SOIL

DIAGRAM FOR WIRING AN ELECTRICALLY HEATED HOTBED

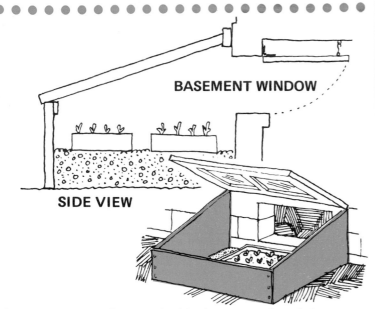

BASEMENT WINDOW

SIDE VIEW

You can heat a cold frame by backing it up to a cellar window.

CARING FOR HOTBEDS

A hotbed must be watched carefully and allowed to get neither too hot nor too cold. On cool nights, your plants have to be put to bed like any other children.

A good old-fashioned method of covering hotbeds at night is to unroll tar paper or roofing paper over the glass or plastic. Then cover with a thick, insulating layer of pine needles. (Pine needles are better than straw or other materials that pack down when wet and rot easily.)

You'll have to learn by experience just how much air to let in on a hot day. Propping one corner of the sash up about five inches is usually adequate. Raise the side or corner away from the prevailing wind. You don't want wind blowing on tender plants.

As the days get nicer, you can gradually expose your plants to more sun, wind, and weather to toughen them up for transplanting to the garden.

Don't overwater. Just keep the soil moist enough to prevent the plants from drooping. HP

ENCLOSING HOTBEDS IN PLASTIC

Here's an idea used by a truck farmer to get excellent germination of seed in his hotbed. After planting and watering, he covers the bed with a glass sash. He then stretches a solid sheet of clear plastic over the sash and seals it down with dirt all around the edges. The plastic-enclosed hotbed provides the warm, humid conditions which seeds love. Watch the temperature during the middle of a hot day. It may be necessary to open one end of the plastic to let excess heat escape.

When covered with plastic, the bed can also be gassed to kill diseases and weed seeds. HP

doors by opening the cover a little at first, and later leaving it off entirely during the day.

A hotbed is the same as a cold frame, except that it has some kind of artificial heat source. You might build a three-sided box by a cellar window, backing it right up against the foundation of the house. If you leave the cellar window partially open so heat can flow out into the frame, you can keep your plants from freezing most of the winter. Some elaborate hotbeds have electric heating cables running underneath them. The cables heat the soil and make the plants grow faster. If you have a large cold frame, you can convert it to a hotbed simply by installing some kind of small heating unit. It would not have to be much. You don't have to keep the temperature in this mini-greenhouse anywhere near as high as you would in your house.

Every home gardener should have some sort of cold frame or hotbed, but there is no reason to spend a lot of money for one. It doesn't have to be very big or very fancy, and scrap lumber is still pretty easy to find.

THE SUN PIT

The greenhouse at my place is actually what I call a "sun pit." It was cheap to build, and it works like a charm. I excavated the side of a large bank that faces south. Once the bank had been dug away, I built an eight-foot cement-block wall on the north side and a partial block wall on the other three sides of the greenhouse area.

After I finished the block walls, I built a frame out of lumber and covered the whole structure with a translucent material called Kalwall. Then I built an entryway or foyer on the east side of the building. I chose the east side because the cold winter winds here in Vermont usually come from the west and north. This foyer is a little like a decompression chamber. You walk in one door, close it, and then open a second door to get into the greenhouse itself. This way, there is no chance of letting the warmer air inside escape as you open the door.

I plant hardy crops in this sun pit. I have many kinds of lettuce, chard, spinach, radishes, celery, chives, parsley, onions, and Brussels sprouts. These are vegetables that require very little heat. The north cement-block wall of the building is painted

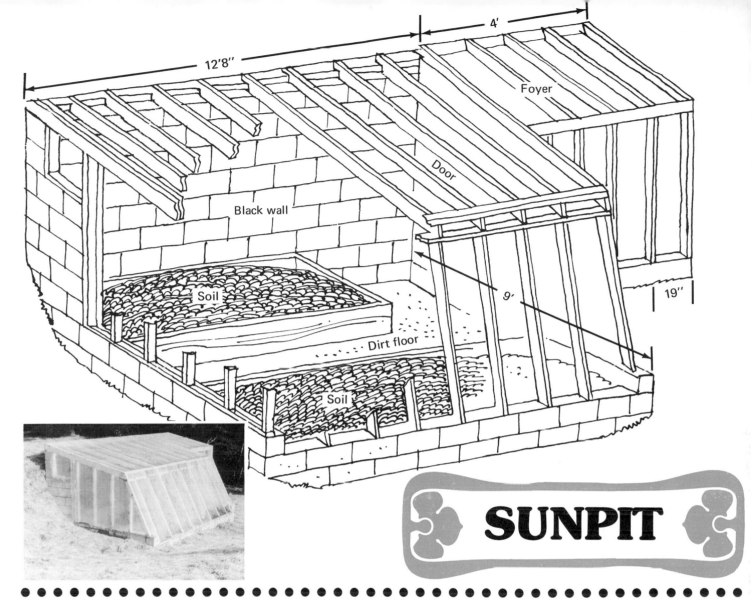

Labels in figure: 12'8", 4', Foyer, Door, Black wall, Soil, Soil, Dirt floor, 9', 19"

SUNPIT

flat black to absorb the heat of the sun. The soil outside this wall remains at a fairly constant fifty-five degrees, which also tends to warm the air inside on cold nights.

I have installed a fan that comes on when the temperature goes above eighty degrees and a heater that will switch on when it gets below thirty degrees. But I find that the heater comes on only rarely. One of the beds inside is sloped four degrees to the south, which exposes it to the sun and makes it much warmer than the flat growing beds. The greenhouse consumes very little energy, but it yields a great deal in the form of vegetables.

In the fall, I bring a few tomato and pepper plants into my sun pit. These will survive and bear fruit until it starts to get really cold in January. The hardy crops will continue to produce right through the winter. A sun pit is also a great place to start plants in the spring. They grow fast and strong because they get so much sun. I have even installed a heating cable under one of the beds; it warms up the soil and will hold the temperature at seventy degrees, twenty-four hours a day, if I want it to.

I have one other trick I use when it gets extremely cold. I have a roll of plastic that is left rolled up against one of the cement-block walls. It hangs about two feet off the ground. On a real cold day or night, when I am afraid that the temperature outside is not going to get much above zero, I roll out the plastic so that it forms a second, lower "ceiling." This leaves only the two feet between the plastic and the beds to be heated. This simple, inexpensive trick cuts down fuel consumption considerably.

I recommend a sunpit to anyone who has the space to build it. You do not have to follow my design exactly, of course. If you can build it in the side of a bank facing south or east, the wind will blow over the top of it, and it will get the maximum amount of sunshine all day long.

Earthworm friends

Earthworms are miniature compost factories. Into these long digestive tubes go minerals and organic matter. And out come "castings," which are rich in nutrients.

Earthworms are about the most important gardening friends you have. They work twenty-four hours a day for you. They tunnel through the soil, permitting the passage of air and water, and they eat all the organic matter in front of them, leaving behind "castings" which are far richer than what they take in.

Have you ever wondered what happens to leaves on the forest floor? There are always lots of them in the fall, but very few by the next summer. Most of them are consumed by earthworms. You can go out in the woods in August or September before the leaves start to fall and see very tiny piles of sticks all over the ground. In many cases, these little "sticks" are the skeletons of old leaves.

We don't fertilize the forest, obviously, so it must be the earthworms that are doing the job.

The roots of the trees go deep into the subsoil to retrieve nutrients that have leached out of the upper layers of earth. The tree pumps these nutrients up its trunk and into the leaves, where they are stored. The earthworms eat the fallen leaves and return the nutrients to the soil in the form of castings. As time goes on, a forest becomes increasingly lush, as more and more nutrients are continually made available to the trees. As the roots are fed better, they help to produce more and more foliage. Try to encourage the same sort of process in your garden.

I have often been quoted as saying, "If an earthworm won't eat it, you should not put it in the garden." This is one reason why I don't like to use sawdust as a mulch and recommend that others use it very sparingly.

EARTHWORMS
By Dr. Henry Hopp

In a forest where a leaf fall takes place every autumn, the earthworm population is regulated by the quantity of leaves which fall and their nitrogen content. The same factor regulates the populations found in prairies and grasslands. The earthworm population will rise above its usual limit only when organics are continuously imported into an ecosystem. Each time a gardener works compost into his soil, he is raising the soil's carrying capacity and ultimately the earthworm population.

Variations in food supply, climate, and soil result in large differences in the size of earthworm populations. There are differences in the size of the population regionally, due to climate, and locally, due to the texture and origin of the soil. There may even be differences in the population from one field to the next due to the method of cropping the land. Hence, an actual examination of your soil is the surest way of knowing whether you are in a locality where earthworms play an important role in maintaining the condition of the soil.

An earthworm examination of your soil can be made quickly. Select an area with ample vegetation on it, such as cover crop, clover, grass, etc. The examination can be made at any season of the year, but it is easiest during a humid period. Dig out a square of earth about one foot across to a depth of approximately seven inches. Count all the earthworms you can find in this sample. Include both mature and young ones. Our experience have given us a fairly reliable thumb rule for judging the earthworm population. If a soil contains at least ten earthworms in such a sample, the population is large enough to be significant in the structural properties of the soil. Sometimes there are only one or two earthworms in the sample. This indicates that the earthworms are playing little if any real part in the physical condition of the soil.

Effect On Aeration

You have probably noticed how poorly crops grow in compact soil. Growth is poor because there are not enough large air spaces in the soil. Not only is the absorption of rain water slow, resulting in its loss by runoff, but aeration of the soil is also deficient. Crops make their best growth where there are large spaces into which the roots can grow. Roots do not grow well in solid soil; they grow primarily in the spaces between the soil particles.

Earthworms are one of the most effective agents for loosening and aerating the soil. Their burrows make large passageways for the roots to grow in. They perforate the topsoil especially and gradually penetrate the subsoil, opening it for root growth and depositing organic matter in it. But even more important is the granulation of the soil which they bring about by their production of casts from the soil and organic debris that they eat. As the soil becomes granulated with casts, it gets looser and looser. These casts are clearly visible in any soil inhabited by earthworms. During damp seasons of the year, cast production is especially prolific. At that time, casts are even deposited on the surface of the ground. However, there are always many more casts underground than there are on top.

Effect On Soil Moisture

The intake of water by fine soil is dependent for the most part on the presence of extraneous channels. Earthworms are highly effective in making such channels. They form an interconnected web of channels which allow rain water to penetrate quickly throughout the topsoil layer.

TOOLING UP FOR GARDENING PLEASURE

There are some gardeners who own as many cultivating tools as a professional golfer has golf clubs. Most of these are unnecessary. All you should really need are a goose-neck onion hoe, a Reisch hoe, an in-row weeder, a regular steel garden rake, one of those small push hoes, and perhaps a rear-end rotary tiller. Whatever you do, don't buy only heavy gardening tools! The only time you need a big, heavy-duty hoe, for example, is when you're hilling or making deep furrows. Treat yourself to a nice light one. Give your back, your arms, and your shoulders a break. There is no reason why any of us should be lame after cultivating our gardens.

GARDENING HAND TOOLS

REISCH HOE

The narrow Reisch hoe is perfect for cultivating between plants. Use the point to loosen the soil deeply; use the side to scrape up small weeds or grass growing close to plants.

ONION HOE

An onion hoe is light and easy to handle. The only task for which you'll need a heavier hoe is hilling.

IN-ROW WEEDER

The in-row weeder does a fine job of weeding wide rows, but, unfortunately, they are not available everywhere. A broom rake with round teeth can be used as a substitute.

DIAMOND-TINED CULTIVATOR

The diamond-tined cultivator makes fast work of weeding the middles between rows. If you use it close to plants, be careful not to damage the roots by cultivating too deeply.

GARDEN RAKE

A good, iron garden rake serves many purposes — thinning seedlings, seedbed preparation, leveling, spreading or removing mulches, and more.

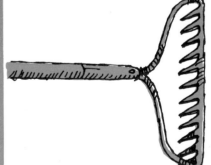

PUSH CULTIVATOR

If you don't have a tiller, you could use a push cultivator to keep the soil in a small garden loose and weed-free.

Roto-tilling for gardening pleasure

A good tiller is plow, disc, cultivator, sheet composting machine, and your best gardening friend — all in one.

If you are planning to have a large garden (quarter of an acre or more), or if you simply want to eliminate a lot of backbreaking work, you should consider buying some efficient power equipment. A rotary tiller is a very good investment. With this machine, you will be able to do many different things. You can do succession planting quickly and easily, you can raise green manures and cover crops, you can sheet-compost leaves, garbage, mulches, trimmings right in the garden, and you can turn your crop residues directly back into the soil. The machine that does this best is a rotary tiller with tines mounted in the rear. I own one that is made by the Troy-Bilt people in Troy, New York.

The Troy-Bilt makes working my acre-and-a-half garden a lot simpler, believe me! I use it to accomplish a lot more than just preparing my soil in the spring. As soon as the first crops have gone by, I use it to till them under and get ready to plant new ones. I cultivate with it constantly and work organic matter into the soil whenever I can. When my sweet corn has all been harvested, I can go right down the row and work the standing stalks into the ground with the tiller. By doing this kind of thing, I am giving something back to the land— taking nothing out of the garden except what my family and I eat.

There are times when I am tempted to say that a rear-end tiller is the only gardening implement you need. I have seen people grow gardens as large as three acres with very little effort, thanks to one of these machines. They are expensive, there is no doubt about that, but they are a much better investment than less costly front-end tillers. These are little more than cultivating machines; they cannot handle heavy jobs like cover cropping and turning under vegetation.

The rear-end tiller is a complete gardening machine that you will use almost constantly—before, during, and after the gardening season. It can be a sheet-composting machine. If you collect a lot of leaves—or any other kind of organic matter —you can spread them on the garden eight or ten inches thick and work them right into the garden soil with the help of the tiller. The machine's tines will not only chop and bury this layer of organic material; they will mix it with the soil particles, making it decompose that much faster.

Preparing the soil for planting.   Furrowing with a tiller.

You can accomplish a lot of garden tasks with a good roto-tiller — preparing the soil for planting, furrowing, cultivating, and tilling under green manures and vegetable plant remains.

Cultivating.

Tilling under green-manure crop.

Preparing the soil for planting

Delicate vegetable-plant roots need a well-prepared seedbed for quick, healthy growth.

The size of your garden, more than anything else, will determine how you prepare the soil. A salad garden or a small summer garden is apt to be a fork-and-shovel garden. In other words, it will be worked by hand—spaded, to be exact. You dig into the earth with a shovel or heavy spading fork, lift out a chunk of sod, and turn it bottom-side-up, so that the grass goes down in the bottom of the hole and the dirt is on top. Spading is hard work, but many people around the world still till their soil this way.

The plow that a farmer uses accomplishes the same thing as spading. It turns the soil upside down. If your garden is big enough, you might want to hire someone to bring in his tractor and plow for an hour or so. The other alternative is to use a rotary tiller. Rotary tillage mixes everything up—roots, grass, organic matter, and soil particles—and it leaves the soil fine and mellow.

If you are starting a new garden, it is best to turn over the soil in the fall and leave it to decompose and be broken up by frost during the winter. If you have to start out with new land in the spring, you can still have success, but it will take more work. If

Man has always known that a bountiful harvest — and frequently his very survival — depends on how well he has prepared his soil, no matter whether he is using a plow, a spade, a tractor, or a tiller.

you want to make a garden where there is heavy sod, till it thoroughly once, let it sit for a couple of days, then till again. The more you till and work the soil, the better job you will do of killing the roots of grasses and weeds. This is one of the most effective ways I know to prevent future weed problems.

You should begin preparing your soil as early as possible in the spring. But don't start work if the soil is still soggy from melting snow and ice or spring rains. When the ground is dry enough to work, you can pick up a clod and easily knock it apart with your thumb. Soil that is too wet won't break apart so easily.

Do not throw away hay, grass, or weeds that you have removed from the garden plot. If you do take off the sod, mow the grass, or pull up the weeds, save them in a compost pile. Once they have decomposed for a while, they will make excellent or-

ganic fertilizer. Rotted organic matter, as you probably know, is called humus— something gardeners are always trying to find or make. Humus should be put back into the soil by plowing, tilling, or working the earth by hand.

Preparing the soil is one of the most important steps in gardening. It should be loose and friable to a depth of at least four to eight inches. The organic matter should be chopped up fine, and there should be no large clods or clumps of earth. The soil, after all, is the foundation for your plants. Your house is only as good as the foundation it sits on, and your plants are only as good as the earth that supports their roots. It is vital that extra time and effort be spent in soil preparation. Once your plants are growing, there is very little you can do to improve the texture of the soil. This should encourage you to work a little harder each spring with your spade, rake, or tiller.

pH REACTION OF VARIOUS SOURCES OF FERTILIZERS

Content and Reaction of Fertilizers Supplying Nitrogen

Fertilizer	Per Cent Nitrogen	Reaction
Urea	46	Acidic
Ammonium nitrate	35	Acidic
Ammonium sulfate	21	Acidic
Calcium nitrate	17	Alkaline
Sodium nitrate	16	Alkaline
Ammonium phosphate	12	Acidic

Content and Reaction of Fertilizers Supplying Phosphoric Acid

Fertilizer	Per Cent Phosphoric Acid	Reaction
Phosphate rock	30-40	Alkaline
Superphosphate	14-20	Neutral
Ammonium phosphate	45-50	Acidic
Double Superphosphate	40-45	Acidic

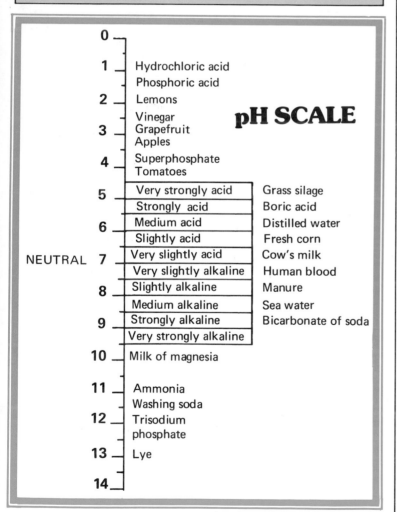

pH SCALE

The hydrogen ion concentration in a solution (such as soil solution) determines its acidity. The hydrogen ion concentration usually is expressed in terms of pH values. pH values lie between 1 and 14, and for soil solutions, mostly between 4 and 8. A pH value of 7 indicates a neutral reaction. Acidity increases as pH values lower from 7 and decreases (alkalinity increases) as pH values rise above 7. Because pH numbers are logarithmic, a soil solution with a pH of 5 is ten times as acid as one having a pH of 6 and one hundred times more acid than a soil solution of 7.

GETTING TO KNOW YOUR SOIL

All kinds of soil benefit from the addition of organic matter. This includes both sand and heavy clay. Light sandy soil consists of tiny round particles. They are able to hold little water. Organic matter will give this type of soil a more spongy texture which allows it to store up moisture and prevents water from draining away so easily. It will also make sandy soil less prone to erosion.

Something slightly different happens when you mix organic matter with clay. Clay particles are much much smaller than pieces of sand, and they are shaped differently. They are flat, like microscopic wafers. The flat surfaces of these tiny, plate-like particles stick together very easily. Bits of organic matter act like wedges which tend to separate the particles and hold them apart so that water and oxygen can pass through the soil. We have all made "Castles of London" from a deck of cards. We set the cards on edge and tried to build a structure using all of the cards in the deck. If one card was taken out, the whole "bridge" would collapse, and the cards would flatten out. Clay without organic matter is like a flattened deck of playing cards. The once-living material that you add tips up the flat "cards," and permits water and oxygen to enter, which in turn encourages all kinds of good things to happen.

MOST GARDENS NEED LIME

Lime is important if you are going to have a healthy, fertile garden. It is used to control the pH—the acidity or alkalinity—of the soil. Without a balanced soil pH somewhere near neutral, fertilizers will not work. Most vegetables require a pH which is somewhere in the neighborhood of 6.3 (slighty acidic) to 7 (completely neutral). This means that if soil tests show a pH above 6.3, you do not need to add lime to your garden. You can do a pH test yourself by buying a kit for as little as two or three dollars. The simple test will give you a fairly accurate reading.

If you use my old stand-by formula, I think you can avoid trouble with soil pH. Spread one twelve-quart bucket of lime on every 1,000 square feet of garden space. If you do this once every three or four years, your soil should stay pretty much within the 6.3-to-7 range. But continue to do a pH test every once in a while just to make sure everything is all right.

There are some plants that like acid soil. Peppers and blueberries are examples. They like soil with a pH from 5.8 to 6. Don't put too much lime on your potato patch either. They do better in slightly acid soil too.

Because we are burning more wood for heat in our homes during the energy crisis, many of us have plenty of wood ashes. These are a wonderful lime substitute, but they should be used sparingly. Spread at the same rate that you would spread lime. Either lime or ashes should be worked into the top three or four inches of soil sometime before planting.

Soil is probably the most marvelous living thing in all of creation; if it is healthy, it is filled with millions and millions of small organisms, all doing different beneficial things. Without these organisms, nothing on earth could survive. All you have to do is see that they are fed and keep the soil in a condition that allows them to breathe. If you do this much, you will have a magnificent garden. Lime, fertilize, and feed your soil with organic matter. The more you feed it, the more it will feed you!

Potatoes prefer a slightly acid soil, so lime your potato patch sparingly if at all. Don't use ashes either.

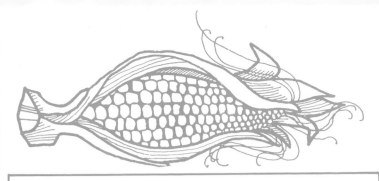

SIX VALUABLE WAYS LIME IMPROVES YOUR GARDEN

by Winston A. Way

1. Lime neutralizes soil acidity.

Soil acidity is due to an overabundance of hydrogen in the soil. Hydrogen in the soil is like a noxious weed, which takes up space but has no value. Hydrogen by itself is not used by growing plants.

Hydrogen, an ingredient common to all acids, is found in vinegar, sour milk, apples, and rainwater. Organic matter produces acids during the process of fermenting or rotting. Rainfall, after entering the soil and picking up hydrogen from acids near the surface, percolates down through the soil and deposits hydrogen on the soil particles below. Since there is only so much storage space within the soil, plant nutrients (which are alkaline) are dislodged and washed away by the drainage water, and hydrogen (which is acid) takes their place. This process, called leaching, makes soils not only more acid, but also less fertile and less productive.

2. Lime supplies calcium and magnesium.

Calcium and magnesium are important nutrients that plants need in large quantities. Both have important functions, and plant growth suffers if supplies are inadequate.

Extra magnesium is needed for potatoes, apples, and garden crops, particularly if manure of compost is not used. The more sandy the soil, the greater the need. If your soil has been properly limed with dolomite limestone, there should be little need for additional magnesium.

3. Lime reduces toxic elements.

Aluminum, manganese, iron, and a few other chemical elements have been shown to inhibit root growth. These toxic elements are most active in acid soil. Liming reduces this effect.

4. Lime makes fertilizers more efficient.

Money spent to fertilize acid soil is money thrown away. This is especially true of fertilizers containing phosphorus, for eighty to ninety percent of the phosphorus may become chemically locked up or fixed by active iron and aluminum. Once fixed, the phosphorus remains unavailable indefinitely — or until the soil pH is changed.

Lime makes nitrogen available by helping soil organisms to decompose organic matter. Commercial fertilizers containing nitrogen in the form of ammonia salts, urea, or protein must be converted to nitrates by nitrifying bacteria. These bacteria need suitable pH levels — around 7.0.

5. Lime aids nitrogen fixation.

Bacteria living on legume roots are able to convert nitrogen gas from the air into substances which furnish nitrogen for the host plant. As roots die or slough off, they rot and make nitrogen available for grasses. A good alfalfa cover crop can produce $60 to $75 worth of fertilizer per acre yearly. The specialized rhizobia bacteria responsible for this thrive best in neutral soil. Inoculation of legume seeds does not insure success; liming is also important. (Continued on next page)

6. Lime improves soil structure.

Calcium helps small clay particles to clump together into crumbs or granules, which are found in soils of good tilth. Once together, a gluing agent is needed to keep them that way, and again lime helps. Properly limed soils contain more humus. It is this sticky substance (nature's soil conditioner) that keeps the granules from falling apart. Numerous small roots, stimulated by lime, act like hairs in plaster to provide strength.

How We Determine Lime Needs

In theory, it's very simple — just measure the amount of hydrogen per acre. Sounds easy, doesn't it? The difficulty comes in measuring the amount of hydrogen per acre. Two methods currently being used are the pH and the lime-requirement test.

pH measures the intensity of hydrogen (acidity) in the soil water. It is expressed in numbers on a scale. The scale goes from 0 to 14, so 7 is considered neutral. A pH above 7 is alkaline; below 7 is acid.

Since pH is a measure of intensity, it might be compared with temperature, pressure, or voltage. None of these measures quantity. For instance, two water tanks might have a pressure of fifty-five pounds per square inch. But this pressure in no way indicates the amount of water, for one tank may hold a thousand gallons and the other only the gallon. pH is an easy method of determining the degree of acidity, but it does not tell how much lime is needed to neutralize it. It is useful only with other knowledge, such as nutrient-holding capacity.

A lime-requirement test gives a truer picture of lime needs than does a pH test, for it measures the acidity of soil particles as well as the acidity of soil water. It is designed to express the amount of ground limestone needed to correct total acidity in any soil, regardless of clay content, organic matter, or pH.

Your state college of agriculture has facilities for performing such a test, or consult your local extension agent.

Using Lime Efficiently

Soils limed for the first time, or soils that have not been limed for five to ten years, respond well to lime mixed in as deeply and completely as possible. Repeat applications of lime are necessary every four to five years to maintain the pH and to replace lime lost by leaching and crop removal.

Sandy soils in areas of high rainfall need reliming more often than heavy soils in areas with less rainfall. Sandy soils hold less lime and lose it faster so they require small, frequent applications.

How Much to Apply

A soil test is the best way to determine the need for liming. Periodic soil tests provide a useful record of progress in building soil fertility. They are also the only way to determine the correct amount to apply.

Soils high in organic matter and clay soils both require large amounts of lime to satisfy their needs, for they have a larger storage capacity. Large nutrient-storage capacity means more hydrogen (acid) to neutralize and more space to fill with calcium. So you can see that two soils of the same pH do not necessarily have the same lime requirement.

You can apply limestone any time of the year when the ground is not frozen. It doesn't burn the plants, it doesn't evaporate, but it may wash off frozen soil. Always try to mix lime with soil before planting.

If you need to change your soil's pH more than one unit, you should make the change gradually. You can add lime every garden season until you reach the desired level. Then remember to maintain that level by soil testing at least once every three years.

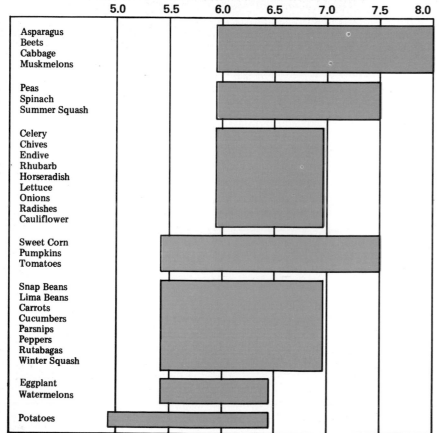

OPTIMUM pH RANGE FOR VEGETABLE CROPS

TO RAISE SOIL ONE UNIT OF pH

	Hydrated Lime	Dolomite	Ground Limestone
Light Soil 100 sq. ft.	1½ pounds	2 pounds	2½ pounds
Heavy Soil 100 sq. ft.	3½ pounds	5½ pounds	6 pounds

TO LOWER SOIL ONE UNIT OF pH

	Sulphur	Aluminum Sulphate	Iron Sulphate
Light Soil 100 sq. ft.	½ pound	2½ pounds	3 pounds
Heavy Soil 100 sq. ft.	2 pounds	6½ pounds	7½ pounds

Note: The amount of lime you use doesn't have to be as precisely measured as this chart suggests.

POTATOES AND LIME

"I was told once to put lime on my seed potatoes when they were cut to make them dry and nice to handle when planting. Then I read where both Irish and sweet potatoes need a slightly sour or acid soil, about 5 or 5.5 pH. Since reading that, I quit drying them with lime. I started fertilizing them with azalea fertilizer, which of course, is a fertilizer for acid-loving plants. I also use one pound of sixty-percent muriate of potash per twenty-five row-feet. That's good for root crops. It does a wonderful job for me. I planted twenty pounds of potatoes and dug at least 1,000 pounds." DR

44

What to feed hungry plants

Plants need good nutrition the same as growing children. Learning to recognize early warning signals of malnutrition will help you ward off garden diseases and will insure maximum production.

To side dress crops, make a shallow furrow down both sides of the row and about 6 inches from it. Encircle hills or mounds with a furrow. Place fertilizer in furrows, then cover it.

What is fertilizer and what does it do for the garden? In garden supply stores, you've probably seen bags of fertilizer with three numbers on them. They might read 5-10-5, 10-10-10 or 5-10-10. There might even be a fourth number, so that the bag reads 5-10-10-2. What does all this mumbo-jumbo mean?

There are three things—besides soil, water, air, and sunlight—that plants need to grow and produce fruit. We call these three things major nutrients. They are nitrogen (N), phosphorous (P), and potassium (K), which is sometimes called potash. The home gardener with average soil needs a fertilizer that contains at least these three elements. The numbers on the fertilizer bag describe the percentage of N, P, and K inside. So, 5-10-10 contains 5 percent nitrogen, 10 percent phosphorous, and 10 percent potassium.

Nitrogen (N) is essential to all growing vegetation. It gives a plant its healthy, dark green color. A plant that lacks nitrogen is apt to look yellow and sickly. When nitrogen is added to the soil, plants may suddenly put on tremendous growth. We have to be careful, though, not to provide too much nitrogen, because if a plant grows too fast—getting quite high and putting out a lot of leaves—the fruit will not be so good. What we are looking for is healthy growth, not overgrowth.

Phosphorous (P) is the major nutrient that helps plants grow strong roots. So obviously it is a must. It is especially important for root crops like carrots, beets, potatoes, and turnips.

45

Then there is potassium or potash (K). This element helps to condition the whole plant. It helps it grow and bear fruit and makes it resistant to disease.

AVOID TOO MUCH OF A GOOD THING

Every home gardener should be careful with commercial chemical fertilizers. Some of the worst gardening failures are the result of adding too much fertilizer. A man might say to himself, "That little handful of fertilizer I used helped me so much last year, I think I'll use two handfuls this year." There are two disastrous things that could happen as a result of this kind of thinking. The plants could be seriously burned and killed by the chemicals in the fertilizer, or the plants could grow large but produce little or no fruit at all.

I use a very simple formula for spreading chemical fertilizer. One day before planting, I take a twelve-quart pail, fill it with 5-10-10 or 10-10-10, and broadcast it over 1,000 square feet of garden space. The fertilizer should be mixed—either with a tiller or by hand—into the top two or three inches of soil. This should be all the fertilizer you need to get plants started. Spreading fertilizer over a broad area like this is safer than putting it down in rows.

Later on, I apply a side dressing—an additional bit of fertilizer that is put into the soil not far from the roots of the plants themselves. If you use this method, you can control the amount of fertilizer that is going into your garden and still have a chance to give individual crops a boost as they need it.

It is probably safe to say that all garden plants benefit from a side dressing just as they begin to blossom. The fertilizer will help the vegetable or fruit to fill out. Vegetables will sometimes let you know when it is time for that extra bit of fertilizer. The cucumber, for example, will stand up and start to blossom just before it lays its vines down along the ground. This brief standing period gives you a chance to reach within three or four inches of the stem so you can get fertilizer right to the roots. Some types of squash will do the same thing.

There is one kind of fertilizer that can be put right in the rows. This is called "super-phosphate" (0-20-0). Superphosphate, or triple phosphate, is an incomplete fertilizer

Cooperative Extension Service of the University of South Dakota

RECOMMENDED TIMES FOR SIDEDRESSING VEGETABLES

CROP	TIME OF APPLICATION
Asparagus	Before growth starts in spring.
Beans	After heavy blossom and set of pods.
Beets	Additional nitrogen might reduce yield or lower quality.
Broccoli	3 weeks after transplanting.
Cabbage	3 weeks after transplanting.
Cauliflower	3 weeks after transplanting.
Carrots	Additional nitrogen might reduce yield or lower quality.
Cucumbers	Apply 1 week after blossoming begins and same amount 3 weeks later.
Eggplant	After first fruit set.
Kale	When plants are about one-third grown.
Lettuce	Additional nitrogen might reduce yield or lower quality.
Muskmelon	Apply 1 week after blossoming begins and same amount 3 weeks later.
Onions	1 to 2 weeks after bulb formation starts.
Parsnips	Additional nitrogen might reduce yield or lower quality.
Peas	After heavy bloom and set of pods.
Peppers	After first fruit set.
Potato	After tuber formation starts (bloom stage).
Spinach	When plants are about one-third grown.
Squash	Additional nitrogen might reduce yield or lower quality.
Tomatoes	Apply 1 to 2 weeks before first picking and same amount after 2 weeks of first picking.
Turnips	When plants are about one-third grown.
Watermelon	Additional nitrogen might reduce yield or lower quality.

Approximate Composition of Fertilizer Materials

Material	Nitrogen (N)	Phosphoric acid (P$_2$O$_5$)	Potash (K$_2$O)
		percent	
Chemical			
Ureaform	30.0–40.0	...	...
Ammonium nitrate	33.5	...	...
Ammonium sulfate	20.5	...	...
Nitrate of soda	16.0	...	...
Urea	42.0–46.0	...	...
Superphosphate	...	16.0–20.0	...
Muriate of potash	...	...	48.0–62.0
Triple superphosphate	...	46.0	...

MEASURING TABLE FOR FERTILIZER

1 pint or 2 cupfuls weigh approximately

Superphosphate	1 pound
Muriate of Potash	1 pound
Limestone	1¼ pounds
Mixed Fertilizer (5-10-5, etc.)	1 pound
Cottonseed Meal	¾ pound
Nitrate of Soda	1¼ pounds
Ammonium Nitrate	¾ pound
Sulphate of Ammonia	¾ pound

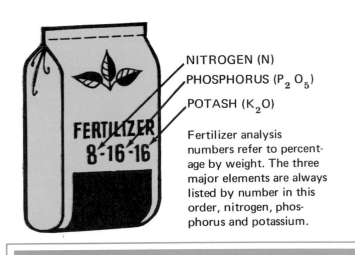

NITROGEN (N)

PHOSPHORUS (P_2O_5)

POTASH (K_2O)

Fertilizer analysis numbers refer to percentage by weight. The three major elements are always listed by number in this order, nitrogen, phosphorus and potassium.

PHOSPHATE IN OLD GARDENS

If a plot has been farmed or gardened for many years, chances are the soil has a reserve supply of phosphate, which is long-lasting in the soil. This means you can use a fertilizer that is high in nitrogen and potash and save money by not adding more phosphate than is needed. But when planting it is good to use a complete, balanced fertilizer to insure the development of a good root system. The plant needs the roots in order to pick up the reserve phosphate. HP

FERTILIZING RYE

It isn't necessary to broadcast fertilizer when planting rye; it will pick up the nutrients remaining in the soil from the previous garden crops.

LIME

Lime does not move from the surface down through the soil as most nutrients do. For this reason, lime should be thoroughly mixed with the soil. UP

BEST SOIL FOR CORN

If you have a choice of soil types, you'd do well to reserve your heaviest soil for corn. Corn likes soil with more clay than sand.

It's best to change the growing location of most vegetables from season to season. This is known as crop rotation. With corn, rotation is not important. Corn produces a lot of organic matter to till or plow under, so it will actually improve the soil from year to year.

Chop the stalks up and work them into the ground as soon as you're through harvesting. Then plant a cover crop (like rye) to be plowed under in the spring. With this kind of program, you can grow corn on the same land year after year. HP

SANDY SOIL

Sandy soil is especially good for garden crops like melons and tomatoes. Surprising as it may seem, sandy soil holds moisture better than heavy soils. The sandy soils and excellent climate along the Chesapeake Bay combine to make it one of the best areas in the nation for truck farming. These conditions are, of course, superb for the home gardener too. HL

because it contains only one of the three major nutrients—phosphorous. Don't be afraid to use superphosphate with root crops if a soil test shows that your garden can use it. You can put it right in a furrow and plant seeds very near it without worrying about the seeds getting burned.

Commercial fertilizers can be combined with or used along with compost, manure, and other kinds of organic matter. In fact, this combination is a very good idea if the quality of your soil is poor. Organic matter can add many nutrients on its own, and by using it, you can reduce the need for chemical fertilizer.

I almost forgot about the fourth number that sometimes appears on a fertilizer package, as in 10-10-10-2 or 5-10-5-1½. The 2 and the 1½ refer to the content of magnesium—one of the sixteen or so minor nutrients that plants also need. Here in the North, our soil is often quite low in magnesium, so a lot of our fertilizers have a high-enough percentage of magnesium to require this last number.

In a 100-pound bag of 5-10-10, by the way, there are five pounds of nitrogen, 10 pounds of phosphorous, and 10 pounds of potassium. All the rest is filler. In other words, if you buy a bag that reads 5-10-10, you are getting twenty-five pounds of fertilizer and seventy-five pounds of soil or some other kind of bulky matter.

NEW LIFE FOR OLD GARDENS

As people get more and more interested in gardening these days, old, forgotten garden plots are being put to use again. A simple rule of thumb seems to work well for a new garden or for one which has lain fallow for four or five years. First, a twelve-quart bucket of lime should be spread over the area and worked into the top four or five inches of soil. Next, a complete fertilizer, such as 5-10-10, should be applied at a rate of one twelve-quart bucket for every 1,000 square feet of garden space. (This is an area measuring twenty-five feet by forty feet.) The fertilizer should be mixed into the top two or three inches of soil. The best time to add fertilizer is a day or two before you are going to plant. If you fertilize too early, much of the nitrogen will be lost. It will drift off into the atmosphere as nitrogen gas if it is not used right away.

MAGNESIUM IN THE SOIL

"I've grown beans on the same land for thirty years. But one year my beans began to die. I had a complete soil test done and found I needed the trace element magnesium. I added this element by applying Epsom salts, and the problem was corrected immediately. The state university soil test, which I use every year, doesn't break the soil needs down far enough to recognize the lack of these trace elements." JLG

PLANT FOOD ELEMENTS

In 1840 the soil scientist Leibig stated his law of the minimum which goes as follows: "Crop yields are determined by the quality of the element that is present in the least abundance."

This means that a plant will not grow properly if the soil is low in one particular element. No matter how much nitrogen you might pour on, if the soil is deficient in magnesium, it still won't show a rich natural green color.

It can be illustrated by this picture of a barrel. If one stave of the barrel is short, the water in the barrel can't rise any higher than the shortest stave.

This is especially important to recognize on some soils. The soil might be rich in all the major food elements, but a deficiency in a minor trace element will stunt the plants. You can guess and add all kinds of fertilizers, but it won't do any good until the soil is brought into balance with the missing plant food element.

This is one important value of organic and natural plant foods. They usually supply a number of trace elements along with the major nutrients nitrogen, phosphorous and potash.

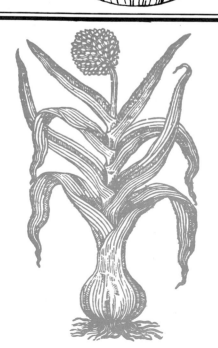

TRACE ELEMENTS

Chemical analysis shows that a plant may contain as many as 40 elements; however, only 15 are necessary to its normal functioning. Three elements, carbon, oxygen, and hydrogen, account for about 90 percent of the dry weight of an average plant. Nitrogen, phosphate, and potash are the primary plant foods found in all complete commercial fertilizers. Though they occur in much smaller quantities than the three essential elements (nitrogen is only 1.5 percent of total dry plant weight), the primary plant foods have tremendous effect on growth and general health. The secondary plant foods (magnesium, manganese, copper, zinc, iron, sulfur, calcium, and molybdenum) occur in even more minute quantities, but they too are very important. For example, a lack of iron, which acts as a catalyst in the enzyme system, causes leaves to turn yellow except for the veins, which stay green. For symptoms of other trace-element deficiencies, see the chart on the facing page. If you suspect your soil of being deficient in elements which don't show up on ordinary soil tests, you might want to send a sample to one of the laboratories listed below.

Prescription Soil Analysis
P.O. Box 80631
Lincoln, Nebraska

Soil and Plant Laboratory, Inc.
P.O. Box 153
Santa Clara, California 95052

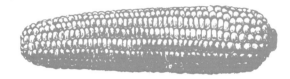

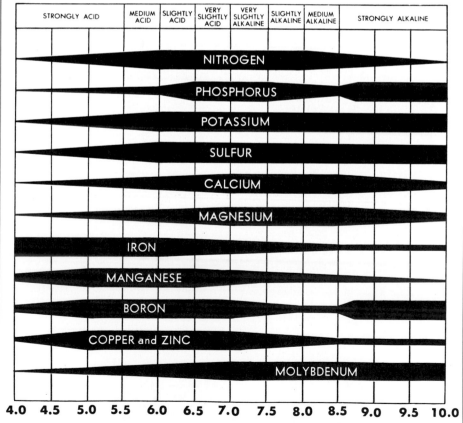

HOW SOIL pH AFFECTS AVAILABILITY OF PLANT NUTRIENTS

| STRONGLY ACID | | | MEDIUM ACID | SLIGHTLY ACID | VERY SLIGHTLY ACID | VERY SLIGHTLY ALKALINE | SLIGHTLY ALKALINE | MEDIUM ALKALINE | STRONGLY ALKALINE | |

NITROGEN
PHOSPHORUS
POTASSIUM
SULFUR
CALCIUM
MAGNESIUM
IRON
MANGANESE
BORON
COPPER and ZINC
MOLYBDENUM

4.0 4.5 5.0 5.5 6.0 6.5 7.0 7.5 8.0 8.5 9.0 9.5 10.0

Availability of above nutrients to plants decreases as width of bar decreases. Soil pH is a key factor in regulating nutrient supply.

KNOW YOUR PLANT FOOD ELEMENTS

PRIMARY PLANT FOOD ELEMENTS

ELEMENT	SYMBOL	FUNCTION IN PLANT	DEFICIENCY SYMPTOMS	EXCESS SYMPTOMS	SOURCES
Nitrogen	N	Gives dark green color to plant. Increases growth of leaf and stem. Influences crispness and quality of leaf crops. Stimulates rapid early growth.	Light green to yellow leaves. Stunted growth.	Dark green. excessive growth. Retarded maturity. Loss of buds or fruit.	Urea Ammonia Nitrates
Phosphorus	P	Stimulates early formation and growth of roots. Gives plants a rapid and vigorous start. Is important in formation of seed. Gives hardiness to fall-seeded grasses and grains.	Red or purple leaves. Cell division retardation.	Possible tie up of other essential elements.	Superphosphate Rock phosphate
Potash	K	Increases vigor of plants and resistance to disease. Stimulates production of strong, stiff stalks. Promotes production of sugar, starches, oils. Increases plumpness of grains and seed. Improves quality of crop yield.	Reduced vigor. Susceptibility to diseases. Thin skin and small fruit.	Coarse, poor colored fruit. Reduced absorption of Mg and Ca.	Muriate or Sulphate of Potash

SECONDARY PLANT FOOD ELEMENTS

ELEMENT	SYMBOL	FUNCTION IN PLANT	DEFICIENCY SYMPTOMS	EXCESS SYMPTOMS	SOURCES
Magnesium	Mg	Aids photasynthesis. Key element in chlorophyl.	Loss of yield. Chlorosis of old leaves.	Reduced absorption of Ca and K.	Magnesium Sulphate (Epsom Salts) Dolomite is 1/3 Mg.
Manganese	Mn	In enzyme system.	Mottled chlorosis of the leaves. Stunted growth.	Small dead areas in the leaves with yellow borders around them.	Manganese Sulphate (Tecmangam)
Copper	Cu	Enzyme activator.	Multiple budding. Gum pockets.	Prevents the uptake of iron. Causes stunting of roots.	Copper Sulphate Neutral Copper

MINOR (OR MICRO) ELEMENTS

ELEMENT	SYMBOL	FUNCTION IN PLANT	DEFICIENCY SYMPTOMS	EXCESS SYMPTOMS	SOURCES
Zinc	Zn	Aids in cell division. In enzymes and auxins.	Small, thin, yellow leaves. Low yields.	None known.	Zinc Sulphate
Iron	Fe	A catalyst. In the enzyme system. Hemoglobin in legumes.	Yellowing of leaves, the veins remaining green.	None known.	Iron Sulphate (Copperas) Chelated Iron
Sulphur	S	Helps to build proteins.	Looks like Nitrogen deficiency.	Sulphur burn from too low pH.	Sulphur Superphosphate
Calcium	Ca	Part of cell walls. Part of enzymes.	Stops growing point of plants.	Reduces the intake of K and Mg.	Lime Basic Slag Gypsum
Molybdenum	Mo	Helps in the utilization of N.	Symptoms in plants vary greatly.	Poisonous to livestock.	Sodium Molybdate
Boron	B	Affects absorption of other elements. Affects germination of pollen tube.	Small leaves. Heart rot and corkiness. Multiple buds.	Leaves turn yellowish red.	Borax

ELEMENTS FROM AIR AND WATER

ELEMENT	SYMBOL	FUNCTION IN PLANT	DEFICIENCY SYMPTOMS	EXCESS SYMPTOMS	SOURCES
Carbon	C	Keystone of all organic substances.	None known.	None known.	Air (Carbon Dioxide)
Oxygen	O	Respiration.	White areas at leaf veins. High Nitrates.	None known.	Air and Water
Hydrogen	H	Necessary in all plant functions.	Wilting.	Drowning.	Water

These charts will help you to adapt fertilizer recommendations for large acreage to a small garden.

For small amounts of fertilizer it is easier to measure by volume than by weight. To convert charts that call for pounds you can figure one pound of common garden fertilizer is equivalent to 2 cupfuls.

Rates of Application of Different Fertilizer Formulas as Recommended for 1,000 Square Feet, for 10 Feet of Row, or for Individual Plants

Fertilizer formula	1,000 sq. ft.	10 ft. row	Single plant
5-10-5	40 lbs.	2 cups	3 Tbsp.
8-32-16	25 lbs.	1½ cups	2 Tbsp.
10-6-4	20 lbs.	1 cup	1½ Tbsp.
12-12-12	17 lbs.	1 cup	1½ Tbsp.

Converting Rate of Fertilizer Application from Pounds Broadcast per Acre to Pounds per Square Feet

Area in Square Feet	Fertilizer to apply, where amount to be applied per acre is:		
	100 lbs.	400 lbs.	800 lbs.
	pounds	pounds	pounds
100	.25	1	2
500	1.25	5	10
1,000	2.50	10	20
1,500	3.75	15	30
2,000	5.00	20	40

Converting Rate of Fertilizer Application from Pounds Broadcast Per Acre to Pounds Per Row

Distance Between Rows in Feet	Row Length in Feet	Fertilizer to apply, where amount to be applied per acre is:		
		100 lbs.	400 lbs.	800 lbs.
feet	feet	pounds	pounds	pounds
2	50	0.25	1.0	2.0
2	100	0.50	2.0	4.0
2½	50	0.30	1.2	2.4
2½	100	0.60	2.4	4.8
3	50	0.35	1.4	2.8
3	100	0.70	2.8	5.6

ORGANIC SOIL BUILDING

Donald Roberts of Kilmarnock, Virginia, hauls in crab shells when they are available from commercial watermen and spreads them on his garden. The shells contain lime and many trace minerals that would be expensive to buy in a bag. He spreads anything on his garden that rots — leaves, straw, manure, all his garbage and grass clippings.

Under his corn this year, he put twenty bushels of frozen fish that had gone bad in a freezing locker. He opened up a furrow, spread the fish down the row, covered it over and planted his corn. He needed very little commercial fertilizer and had a bumper productive crop.

At planting time, Mr. Roberts opens up a double row with his plow, fills the furrow with plenty of cow manure and throws the dirt back over it. That's what he plants his tomatoes, cucumbers, squash, and eggplant on. They take off fast and don't know when to quit growing.

SOME ORGANIC SUBSTITUTES FOR CHEMICAL FERTILIZERS

Most commercial fertilizers are made with chemicals. But there are other kinds of fertilizer, and they do not come from a garden-supply store in a bag. I mean natural, organic fertilizers. They are easy to find and are usually cheap, sometimes free. I am talking about manures, compost, soybean and cottonseed meal, seaweed, decomposed hay and straw, crop residues, leaves, and grass clippings. As I have said before, when you mulch with these materials, you are adding fertilizer to your garden at the same time.

Anyone knows that there are as many kinds of manure as there are animals. Cow manure is one of the most common, but horse manure, rabbit manure, chicken manure, duck manure, sheep and goat manure are sometimes available too. Some manures are very strong. Cow manure, for instance, should be aged before it is put on the garden. It should be piled up outside for three to six months. If you can't wait this long, spread fresh manure over the garden a couple of weeks before planting, and then mix it into the top two or three inches of soil very, very thoroughly—either with a tiller or with a plow and harrow. It's best not to use fresh manure in a row or as a side dressing. If you do, you are likely to burn your seeds or injure your plants. Fresh manure has a very high percentage of water, so a bushel of aged and dried manure contains more organic matter and more nutrients than a bushel of fresh.

Cow manure is available to more people than any other kind. You can use quite a bit of it without worrying about over-fertilizing.

I like to put aged cow manure in the bottom of a furrow and plant seeds on top of it. The only drawback is that cow manure contains some weed seeds. Whenever you broadcast it over the entire garden, you are making work for yourself by planting some extra weeds. But I have found that putting it in furrows virtually eliminates this problem, possibily because the weed seeds are too deep to germinate successfully.

Chicken manure is very high in nitrogen because chickens have a high-protein diet. Use it very sparingly. If you use too much, it will either burn your plants or make them grow huge tops with few good vegetables. Chicken manure from poultry farms is usually mixed with sawdust or wood chips, and this dilutes the potency of the manure. Even so, the safest way to use it is to sprinkle it lightly over the soil and work it in.

There is no danger of burning your plants when you till old hay, grass, leaves, and similar organic substances into the soil. In fact, it is impossible to use too much of these things. They will use up some nitrogen in the soil for a while as they continue to decay, but this debt will be repaid as soon as the microorganisms have had a chance to do their work.

Compost is a wonderful fertilizer, although it varies in strength depending on the ingredients put into it. Most plants will thrive in compost. It may be all the fertilizer they need.

A garden which has been fertilized only with manures, compost, or organic matter will probably show a lack of phosphorous before too long. A light application of rock phosphate, an organic fertilizer, or a sprinkling of superphosphate, a chemical fertilizer, will be helpful from time to time. On the other hand, if you are careful about making compost from a wide range of different things, you may be producing a more or less complete fertilizer capable of fulfilling all your plants' needs.

It all boils down to this: adding natural fertilizers makes your soil healthy. If your soil is healthy, your plants are going to be healthy too. It is just that simple. It is a fact that diseases and insects are less likely to attack strong, healthy plants than weak, spindly ones. If you use commercial fertilizers year after year without putting in any organic matter, you are making a serious mistake. You are sapping the soil and are leaving yourself open to all sorts of trouble. You are providing the immediate chemical nutrients but not doing anything for the texture and structure of your soil or providing a favorable environment for the important soil organisms.

APPROXIMATE COMPOSITION OF NATURAL FERTILIZER MATERIALS

Material	Nitrogen (N)	Phosphoric acid (P)	Potash (K)
BULKY ORGANIC MATERIALS			
Alfalfa hay	2.5	.5	2.0
Bean straw	1.2	.3	1.2
Grain straw	.6	.2	1.0
Olive pomaces	1.2	.8	.5
Peanut hulls	1.5	—	.8
Peat	2.3	.4	.8
Sawdust	.2	—	.2
Seaweed (kelp)	.6	—	1.3
Timothy hay	1.0	.2	1.5
Winery pomaces	1.5	1.5	.8
MANURES			
Bat guano	10.0	4.5	2.0
Cow manure, dried	1.3	.9	.8
Cow manure, fresh	.5	.2	.5
Hen manure, dried, with litter	2.8	2.8	1.5
Hen manure, fresh	1.1	0.9	.5
Horse manure, fresh	.6	.3	.5
Pig, fresh	.6	.5	.4
Sheep manure, dried	1.4	1.0	3.0
Sheep manure, fresh	.9	.5	.8
ROCK POWDERS			
Basic slag	—	8.0—17.0	—
Greensand (Glauconite)	—	1.4	4.0—9.5
Hybro-tite	—	.002	—
Rock phosphate (apatite)	—	38.0—40.0	4.5
VEGETATIVE & ANIMAL CONCENTRATES			
Bonemeal, steamed	2.0	22.0	—
Castor pomace	6.0	1.9	.5
Cocoa shell meal	2.5	1.5	2.5
Cottonseed meal	6.0	3.0	1.0
Dried blood meal	13.0	1.5	.8
Fish meal	10.0	6.0	—
Fish scrap	5.0	3.0	—
Garbage tankage	1.5	2.0	.7
Hoof & horn meal	12.0	2.0	—
Sewerage sludge	2.0	1.4	.8
Sewerage sludge, activated	6.0	3.0	.1
Soybean meal	7.0	1.2	1.5
Tankage, animal	9.0	6.0	—
Tankage, processed	7.0	1.0	.1
Tobacco dust and stems	1.5	.5	5.0
Wood ashes	—	1.8	5.0

WINTER LETTUCE

"I plant lettuce along with the turnip greens about the end of September. The cold hardy turnip tops protect the more tender lettuce from the frost. Our winters are mild enough that I have small lettuce plants among the turnips to transplant in early spring." DR

Finally — it's time to plant!

The sowing of seed is one of the most fulfilling of life's pleasures. The warm spring sun on your back and the promise of future harvest brings true satisfaction.

Planting time is one of the most exciting and critical periods of the gardening season. Your crop will be abundant only if you plant carefully.

First, let's talk about setting out plants you've started early in your hotbed or bought at a garden center.

Taking a plant out of its container and placing it in the ground gives it a terrible shock. The best time to do this is in the late afternoon or evening if the day is sunny. A cloudy day would be better still.

Soak the flats thoroughly before you remove the plants. The soil should be pure mud. The muddier the potting soil, the less the roots will be exposed to the air as they are removed from the containers. Try to have your rows laid out, your furrows or holes dug, and your fertilizer applied, so that everything is ready before the actual transplanting takes place. Use your fingers or a spoon to take a plant out of its container. Try to keep as much mud around the roots as you can. Set the plant in the prepared furrow or hole immediately, cover the roots with soil, and firm it down thoroughly. Don't be afraid to water recently transplanted vegetables generously. It is impossible to overwater when you are moving plants from pots to garden soil.

New transplants must be protected from wind and frost. If you use "hot caps," you can steal some time from Mother Nature by transplanting a week or two before the average date of the last killing frost.

Be sure to check all purchased plants for bugs. Any plants raised in a greenhouse may have aphids, spiders, or white flies on

IDEAS FOR SETTING OUT PLANTS EARLY

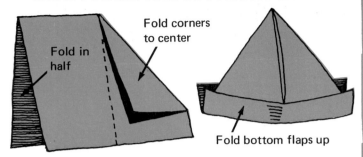

Fold in half

Fold corners to center

Fold bottom flaps up

PUT A "SOLDIER'S HAT" OVER PLANTS FOR FROST PROTECTION

Remember as a kid making a play soldier's hat to march around in? Now you can put such hats to good use. Take a newspaper and fold it in half. Take the two upper corners and fold them so that they meet at exact center. Now fold the bottom flaps up, one on each side. Open hat out and place over young plants when frost threatens, hold down with small stones or dirt at each end.

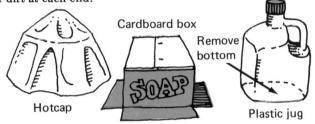

Cardboard box

Remove bottom

Hotcap

SOAP

Plastic jug

Hotcaps are wax-paper cones placed over individual plants to protect them from frost and wind. Hotcaps cost a dime apiece or less, depending on the quantity bought.

You can save money by using paper "soldier's hats," old boxes, fruit baskets, or plastic jugs with the bottoms cut out instead of hotcaps.

MINI-GREENHOUSES

This plastic, three-piece container is a miniature greenhouse for setting out tomatoes at least two weeks earlier than you can under a hotcap. It has a plastic dome with a shower-cap-like cover that goes over the top. It will take temperatures down to about 10° F.

As the plant grows, you take off the dome, leaving the plastic ring as a support for the vines. ST

See page 117 for some good ideas on getting an early crop of corn.

SPACING ROWS FAR APART

Planting long vine crops such as watermelons and pumpkins closer than recommended will make working them easier. Space them two to three feet apart in the row instead of the normal six to eight feet. But make the rows fifteen to twenty feet apart to give the vines plenty of room to spread out.

You can plant a fast-maturing crop like radishes or lettuce between the rows, harvest them, and till the remains before the vines reach the middles. HP

them. These insects can do a lot of damage, so you will want to dust the plants with rotenone or some other insecticide before setting them out in the garden.

In the spring, there is always the danger of cutworms—small creatures that chew off plant stems flush with the top of the ground. Protecting your young plants against them is not much of a problem. Tear newspaper into pieces about the size of old-fashioned cigarette papers, two inches by three inches. Wrap one of these around each plant stem so that about half the paper shows above the soil and half is below. The paper will last long enough to keep cutworms away during the critical early growing period. By the time the plant is strong enough to stand on its own, the newspaper collar will have rotted away.

RULES TO REMEMBER AT PLANTING TIME

1. Hardy vegetables can stand some shade and "wet feet" because they are cool-weather crops.
2. Root crops can tolerate some shade and damp, but not very wet, feet. The same is true of cabbage, broccoli, Brussels sprouts, and cauliflower.
3. Vine crops, like cucumbers, melons, and squash, as well as tomatoes, peppers, corn, eggplant, and beans all require a lot of sunshine and dry feet.

WIDE ROW PLANTING

There are two ways to plant—in single rows or in wide rows. Single-row planting means that you make an indentation in the soil—a furrow or a small trench—and plant your seeds in a single line. If you plant in wide rows, on the other hand, you would take two lengths of string and mark off a row which is about ten inches wide, or about the width of a normal steel rake. I use this width because I don't like to rake the whole garden; I rake only where I am going to plant—that is, the area between the two strings. I find that if I rake the whole garden area, I tread the soil down with my feet too much, making it very hard and compact. Packed-down soil does not make a good seedbed. I make no indentations at all between the strings. I simply

SINGLE-ROW PLANTING

1 RAKE SMOOTH

Rake over the area to be planted. A smooth seedbed is particularly important with very fine seeds.

2 STAKE AND MAKE ROW

Drive a stake at each end of the row and stretch a string between them. To make a furrow, lay your hoe directly under the string and step on it. Repeat down the length of the row.

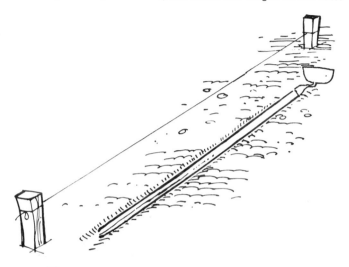

3 DROP SEED

Drop seed into the row, spacing them correctly. (See chart on pages 150 and 151.)

4 COVER WITH SOIL

Firm the soil by walking down the row or by tamping with a hoe or a rake.

Wide-row planting

1 STAKE WITH STRING

Use two lengths of string and four stakes to mark off an area about ten inches wide, or the width of a normal steel rake.

level and smooth the soil with my rake. It always helps to work from the same side of a row. This way the soil between rows stays looser.

Now I am ready to plant. Take lettuce, for example. I broadcast the seed over the area between the strings. You should do this in much the same way that you would seed a lawn; just remember to spread the seed somewhat thinner than grass seed.

After I have planted lettuce seed, I sprinkle a few radish seeds in the same row. This serves two purposes: (1) The radishes will come up in three or four days —much earlier than the lettuce. They will mark the rows and can be harvested long before the lettuce is ready. (2) When the radishes are pulled, the row will automatically be thinned and cultivated. Each

time a radish is pulled out, a little cavity is left in the soil. The roots of the other plants can then grow into the loose soil around the cavity.

If you have heavy clay soil and want to raise carrots, beets, or other root crops, try planting icicle radishes along with them. I don't harvest them to eat; I wait until they get about twice as big as my thumb and then pull them. Because they are long, they leave a deep cavity in the soil. As the beets and carrots expand, they can fill up the holes left by the radishes.

Radishes can be planted with many crops. Just this morning before I came to work, I pulled radishes out of my spinach. I noticed that many of the radish leaves had been eaten by insects, but the spinach leaves had hardly been touched. It isn't that

2 RAKE SMOOTH

Rake over the area between the strings until it is smooth. Make no indentations or furrows.

3 BROADCAST SEED

Broadcast seed over the raked area as if you were seeding a lawn; remember to plant vegetable seeds a little thinner than grass seed.

radishes keep bugs away from spinach. Bugs just like radishes better.

DON'T LET PLANTS GET TOO CLOSE FOR COMFORT

Vegetable plants that grow too close together will be stunted and sickly. They need elbow room. It is hard to pull up little plants that are growing well, but it needs to be done. Spacing plants properly by removing others is called thinning. How do we thin? I use an iron rake with stiff teeth to do my first thinning. I drag it slowly across the wide row, taking out a good share of the plants. I try to do this when the plants are anywhere from half an inch to an inch high. I do this first thinning in both single-row and wide-row plantings.

You don't have to thin peas or beans; the

4 COVER SEED

After sowing fine seeds of vegetables such as lettuce, chard, and beets walk over the seeded plot, then smooth down the spaces between your tracks with the back of a rake. Firm the soil with a hoe. Instead of walking fine seeds into the soil, you can use a regular iron rake to tamp down the seeded area. Again, take a hoe and firm down the soil surface.

If you're planting larger seeds such as peas or lima beans in wide rows, you can either walk on them or push them in with a rake. Either way, you'll have to rake extra soil from the sides of the row over the seeds. Finally, firm it with a broad hoe. When planting large areas of peas and beans for cover crops, till the soil, sow the seeds, and then run a roto-tiller over the area. Don't till too deeply. Finally, firm the soil, either by walking on it or with a hoe or a roller. If you do plant with a roto-tiller, sow your seeds a little thicker; some of them won't get deep enough to germinate.

5 THIN WITH A RAKE

Use an iron rake with stiff teeth to thin seedlings when they are ½ to 1 inch tall. Drag the rake slowly over the row, taking out quite a few plants. Large-seeded plants probably won't need thinning.

seeds are larger, so it is fairly easy to control how close you plant them. Smaller, finer seeds are harder to space because they roll off your hand so fast as you plant them.

The second thinning, of course, is the pulling of the radishes. The third thinning takes place when you start harvesting. You can make the first fresh salad of the season with thinnings from your lettuce patch. Thin by pulling the biggest, most edible plants. The smaller ones will grow to replace the ones you remove. Keep doing this until the spacing is about right.

You can do the same thing with carrots. When they are about the size of your little finger, they make good eating. This is when they are really succulent. It is easy to select the largest ones; they are almost always the ones with the largest, greenest leaves.

VEGETABLES THAT CAN BE GROWN IN WIDE ROWS

Here is a list of crops that I like to plant in wide rows: carrots; beets; lettuce; dill; chard, spinach, collards, and all other greens; onions, both from seed and from sets; Chinese cabbage; rutabagas; turnips; beans; and especially peas.

CARROTS AND BEETS—These root crops are slow in coming up. Icicle radishes mark rows early and do a good job of cultivating when they are pulled.

ONION SETS—These are easy to plant. Grip each bulb by the top (the pointed end) and push it into the soil. In a row that is ten inches wide, you can plant four or five onion sets side by side, move down the row two or three inches, plant another four or five, and so on. There is no need to make any sort of trench in the soil. Pushing the bulbs in with your fingers works fine.

LETTUCE—A good rule of thumb for planting any seed is that its depth be three or four times the diameter of the seed itself. So lettuce seed should be covered with a very small amount of soil. Then gently tamp down the seedbed so the seeds will have good contact with the soil. This also shuts out air and protects tender sprouts from drying out.

PEAS—The only way I know to get a decent crop of peas is to plant them in a wide row. A rake-width row may not be broad enough. In fact, I have often used rows four feet wide. I simply broadcast the seed in wide bands and then walk on the soil. Next, I turn the rake upside down and drag it back and forth over my footprints. Occasionally, I reach over to the side and pull a little extra dirt over onto the seeds. It doesn't take much; walking on the seeds usually pushes them far enough into the soil. This is especially true if the soil has been carefully prepared for planting and has what we call good "tilth."

BEANS—You can grow a tremendous crop of snap beans in a wide row. I usually plant them in rows that are ten inches wide. I plant three or four beans across the row, move down the row to plant another two or three, and so on. The main advantage to this method is that you can produce four, five, even six times as many beans as in a single row because you don't have so much

This photograph vividly illustrates the difference in yield between wide and and single rows

Dick Raymond has invented a tool which he calls an in-row weeder. As you can see, it does a fine job of keeping wide rows weed-free.

walk area, which is actually wasted growing space. I sometimes plant beans in rows as wide as three or four feet.

Wide-row planting has an advantage when you are weeding, too. When you weed a single row, you can reach only about three feet of row from one position. If you have a three-foot-wide row, which is equivalent to five or six single rows, you can figure that each time you weed three feet down the row, you are weeding a space which is equivalent to nine to fifteen feet of single row! The same proves true at har-

Using wide rows, you can grow 4 to 7 times more produce than you can grow in single rows in the same space.

If you never get enough garden-fresh peas, try growing them in wide rows as Dick Raymond does.

vest time. Each time you stoop down beside the wide row, you can reach a three-foot area. But in that three-foot area, you can probably pick a peck of produce without having to move!

Wide-row planting really works. The average gardener, using the single-row method, might plant a twenty-foot row of lettuce. If he plants a row ten inches wide instead, he can plant enough in twenty feet to equal 100 feet the old way. A family of four needs only about six feet of lettuce planted in a wide row. Try putting in three feet of one variety and three feet of another. You won't be able to keep ahead of it all! In the rest of the row, you might plant beets, chard, or carrots.

There is still another advantage. We know that weeds don't grow well on shaded ground. When you plant crops in wide rows, you automatically shade the ground. Very few weeds, if any, will do well within the rows—with the exception of a few grasses which grow tall and are easy to pull. Most weeds will be smothered out. This is what I call a shade mulch because the leaves of the plants themselves shade the soil. This saves many hours of backbreaking weeding.

Experiment with wide rows this year. You can grow four to seven times more produce than you can grow in single rows using the same amount of space. It makes thinning, weeding, and harvesting simpler because the whole area is laid out right in front of you—within easy reach.

Cultivation and keeping out weeds

One of the most common causes of garden failure is letting the weeds and grass get a head start. Cultivation at the right time is a basic rule of success.

Cultivation is important! Most gardening books don't stress this enough. Cultivating lets oxygen get to the tiny microorganisms at work in the soil. They, in turn, will decompose the organic matter in the ground, releasing nutrients which the plants can use. Soil, just like people, must be allowed to breathe. Cultivating once a week or so also creates a dust mulch, which will hold moisture in the ground.

You should begin to cultivate the soil as soon as your seedlings appear aboveground. This is the time when they need it most.

As you cultivate, remember that you should hoe, till, or scratch just the surface of the soil because so many garden plants have shallow feeder roots. Pull any weeds that don't fall victim to your cultivating tool. If they are allowed to grow, they will steal moisture and plant food from your vegetables. A garden filled with weeds will yield just about half as much as a well-kept garden of the same size.

Killing weeds between rows is no problem. You can do it with a rotary tiller or with a hoe. Weeds within the row have to be pulled. As you pull them, keep a sharp eye out for diseased and dying vegetable plants. Pull these up too and dispose of them. If there seem to be a lot, try to find out what disease they have. Gardening books can be helpful, and so can the Agricultural Extension Service. They can tell you if you have a serious problem and can suggest what you should be doing about it. Don't panic if a few plants die. This may be normal attrition. There is probably little danger that a major outbreak of disease will destroy your whole crop.

A lot of people have asked me, "How do you tell the plants from the weeds?" This is not as silly as it might sound. It can be a big problem for inexperienced gardeners. Weed and vegetable seedlings are apt to come up at exactly the same time. One thing you can do is keep the packet the seeds came in. This will give you a good picture of what the vegetable looks like when it is mature. From this, you can get some idea of what it looks like when it is very young.

It's also a good idea to carefully mark both ends of your rows with small wooden or plastic stakes. These should remind you where you have planted what. The greenery coming up elsewhere is probably weeds. If you plant in single rows, check to see which seedlings are coming up in a line. Weeds, naturally, don't grow in a straight row. In a wide row, the largest number of seedlings of the same type are probably your plants.

One of the best times to weed and cultivate is a few hours after a rain shower. Wait until the plants have dried off, then go into the garden before the ground gets too dry. Weeds pull up very easily at this time because the ground is soft, and you will not risk disturbing the roots of neighboring vegetable plants. This is also an excellent time to cultivate. Weed seeds near the soil surface may have started to germinate as a result of the rainfall. If you expose them to the dry air and sun, they will die.

THE IN-ROW WEEDER

I have invented a tool which I call an in-row weeder. It is very handy, especially in wide-row plantings. You can rake right over the tops of plants with it. (You can also use a regular broom rake with round, spring teeth, but it won't work quite so well.) You can use the in-row weeder whenever the plants get to be half an inch to an inch tall. I start going over the plants once or twice a week at that time.

You can understand how the in-row weeding tool works if you understand a little about the way plants grow. When a seed begins to germinate, it sends down a deep root called the "tap root." Then the plant itself starts to grow upward. By the time it reaches the soil surface, tiny weeds have had time to grow too. Unfortunately, these are too small to pull. What is fortunate is that the roots of these weeds grow very near the surface of the ground. Raking over a wide or single row with the weeder will pull up or disturb the roots of these little weeds before they have a chance to establish themselves. You will find that you will not pull up the vegetable plants because they are anchored by deep roots— unless they are planted too thick, in which case the tool does a fine job of thinning. You will find that this little device can cut your weeding time in half.

MULCH AWAY THE WEEDS

A mulch is a layer of material spread on the garden so that it shades the ground completely. It prevents weeds from growing by depriving them of sunlight. It holds moisture in the soil by reducing evaporation, and it keeps the soil cooler on hot days and warmer on cool nights by acting as insulation.

There are any number of things that you can use for mulch. You could try paper, concrete slabs, sawdust, wood chips, grass clippings, hay, or polyethylene plastic. Mulching is a particularly good idea in a small garden, where it will really cut down on labor. It is a little harder to do in a very large garden simply because it is difficult to get enough mulch materials.

Grass clippings are one of the best and most common mulches. They contain no weed seeds, but don't use them fresh. Let them dry for a day or two by spreading them in the sun. If you don't, they will get slimy and foul-smelling. Be careful about using old hay and straw as mulch. Try to get hay which was harvested before it had time to go to seed.

One thing to remember about mulch is that if it has weed seeds in it, it will surely add weeds to your garden. It will also attract rodents eager to feed on the seeds. Seedless, organic mulches include grass clippings, leaves, woodchips, and salt marsh hay.

It is particularly important to use a seedless mulch around fruit trees and berry plants. Seeds will encourage rodents to crawl into the warm mulch for the winter. Once they have devoured the seeds, they

Both the black plastic mulch around the pepper plants and the straw mulch under the cucumber vines will keep the soil moist and weed-free. The black plastic is easier to apply and maintain, but it doesn't provide the soil-conditioning effects of straw.

GROWING POTATOES UNDER LEAVES

As just a boy, I used to help my great-grandfather haul leaves to put on the potato patch every fall. Now, I had no idea what, the leaves were really for, but we had a high-heeled time getting in the leaves with Grandpa. We would scatter them on the plowed patch, filling the rows level with leaves. Then in mid-February, when the leaves had settled to about half their original thickness, Grandpa would drop cut pieces of potato on top of them. Then he would plow the ridges over onto the top of the bed of leaves, giving the seed potatoes a covering about four inches thick.

I knew that Grandpa always had the largest, smoothest spuds of anyone in the area, but I didn't understand the principles behind his practices. Those leaves would half-rot and hold moisture like a sponge. And if potatoes have plenty of moisture, they will not fail to produce a good crop. At the same time, the bed of leaves provided good drainage in case of a wet spring, so the potatoes would not drown and go sour as they sometimes do. The yearly covering of leaves also contained minerals which the tree roots had brought up from deep within the earth. J A

HARVESTING SPUDS AND ROSEBUDS

"One year, my wife had about 400 roses which we mulched with shavings and hay. One spring, I bought 45¢ worth of seed potatoes and hid them in the rose mulch. At first, my wife was displeased with this, but when she discovered what lovely, clean potatoes were there, without digging, her mind was changed. She soon began moving the mulch, picking up the spuds, and hiding the smaller ones away in the mulch. We had plenty of potatoes the next year with no plowing or hoeing, and a new crop was harvested that way every year thereafter. I think that was about the best 45¢ I ever spent. JG

MULCH GARDENING WITH GRASS CLIPPINGS

Charlie E. Hunt of Goodlettsville, Tennessee, is a mulch gardener. When he began this practice three years ago, his garden land was mostly clay; therefore, it was hard to work. Now it is rich, friable soil.

Mr. Hunt mows three yards in his neighborhood with a Sears 10XL machine. The clippings are blown into an enclosed trailer, which holds twenty-eight bushels. He makes a large heap of the clippings, adding leaves in the fall. He lets this heap stand for one year. In the spring, the clippings and leaves are ready to be used as mulch or as compost. After the garden is through producing in the fall, the mulch is worked into the ground with Mr. Hunt's Troy-Bilt tiller. He doesn't think any other tiller could do this job so well.

The first time Mr. Hunt tried mulching, he did not have grass clippings ready to use, so he used a mulch of four layers of newspapers. He had a good garden that year also.

Mr. Hunt is very pleased with his mulched garden. He finds that he doesn't even have to plow to uncover his potato crop now, he just lifts the mulch with his pitchfork and there they are! Kennebec potatoes are Mr. Hunt's favorites, and he saves his own seed from year to year.

Even if an especially dry season comes along, he doesn't worry much about his garden. His mulch holds moisture in the soil, and he always has a reserve supply of free water — in his cistern. All rain water from the roof of his house runs into gutters and through two spouts into the large cistern built above the garage. This stored water supplements the city water used by the family.

Mr. Hunt uses no chemical fertilizer. Weeds are kept under control by the heavy mulch. He avoids insecticides but will dust if some bugs get out of hand.

MULCHING TOMATOES

"I've found a good mulch for tomatoes. I collect large sheets of cardboard, and after cutting holes and slits to put the plants through, I cover the ground around the plants with it. I never stake. This cardboard mulch keeps down weeds, holds moisture, keeps the fruit clean, and you can pick tomatoes without getting your feet dirty. In the fall, the cardboard will till into the soil."
SWR

will start to eat the berry canes or the bark from the trunks of the fruit trees.

Rodents sometimes damage vegetable crops too. I like to grow at least some of my potatoes under a hay mulch. One year, when I used a seedy hay, I found that I had also raised several families of field mice in my potato patch. Those little fellows ate all the seeds in the hay, then chewed up almost all my potatoes.

If you mulch too early in the spring, you may find that it sets your crops back a week or two. Wait until the soil has warmed up in the late spring, then put mulch right around the stems of your plants, covering the ground completely. This should eliminate all weeding and cultivating.

The very best time to mulch is right after a heavy rain. If the mulch is thick enough, it will help the soil to retain most of this moisture for the entire growing season.

A FULL-TIME MULCH

To build a permanent-mulch garden, stake off the boundaries of your plot, and till the soil until it is very loose and fine. Plant or transplant your vegetables as usual the first year. As soon as they come up and look healthy, spread mulch everywhere—in the rows, between the rows, and right up to the stems of the plants themselves. Protect the whole garden with it. As times goes on and the organic matter starts to decompose, add more mulch.

What you are doing is making it very difficult for weeds to grow. Those few that manage to poke through this heavy layer of organic matter will be easy to pull. When you do pull them up, drop them right in place so that they can become part of the mulch. A good mulch also provides a barrier which slows down evaporation. Permanent-mulch gardens almost never have to be watered.

Don't bother to till the soil at all the second year. You can lay out your rows and rake the mulch back just enough to make plantings. Once the plants have sprouted and grown a couple of inches tall, pull the mulch back around them. You will find that the soil beneath the mulch has stayed loose and friable because you have created an environment which is both appetizing to earthworms and hospitable to beneficial microorganisms of all kinds. If the mulch is heavy enough to keep the garden from freezing, they will work happily in your soil all year long.

To have a permanent-mulch garden, you have to have enough mulch! I mean enough to spread as much as eight to ten inches of it everywhere. It will settle to a depth of four to seven inches. Use hay, straw, grass clippings, or leaves. I don't recommend using sawdust. If you do, you will have to add fertilizer to replace the nitrogen that the sawdust will use up as it decomposes. Most gardens with a permanent mulch don't require a lot of fertilizer, but there is no harm in adding a little when you pull the mulch back from the rows in spring.

It is hard to maintain a permanent mulch in a very large garden because it takes mountains of material to keep the area covered. A permanent mulch might also shorten your growing season a little. Mulched soil will stay cold and wet in the spring because the warming rays of the sun never strike it directly. This will delay the planting of heat-loving plants like tomatoes.

Year-round mulching has its advantages and disadvantages. In a small garden where you don't have to constantly scramble around to find enough mulch, it will certainly save you lots of work. The idea of permanent mulching was made famous by two books, "How to Have a Green Thumb Without an Aching Back" and "Gardening Without Work," both written by a lady named Ruth Stout.

It is a good idea to mulch some portions of a large garden. Whenever plants get to be five or six inches high, you can bring mulch up around their stems. This will save you a lot of weeding, hoeing, and cultivating in the rows. If you do not have enough material to mulch between the rows, limit yourself to mulching around the plants. Most organic mulches add nutrients to the soil; so when you mulch you are also side dressing. Earthworms and microorganisms will eventually devour organic mulches and turn them into good humus. When the gardening season is over, you can simply

turn under all remaining mulch along with crop residues if you don't want to maintain a permanent mulch.

Some crops are a lot easier to take care of when they are mulched. Mulching the area where your cucumber or squash vines are going to grow, for instance, will save you the headache of having to weed later on, when the plants are spread out over the ground. Once the soil has warmed up, you will probably want to mulch at least some of your tomato and pepper plants. The mulch will keep the earth around these plants' roots at a more even temperature, which they like. You might also want to mulch your sweet corn. Some plants are not worth mulching. Carrots and beets are difficult because you can only put mulch on either side of the row. You can, of course, mulch the plants with some sort of finely chopped material, but I think it is more work than it is worth. There is no reason to mulch most peas; they ripen early in the spring and are usually finished by the time the heavy weed season comes along. Pea vines themselves, however, make a nourishing mulch for other plants, especially if they are shredded or chopped. You might want to use them on your tomatoes. The timing is just about perfect. The peas will be spent by the time the tomatoes are ready for mulch.

The very best mulches are alfalfa, clover, and all the other legumes, including peas and beans. All legumes have a high nitrogen content and contribute nitrogen to the soil both when they are growing and after they are dead. This is why they are the most nearly perfect mulch you can use. The plants are almost as precious as the food they produce. I think trying to find some alfalfa or clover hay would be worth your while, even if you have to pay a little for it.

Some people call mulching a "sophisticated" gardening technique. I don't agree. It can be as simple or as complicated as you want to make it. Almost every good gardener mulches some things. Some do a lot more than others. You should do as much as seems practical to you.

If you live in a particularly dry part of the country, you may have to install a permanent sprinkler system in order to have a productive garden. Before doing so, you might ask your county agent how much water will be required per week so you will know how much your water bill will jump or if your well or spring can supply your needs.

If you water your garden with a sprinkler, you should know how long it must run to deliver an inch of water. To find out, set a few cans at various distances from the sprinkler and turn it on. Measure the water in the cans periodically, and take note of how long it takes for an inch of water to accumulate in the various cans. (It will probably take longer than you think.)

WATERING

Ideally, a garden should get one inch of rain or applied water per week. Applying one inch of water to an acre takes 27,000 gallons. You can use this figure to determine the cost of applying an inch of water to your garden if you know its approximate size. RR

WATERING CORN

Corn can use plenty of water, but this isn't true of all crops. Cantaloupes don't like an abundance of water. They crack and the flavor is not good if they are given too much water. Tomatoes shouldn't be overwatered either. HL

KEEPING OUT THE WEEDS

If you have water running down a weedy field or pasture, then across your garden, you'll have lots of weeds regardless of how clean you keep your garden. Weed seeds will be carried by the water. JLG

Take care of your plants

Know when and how to water. Give your garden lots of love.

Would you believe me if I told you that I never water my garden? It's true. The only time I water is when I transplant. I give new plants water for a couple of days after they have been set out, then I leave them alone. I guess I am fortunate to have excellent soil which is rich in humus and holds moisture well.

I will grant that most gardens need to be watered at one time or another, but I am discouraged to see so many gardeners watering unwisely. Too many people look out the window, see some of their plants wilting on a hot afternoon, and immediately rush out to water them. A lot of plants will droop in a strong, hot sun late in the day. This is normal. It is a different story if the plants still look wilted when you get up in the morning. When plants look drought stricken early in the day, you should give them some water.

But don't water just for the sake of watering. Water only when it is really necessary. You are doing more harm than good when you sprinkle water on the garden just to keep the dust down or to moisten the soil surface. You should encourage your plants' roots to grow as deep as possible. If the plants get used to finding water near the soil surface, they will grow only shallow roots. When it really gets dry, these plants will not survive. If you are going to water, don't pussy-foot around. Soak the soil. Make sure that it is very wet at least three to six inches below the surface.

One good way to water is with a "soaker," a perforated canvas hose which allows water to run directly into the ground. An overhead sprinkler works well if you leave it in one place long enough, but I don't use these if I can help it, especially on a hot day. Sprinklers seem to use up a lot more water because so much moisture evaporates before it reaches the ground.

FURROW OR ROW IRRIGATION

Row irrigation, which is done by running water in furrows between rows of plants, is an excellent method of watering where conditions permit. The only equipment necessary is a hose or pipe and a wooden trough for distributing water to several furrows at once.

Row irrigation works best on land with a slope of 2 to 6 inches of fall per 100 feet, but it can be adapted to land with more or with less slope. On very steep slopes, small furrow streams must be used to prevent erosion. If the soil surface is uneven or extremely flat, you may have to grade the garden (move soil from one area to another) to make row irrigation possible.

The size of the wooden trough will vary according to the number of rows you want to irrigate at once and the capacity of your hose or pipe. Usually, a flow of 1 to 5 gallons per minute for each hole will be necessary. Drill holes (1 inch in diameter) on one side of the trough near the bottom. The holes should be the same distance apart as the furrows. It is also a good idea to attach a wooden knob just above each hole so the flow of water can be easily adjusted or stopped.

In order to get an even distribution of water in the furrow, adjust the flow so that water reaches the end of the furrow in about one-fourth of the time it takes to irrigate the whole row. Water is therefore on the lower end of the row three-fourths as long as it is on the upper end.

Start irrigating with a heavy flow of water; then turn back the water so that an even flow is maintained in the row with no puddling or washing at the end of the row. Check the depth to which the water has penetrated with a shovel, a steel rod or a stick. Water that seeps down deeper than the root zone is wasted.

PRUNING MELONS, SQUASH, AND PUMPKINS

You may not know that these vegetables benefit from pruning, too. Pruning consists simply of picking the fuzzy, green growing tips off the vines. This keeps the plant from taking up too much garden space and forces it to devote more of its growing energy to fruit production. If the climate in your part of the country is so cold that frost frequently destroys a large part of your melon harvest, you can speed up the ripening process by pruning judiciously. About the first week in August (when the melons are probably just starting to ripen), pick the fuzzy ends off all the vines. Then, during the last week in August, pick off any melons that are too small and green to ripen before frost. All the plant's energy can now go to the fruit still on the vine. (Keep picking off the fuzzy vine ends.)

GROWING CARROTS IN RICE HULLS

This spring we purchased several bales of rice hulls to put around our strawberries. During this time we were planting our garden.

Since our ground gets hard and is very difficult to grow root crops in, we thought we would try something different. We planted carrots, beets, and radishes in the following manner: After tilling the ground, we used our furrowing attachment to dig a furrow approximately 6 to 7 inches deep. We filled this to about 3 inches from the top with rice hulls. Then we spread a very thin layer of dirt to lay the seed on. I planted the seed and covered with another layer of dirt. And then the harvest! We had the best crop of beets and carrots we ever raised!

The rice hulls hold moisture and keep the ground loose so the root crops can grow bigger. P S

PRUNING TOMATOES

Pruning and training tomato plants properly keeps them producing longer and favorably affects the size and quality of the fruit. There are many different methods of training, but the most common is staking. As the plant grows, it is tied with strips of cloth, old nylon stockings, or soft cord to a six-foot-tall wooden stake. Early in the growing season, probably in June, pruning should begin. In the angle where each leaflet branch joins the main stem, a sucker or side shoot will grow. All of these should be pinched out as soon as they appear. At first, you may have to prune once a week; later, once every two weeks may be adequate. once the plant reaches the top of the stake, you can pinch out the growing tip to stop further vertical growth. Or you can discontinue pruning, and allow all new suckers to grow without staking. They will fall over, set some fruit, and provide shade for the fruit on the rest of the plant.

The "Missouri Method" of pruning is very similar to the one described above. Its advocates claim that this method produces yield increases of 15 to 25 percent (as a result of larger fruits.) Stake, tie, and remove suckers as above, but do not remove any sucker that is growing directly below a flower cluster. As soon as each of these remaining suckers gets about six inches long, pinch off the growing tip. These extra branches increase the plant's food-producing capacity and provides some shading of the tender fruits.

Still another variation is the double-stem system, in which all suckers except the first one directly below the first flower cluster are removed. This first sucker is allowed to develop into a second stem. Both stems are tied to the same stake, and all other suckers are removed as soon as they appear.

Tomato plants grown in wire cylinders or similar support structures don't need to be pruned. Neither do unsupported tomatoes.

Some varieties have what is called a determinate growth habit, which means they form short, bushy plants usually less than three feet tall. These plants require little or no pruning. Some determinate varieties are: Springset, Roma, Small Fry, Fireball, New Yorker, and Spring Giant.

GARDEN PROBLEM GUIDE

SYMPTOMS	POSSIBLE CAUSE	POSSIBLE CURES
Dying young plants	Fertilizer burn	Mix fertilizer thoroughly with soil.
	Disease (damping-off)	Treat seed; don't overwater.
Stunted plants pale to yellow	Low soil fertility	Soil test for fertilizer recommendations.
	Low soil pH (too acid)	Soil test for lime recommendations.
	Poor soil drainage	Drain and add organic matter.
	Shallow or compacted soil	Plow deeper.
	Insects or diseases	Identify and use control measures.
	Nematodes	Soil test for treatment recommendations.
Stunted plants purplish color	Low temperature	Plant at recommended time.
	Lack of phosphorus	Add phosphorus fertilizer.
Holes in leaves	Insects	Identify and use control measures.
	Hail	Be thankful it was not worse.
Spots, molds, darkened areas on leaves and stems	Disease	Identify, spray or dust, use resistant varieties.
	Chemical burn	Use recommended chemical at recommended rate.
	Fertilizer burn	Keep fertilizer off plants.
Wilting plants	Dry soil	Irrigate if possible.
	Excess water in soil	Drain.
	Nematodes	Soil test for treatment recommendations.
	Disease	Use resistant varieties if possible.
Weak, spindly plants	Too much shade	Remove shade or move plants to sunny spot.
	Too much water	
	Plants too thick	Seed at recommended rate.
	Too much nitrogen	Avoid excess fertilization.
Failure to set fruit	High temperature	Follow recommended planting time.
	Low temperature	Follow recommended planting time.
	Too much nitrogen	Avoid excess fertilization.
	Insects	Identify and use control measures.
Tomato leaf curl	Heavy pruning in hot weather	Don't.
	Disease	Identify and use control measures.
Dry brown to black rot on blossom end of tomato	Low soil calcium	Add liming material.
	Extremely dry soil	Irrigate.
Misshapen tomatoes (catfacing)	Cool weather during blooming	Plant at recommended time.
Abnormal leaves and growth	2,4-D weed killer	Don't use sprayer that has previously applied 2,4-D. Don't allow spray to drift to garden.
	Virus disease	Remove infected plants to prevent spreading. Control insects that transmit.

Single-virus streaking of tomato

Fusarium wilt

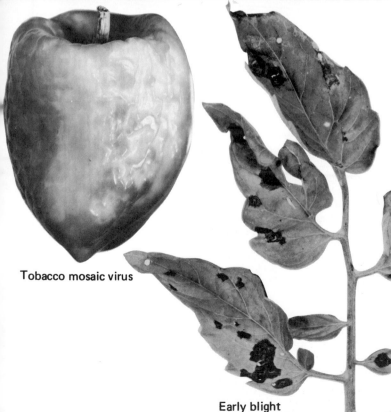

Tobacco mosaic virus

Early blight

Prescription for sick plants

Learn to identify plant ailments and to give them the necessary protective medicines.

Most plant diseases, like animal diseases, are caused by microscopic bacteria and fungi called pathogenic organisms. No garden is free of potential disease organisms. They are everywhere. The trick is to keep them from becoming active and to prevent them from spreading. An unhealthy plant is far more subject to disease than a strong specimen. If you keep your crops well nourished and well tended, they will continue to ward off disease just the way a healthy human body will.

Plant diseases are spread by excessive handling of plants and by insects traveling from one plant to another. Some diseases, like leaf blight and leaf spot, attack the leaves of plants. Others get into the stem and cause plant rot or wilt from within. Bacterial wilt starts inside and cuts off the supply of moisture and nutrients. A lot of pathogenic fungi get into a plant through the roots. Damping off is an example of a disease that enters a plant through its roots.

Most diseases are easy to prevent. I have rarely seen many diseased plants in a well-kept garden. Keep your plants healthy. As I have said before, if there is a problem with disease, contact an expert for advice. Let him recommend some ways to treat the disease, but try to use the least amount of the weakest chemical remedy that will solve the problem.

There are a number of other ways to keep diseases from getting the upper hand.

1. You can keep your garden well drained. This means that you must give it

all the organic matter you can and cultivate it as often as possible.

2. You can keep the soil well fed with fertilizer. This will keep the garden plants vigorous and disease-resistant.

3. You can be selective when you choose your seeds and plants. Study the seed catalogs and read the backs of seed packets. The brief descriptions may tell you something about a particular variety's susceptibility to disease.

4. Use seeds that are treated with fungicide. They are more difficult to find than they used to be, but getting them is not impossible. Treating seeds yourself is no problem either.

5. Rotate the crops in your garden. Don't plant cabbage, for example, over and over again in the same spot. Leaving the same plant in the same place year after year gives disease spores a chance to accumulate.

6. Leave as much distance between rows as you can. This will allow good air circulation. If one row is allowed to grow right into the next, the plants will never have a chance to dry out properly after a rain shower. Constant moisture above ground level stimulates disease.

7. Place your garden in the sunniest spot possible. Sunlight is one of the best fungicides around. Ultraviolet rays kill many pathogenic organisms.

8. Avoid going out to cultivate, pull weeds, hoe, or thin when the plants are still wet. Disease organisms cling to your clothing and hands, and these can easily be transferred to the plants when they are damp.

9. Keep the insect population down. Insects are disease carriers, and they are constantly moving to and from the various plants.

10. Till under or compost all plant residues after your annual plants have stopped bearing fruit. Leaving them to wither in place provides a place for pathogenic organisms to multiply.

11. Avoid watering your crops on muggy, overcast days when there is no sunshine. Watering sometimes splashes disease spores from the soil onto a plant's leaves.

BLOSSOM-END ROT OF TOMATOES

Blossom-end rot is a tomato disease that appears as a sunken scar or rot on the end of the fruit. It is caused by a dry spell following an extra wet period. Regular watering will help control this disease. So will a good mulch, which will keep the ground moist and cool.

Lack of calcium can also contribute to this problem. Lime is a good source of calcium. Add five pounds per 100 square feet to correct a calcium deficiency. RR

CUCUMBER DISEASES

Phaltin and Captan are good for controlling diseases of cucumbers. Sevin is best for insects. RR

TOMATO BLIGHT

When tomato plants begin drying up and dying, gardeners may think it's a blight. Often it's a tobacco mosaic disease that's brought into the garden on the hands of people who smoke. If you smoke, wash your hands thoroughly or dip them in milk before going into the garden so you won't risk infecting your plants with tobacco mosaic. JLG

BEAN RUST

When you have cold nights and heavy dews late in the season, you have trouble with rusts on beans. Wettable sulfur is the best spray to control bean rusts. JLG

CANTALOUPE DISEASES

Use Karathane or Captan to control diseases of cantaloupes.

CUCUMBERS

"My cucumbers were all yellow and dead looking, it looked like the entire crop was gone. I sprayed them with sulfur and captan, with double the strength recommended for my fruit trees. It won't burn. They came back and I had a lovely crop." DR

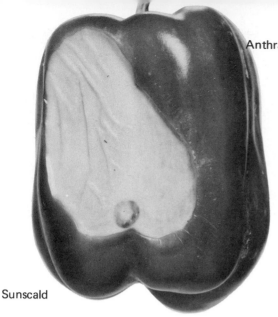

Sunscald

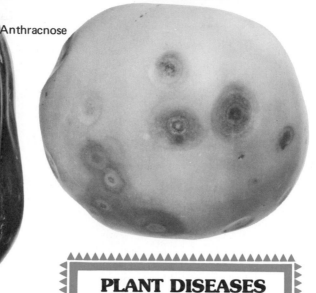

Anthracnose

Cercospora leaf spot

PLANT DISEASES

DISEASES OF SPECIFIC VEGETABLES*

ASPARAGUS
Rust

BEANS (snap)
Anthracnose, Powdery mildew, Bacterial blight, Curly top, Fusarium root rot, Gray mold, Mosaics, Rust, White cottony rot

BEANS (lima)
Stem anthracnose, Root-knot nematodes

BEETS
Curly top, Mosaic, Downy mildew

BROCCOLI, CABBAGE, CAULIFLOWER, COLLARDS
Club root, Downy mildew, Ring rot, Wirestem, Blackleg, Yellows, Alternaria leaf spot, Bacterial soft rot, Late blight

CELERY
Smut, Stewart's disease, Maize dwarf mosaic

CUCUMBERS
Anthracnose, Angular leaf spot, Curly top, Fungus leaf spot, Mosaic, Downy mildew, Powdery mildew, Scab, Wilt

EGGPLANT
Blight, Fruit rot

LETTUCE
Downy mildew, Drop, Mosaic, Slimy rot, Aster yellows

MUSKMELON
Anthracnose, Curly top, Wilt, Angular leaf spots, Mosaic

OKRA
Root-knot nematodes, Verticillium wilt

ONIONS
Bulb rot, Downy mildew, Neck rot, Smut, Soft rot, White rot

PEAS
Bacterial blight, Downy mildew, Fungus blight, Virus diseases, Wilt, Powdery mildew, Root rots

DISEASE OR CAUSE	VEGETABLES	LOOK FOR	HOW TO CONTROL
Downy Mildew	Beans Cucumbers Cantaloupes	Yellow to dark areas that may be vague or sharply defined, occur on upper surface of older leaves. White to dark cottony mold found on underside of leaves and on bean pods. Vines may be scorched and killed.	Same as for Powdery Mildew, except use maneb on beans and maneb or Bravo (chlorothalonil) on cucumbers and cantaloupes.
Blossom End Rot	Tomatoes Peppers Watermelons Squash	Blossom end of fruit becomes dry, sunken, leathery and brown-black; or light colored and papery in pepper. One-half of fruit may be affected.	Maintain even soil moisture by watering during dry periods. Mulch or cultivate shallowly during drought. Fertilize properly based on a soil test.
Root Rot	Many vegetables	Plants may become pale, yellow, and/or stunted. May wilt, die back or collapse. They do not respond to water and fertilizer. Decayed roots may be mushy or firm and covered with mold.	Practice rotation. Avoid wet, poorly drained soils. Remove and destroy affected plants. Control nematodes and prevent injury.
Nematodes	Cucumbers Cantaloupes Tomatoes Many others	Plants may be stunted, yellow, and have galls or swelling on roots. Or roots may be stunted, bushy and discolored. Plants may suddenly wilt in dry weather.	Move garden to a different area or treat soil with a material such as Vapam, Nemagon or Fumazone.
Viruses	Many vegetables	Symptoms vary considerably. May consist of yellowing, stunting, spotting, mottling, mosaic pattern, streaking, etc.	Use resistant varieties where possible. Control weeds, insects and nematodes.
Sunscald	Peppers Tomatoes Others (occasionally)	Large, irregular white areas on fruit that may appear paperlike in texture. White or reddish spots may develop on leaves. Affected areas often covered with dark molds.	Use varieties with more foliage. Fertilize and water properly. Control defoliating diseases.
2-4-D and Dicamba Injury	Tomatoes Beans (most susceptible) All vegetables may be affected	Leaves and stems curl, become distorted and twisted. Leaf margins are wavy or frilled. Tomato fruit may be cracked and distorted.	Do not use 2-4-D near the vegetable garden.

68

FUNGICIDES

Fungicides can be a great help in preventing diseases when properly applied to the plant foliage. Since fungicides have a preventative function, they should be applied before the disease occurs or as soon as the first symptoms appear.

Fungicides are available primarily as wettable powders and as dusts, but a few are sold as emulsifiable concentrates. Wettable powders are formulated to be readily suspendable in water. Dusts should not be mixed with water, but applied directly to the plant. Emulsifiable, concentrate-type fungicides contain an emulsifying agent which makes them readily suspendable in water.

Some soil fungicides are now available in granular form and are applied in the furrow at planting time. Dusts and spray materials can also be used as in-furrow treatments to control seedling diseases.

Nematicides (for nematode control) are available as liquids and as granules, they should be applied at or prior to planting time.

Powdery mildew

DISEASE OR CAUSE	VEGETABLES	LOOK FOR	HOW TO CONTROL
Anthracnose & Other Leaf Spots	Beans Cucumbers Cantaloupes Watermelons Peppers Tomatoes	For anthracnose, check for reddish-brown or black sunken spots or blotches on leaves, stems, pods, and/or fruits. Other leaf spots may vary greatly in shape and color. Leaves may wither and fall early.	Practice two year rotation or longer. Avoid overcrowding and keep weeds removed. Destroy residue after harvest. Spray or dust with maneb or zineb.
Fusarium & Verticillium Wilt	Tomatoes Watermelons Cantaloupes	Seedlings wilt and die. Older plants are stunted while leaves wilt, turn yellow, wither and drop. Dark streaks appear in lower stem and roots.	Plant in well-drained, wilt-free soil and follow a 3-4 year crop rotation. Use resistant varieties where possible.
Early Blight or Target Spot	Tomatoes Potatoes	Brown to black spots on leaves and stems. Spots are angular to round with concentric rings (targets). Spots may merge to kill portions of leaves and defoliate the plants, starting at the base. Tomato fruit may sunscald and show sunken leathery spots near the stem.	Practice crop rotation and destroy residues after harvest. Use well-drained soil and keep weeds down. Use resistant varieties. Spray or dust with maneb or Bravo (chlorothalonil).
Late Blight	Potatoes Tomatoes	Develops during wet humid season. Irregular, greenish-black, water-soaked spots develop on leaves, petioles and stems. May resemble sunscald or frost damage in advanced stage. A sparse whitish mold appears on underleaf surface. Fruits and tubers also affected.	Same as for Early Blight. See above.
Powdery Mildew	Squash Pumpkins Watermelons Cantaloupes Cucumbers	White or brown mealy growth on leaves and young stems (especially on the upper surface and occasionally on the fruit). Plants may yellow, wither and die while fruit sunscalds or ripens prematurely.	Use resistant varieties. Practice rotation and good weed control. Space plants well. Destroy crop residue. Spray or dust with Karathane when disease first appears.

PEPPERS
Curly top, Blossom-end rot, Bactcrial leaf spots, Mosaic, Southern blight, Root-knot nematodes

POTATOES
Black leg, Black scurf, Early blight, Late blight, Scab, Verticillium wilt, Virus diseases, Rhizoctonia, Ring rot

SPINACH
Anthracnose, Downy mildew, Cercospora leaf spot, White rust

SQUASH
Curly top, Powdery mildew, Storage rot, Blossom-end rot

SWEET POTATOES
Soil rot, Scurf, Stem rot, Black rot, Internal cork

TOMATOES
Anthracnose, Leaf spot, Tobacco mosaic, Bacterial canker, Blossom-end rot, Curly top, Fruit rot, Late blight, Leaf roll, Early blight, Fusarium wilt, Verticillium wilt

WATERMELON
Anthracnose, Fusarium wilt

*The average home gardener will have few problems with any of these diseases. Some of the diseases listed exist only in a few specific areas of the country.

Plant diseases vary greatly from one locality to another, so it's a good idea to get a specific diagnosis and recommendation from the local agent of your agricultural extension service before using toxic sprays and dusts. A good all-purpose garden dust or spray may be all you need to use.

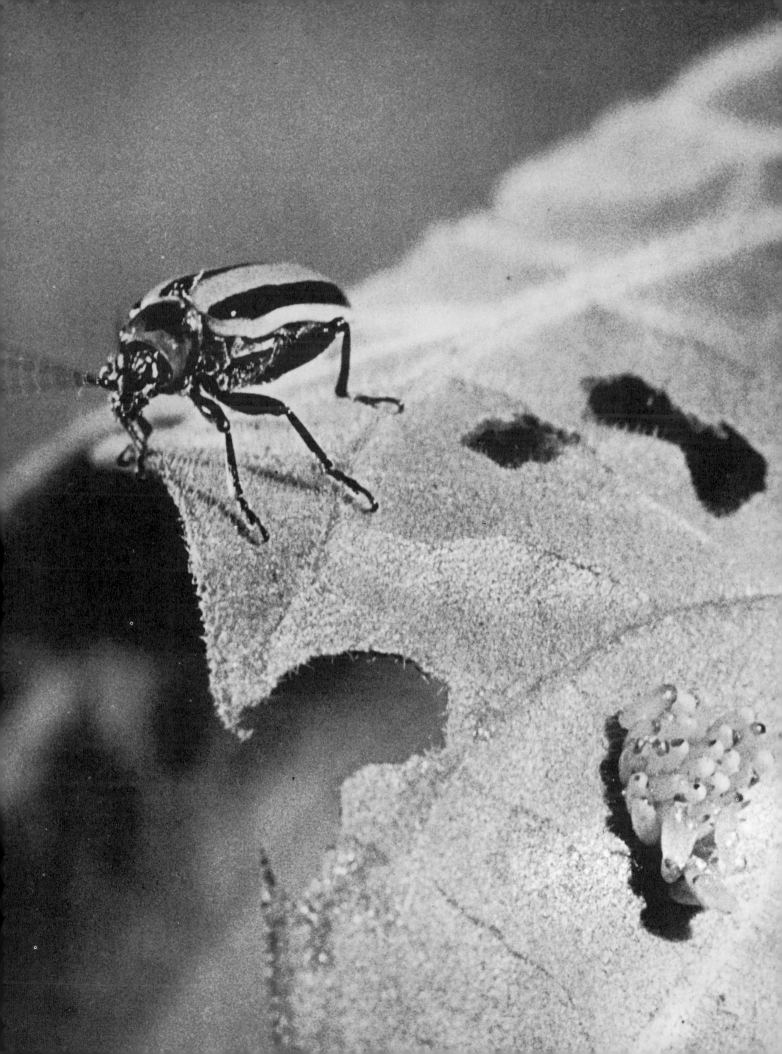

Getting the bugs out of your garden

Insect-pest control is not difficult if careful observation is regularly made and simple measures are taken to destroy pests before they launch a full-scale invasion.

If you are going to garden, there will be times when you are bugged by insects and diseases. There is no way to escape them. No matter where your garden is located, they will search you out and do their best to destroy anything they can.

Infested gardens and sick plants are discouraging, but they are not difficult to cope with if you are prepared to fight. The best way is to get a head start on them—catch them just as the insect larvae are starting to hatch or just as the disease is starting to take hold. It is much harder to defeat them once they have had a chance to do some damage.

Generally, there are three kinds of insects:

1. Bugs that eat leaves or suck plant juices from stems,
2. Bugs that feed from within the stems themselves, and
3. Insects that attack at ground level or below the surface of the soil.

There are two good weapons you can use to kill insects that eat stems and leaves —rotenone and Sevin. Try rotenone first; it is much less toxic and less dangerous than Sevin.

Another safe weapon for the home gardener is pyrethrum. Pyrethrum is a dust made from ground-up flowers—chrysanthemums, to be exact. It is perfectly safe to humans, but it is deadly to leaf-eating insects.

Insects that suck juices from the stem, such as plant lice, aphids, and leaf hoppers, cannot be killed with a residual poison like rotenone. They have to be hit with a contact spray—something that will actually touch their bodies.

Try not to become paranoid about bugs. Don't try to wage an all-out war against them. Your garden can survive a little insect damage. Don't fall into the trap of using stronger and stronger insecticides every year. You will not only be poisoning yourself; you will also be giving the insects in your garden an opportunity to build up an immunity to weaker remedies. And you will be killing off many helpful insects, such as the ladybug and the praying mantis, which feed on some of the harmful insects.

If you are going to use strong sprays or chemicals, be very careful! Contact your county Extension Service agent for advice, read the label on the package very carefully, and be sure you know exactly what you are doing.

Don't forget that certain pests, such as slugs, potato beetles, tomato worms, and cabbage worms are easy to spot, trap, or pick off the plants with your fingers.

Following is a list of the main insects to look out for in the garden.

Aphids—These are very tiny bugs—about one-sixteenth of an inch long—which can be found on the bottom sides of leaves and on tender, new growth. They are very light green in color, so they look almost white against the leaf. The problem with aphids is that they multiply so rapidly. They can do a lot of damage in a very short time. They can also cause a lot of problems indoors, in a greenhouse, or with houseplants. Check under your plants' leaves as often as every couple of days to see if there are aphids. They can be found on almost any kind of vegetable plant. Fortunately, a non-toxic dusting will usually take care of them.

Asparagus Beetles—These are blue-black beetles with lemon-colored spots. They measure about one-fourth of an inch long. They only attack asparagus, but they can do a lot of damage. Asparagus beetles can be foiled with either rotenone or pyrethrum.

Bean Beetles—Bean beetles are the black sheep of the ladybug family. They are coppery-brown and have eight black spots

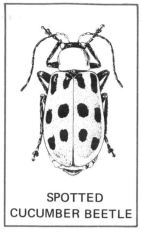

SPOTTED CUCUMBER BEETLE

CUTWORM

POTATO BEETLE

CABBAGE WORM

Cabbage being attacked by Cabbage loopers.

on each wing. They lay clusters of eggs which will hatch into larvae with voracious appetites! Spray for them on the underside of bean leaves. Spraying is more effective than dusting. Dusting should be done when there is dew on the plants.

Cabbage worms—If you see little white butterflies around your garden, you can be sure that you are going to have a problem soon. Catch them and kill them if you can. In a few days, they will produce green worms which are an inch or an inch and a quarter long. You can find them on any member of the cabbage family, but you will have to look closely to see them because they are beautifully camouflaged. Pick them off if you can find them, or spray with rotenone or Sevin. Salt sometimes discourages them too.

Corn earworms—The corn earworm is a two-inch-long caterpillar with green and brown stripes. Earworm eggs are laid in corn silk. Later, the larva bores his way into the ear itself and eats the young kernels of corn. If you don't have a whole lot of corn, you can put a few drops of mineral oil in the silk of each ear. Spraying rotenone or

Sevin on the plant also works quite well.

Cucumber Beetles—These are among the worst garden pests, as far as I am concerned. A cucumber beetle is very small and has three black stripes down his back. He will begin to eat a cucumber plant as soon as it appears above the ground, and he will never let up if he is not destroyed. He will breed on the blossom end of the vine and may not be content to restrict himself to cucumbers. He may get interested in squash, pumpkins, and other vine crops.

To make matters worse, cucumber beetles also spread disease, and this may cause a bigger problem than their insatiable appetites. Begin to examine your vine crops as soon as they are an inch tall. If you see any evidence of the cucumber beetle, dust and spray for them immediately before they have a chance to multiply.

Plant a few radish seeds in every cucumber, squash, or pumpkin hill. The beetles will devour the radish leaves and, hopefully, leave your other crops alone.

Cutworms—I have already said a lot about cutworms and have suggested a way to combat them—by putting a paper collar

FLEA BEETLE

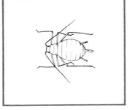

APHID

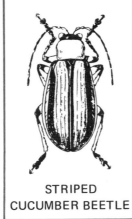

STRIPED
CUCUMBER BEETLE

SLUG

CORN EARWORM

SQUASH BUG

LEAF HOPPER

ASPARAGUS
BEETLE

around the stem of a plant just before setting it out. A cutworm is a small caterpillar-like animal that likes to gnaw off plant stems just at ground level. Once healthy plants get established, cutworms will leave them alone. There is no need to spray for them.

Flea Beetles—The flea beetle looks like a tiny black fly. He is so small that he is tough to spot, but you will know he is around if your plant leaves are riddled with little holes. Flea beetles seem especially fond of eggplant leaves, but they will also devour the leaves of tomatoes, potatoes, turnips, Chinese cabbage, and a lot of other vegetables. They will even get into radishes. Don't worry though; they are fairly easy to get rid of. Almost any mild dust or spray will do the job.

Potato Bugs—The striped potato bug lays eggs on the underside of potato leaves. These eggs will show up in small, orange clusters. If the clusters are allowed to hatch, there will suddenly be hundreds and hundreds of little red beetles with soft shells. These fellows can eat up a lot of greenery in a short time, and they may not stop at the potatoes. They will go on to tomatoes and eggplants too. If you get potato bugs, you may have to pick them off, or spray or dust for them several times. Keep after them!

Potato Leaf Hoppers—A potato leaf hopper is a pale green bug about an inch or an inch and a half long. You can see them flying off potato leaves as you walk down the row and touch the plants. Rolled-up, wilted-looking leaves are evidence of their work. Potato leaf hoppers should be no problem once the plants have been sprayed.

Squash Bugs—These are red-brown insects about three-fourths of an inch long. They lay eggs on the underside of leaves. It is good to be on the lookout for them, but like so many other bugs, they are very easy to control with non-toxic chemicals.

Tomato Worms—A tomato worm is a huge, green caterpillar—three or four inches long—with a horn on his rear. His ugliness is almost as amazing as his appetite. If you see tomato worms ravaging the leaves of your plants, you can spray them. They are so easy to spot, though, that it is almost as easy to pick them off by hand.

PURPLE MARTINS

Purple Martins are nature's bug catchers. It is claimed that one martin will consume 2,000 mosquitoes a day, along with a host of other flying insects. They are the largest members of the swallow family. You might like to invite a family to stay at your house. You'll enjoy watching their graceful, aerial acrobatics.

Martins love shiny walls in their homes. Studies show that they are attracted to flashy, metal houses. If you have a dark, wooden martin house that hasn't worked, perhaps you could line it with tin or aluminum foil. They also like an open site for their home. ST

INSECTICIDE AND MOLASSES

One of the best all-purpose insecticides is Sevin-Mol-4. It's a liquid Sevin spray containing molasses, which makes it stick to the leaves and also encourages insects to eat the insecticide. Always spray late in the evening after the sun is weak. Never spray in the morning when dew is on the plants or in the heat of the day. It is all right to use an insecticide dust while the plants are wet with dew. JLG

COOPERATE WITH THE BEES

You get a bigger harvest when you have a lot of bees to pollinate your crops. It's worth keeping bees for this reason alone. It's important not to spray anything that will kill off the bees. Spray insecticides late in the day when the bees are not working. JLG

VEGETABLE INSECTS

INSECTS ATTACKING SPECIFIC VEGETABLES

ASPARAGUS
Asparagus beetle, Cutworm, Garden centipede

BEANS SOUTHERN PEAS
Aphids, Mexican bean beetle, Bean leaf beetle, Flea beetle, Leafhopper, Seed corn maggot, Spider mite, Lesser cornstalk borer

BEETS
Aphids, Wireworm, Flea beetle, Leaf miner

SWISS CHARD
Spinach leaf miner

BROCCOLI BRUSSELS SPROUTS CABBAGE CAULIFOWER CHINESE CABBAGE COLLARDS KOHLRABI SPINACH ALL GREENS
Aphids, Cabbage root maggot, Cabbage worm, Cabbage looper, Cutworm, Flea beetle, Thrips, Mites

CARROT
Celeryworm, Carrot rust fly, Leafhopper

CORN
Aphids, Corn earworm, European corn borer, Seed-corn maggot, Sap beetle, Flea beetle, Spider mite, Wireworm

CUCUMBER
Spotted and striped cucumber beetle, Squash bug, Aphids, Corn maggot, Spider mite, Squash-vine borer, Mites, Blister beetle, Darkling beetle, Pickle worm

EGGPLANT
Aphids, Colorado potato beetle, Flea beetle, Tomato hornworm, Mites

LETTUCE ENDIVE
Cabbage looper, Aphids, Slugs, Wireworm, Leafhopper

MUSKMELONS
Cucumber beetle, Aphids, Mites, Squash bug, Seed corn maggot

Insect	Crop	Dust Formula	Spray Formula	Remarks
Aphid	Cabbage Cucumbers Melons Peas Potatoes Tomatoes	5-percent malathion	2 Tsp. 50-57-percent emulsifiable malathion *or* 1 Tsp. 64-percent emulsifiable dibrom in 1 gal. water	Apply on foliage when aphids appear. Repeat weekly as needed.
Blister beetle	Potatoes Corn Tomatoes Beans	5-percent sevin	2 Tb. wettable sevin in 1 gal. water	
Cabbage worms	Broccoli Cabbage Cauliflower Greens	4-percent dibrom	1 Tsp. 64-percent emulsifiable dibrom in 1 gal. water *or* *Bacillus thuringensis* biological insecticide	Thorough treatment is necessary. Repeat weekly as needed. Begin treatment when worms are small.
Corn earworm (⅔ nat. size)	Sweet corn Tomatoes	5-percent sevin	Inject ½ medicine dropperful of mineral oil into silk channel as silks start to dry *or* 2 Tb. wettable sevin in 1 gal. water	Dust or spray silks with sevin every other day for 10 days. Dust or spray tomatoes with sevin 3 to 4 times at 10-day intervals; begin when first fruits are small.
European corn borer	Sweet corn	5-percent sevin *or* 5-percent sevin granules	2 Tb. wettable sevin in 1 gal. water *or* 2 Tb. 25-percent diazinon in 1 gal. water	Apply insecticide four times at 5-day intervals beginning with egg hatching near mid-June. Avoid early spring plantings. On late corn dust as for corn earworm.
Striped cucumber beetle	Cucumbers Melons Squash	5-percent sevin	2 Tb. wettable sevin in 1 gal. water	Treat as soon as beetles appear. Repeat when necessary.
Cutworm	Most garden crops		2 Tb. 25-percent diazinon in 1 gal. water	At transplanting, wrap stems of seedling cabbage, pepper, and tomato plants with newspaper or foil to prevent damage by cutworms.

NATURAL PEST CONTROL

Pest	Birds	Oil	Pyrethrum	Rotenone	Ryania	Sabadilla	Bacillus Thuringiensis	Sulfur	Beneficial Insects
Ants	X		X						X
Aphids	X	X	X	X	X				X
Mealybugs	X	X							X
Scale	X	X							X
Mites		X		X	X			X	X
Caterpillars	X		X	X	X	X		X	X
Moths	X				X		X		
Leafhoppers	X		X	X	X	X		X	X
Borers					X				X
Snails and Slugs	X								
Thrips		X	X	X	X				X
Beetles and True Bugs	X		X	X	X	X			X

Cooperative Extension Service of the University of Maine

Insect	Crop	Dust Formula	Spray Formula	Remarks
Flea beetle	Most garden crops	5-percent sevin	2 Tb. wettable sevin in 1 gal. water	Apply as soon as injury is first noticed. Thorough application is necessary.
Grasshopper	Most garden crops	5-percent sevin	2 Tb. wettable sevin in 1 gal. water	Treat infested areas while grasshoppers are still small.
Hornworm (½ nat. size)	Tomatoes	5-percent sevin	2 Tb. wettable sevin in 1 gal. water	Ordinarily hand-picking is more practical in the home garden.
Leafhopper	Beans Carrots Potatoes Cucumbers Muskmelons	Use sevin dust or 5-percent methoxychlor dust	2 Tb. wettable sevin in 1 gal. water	Spray or dust once a week for 3 to 4 weeks, beginning when plants are small. Apply to underside of foliage.
Mexican bean beetle	Beans	5-percent sevin	2 Tb. wettable sevin in 1 gal. water	Apply insecticide to underside of foliage. Also effective against leafhoppers on beans.
Potato beetle	Potatoes Eggplant Tomatoes	5-percent sevin	2 Tb. wettable sevin in 1 gal. water	Apply when beetles or grubs first appear and repeat as necessary.
Squash bug	Squash	5-percent sevin	2 Tb. wettable sevin in 1 gal. water	Adults and brown egg masses can be hand-picked. Trap adults under shingles beneath plants. Kill young bugs soon after they hatch.
Squash vine borer	Squash	5-percent sevin	2 Tb. wettable sevin in 1 gal. water	Dust or spray once a week for 3 to 4 weeks beginning in late June when first eggs hatch. Treat crowns of plants and runners thoroughly.

Where two drawings are shown, the smaller one is natural size.

ONION
Onion maggot, Onion thrip, Wireworm

PARSLEY
Aphids, Celeryworm

PEAS
Aphids, Pea weevil

PEPPERS
Aphids, Corn borer, Flea beetle

POTATOES
Aphids, Colorado potato beetle, Flea beetle, Spider mite, Wireworm, Leafhopper, White grub, Cutworm

PUMPKIN
Cucumber beetle, Squash bug, Aphids, Vine borer

RADISH
Aphids, Flea beetle, Cabbage root maggot

SQUASH
Cucumber beetle, Squash bug, Aphids, Seed-corn maggot, Vine borer

TOMATO
Tomato hornworm, Flea beetle, Aphids, Cutworm, Blister beetle, White fly, Sap beetle, Fruitworm

TURNIP
Flea beetle, Aphids

*The home gardener will probably see few of the many insects listed here. This list includes insects that infest vegetables over the entire United States. Some of these insects may not even exist in your area.

Animal-pest control

If you have squirrels, woodchucks, raccoons or skunks in your area, you may have a problem. These animals seem to have an amazing ability to get into your garden and eat the corn the night before you were planning to pick it. Discouraging! A three-foot chicken-wire fence will keep some of these pests out. It should also give your garden a little protection from children and wandering neighborhood dogs and cats.

Unfortunately, chicken wire will not keep raccoons and squirrels out. An electrified strand of wire on top of the chicken wire might be a worthwhile investment. The wire should be run approximately three inches above the top of the fence. If an animal crawls up and gets a shock from the wire just once, he is not likely to try it again.

You probably don't need an electric fence for protection against woodchucks and skunks. Some woodchucks will climb fence posts to get over chicken wire, but usually they dig a tunnel under it. One way of keeping them away is to sprinkle blood meal, mothballs, or lion dung in the garden. They will be frightened by the smell. I am serious about the lion dung. Most people would consider this a hard-to-find item—obviously. But if you live near a zoo and can get lion dung, sprinkle some around the perimeter of your garden. Pests will never bother it again. Remember that mothballs are dangerous to children and that they look like candy.

There is another tactic that works well against those animals hungrily eying your vegetables. Allow some tall grass to grow around your garden plot. Then make up a mixture of half diesel fuel and half kerosene, and spray it lightly on the grass. Remember that a heavy application will kill it. When the animals start to sneak through the grass, they will get this smelly petroleum on their fur and will hate its taste when they try to lick it off. One trip through the oily grass, and they will stay away from your garden for a while.

If your garden is near a wooded area, you'll probably have to build a strong fence with an electric wire on it to keep out raccoons, squirrels, and other four-legged marauders.

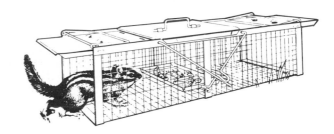

If you can't bear to kill the small animals raiding your garden, you might consider buying one of the many humane traps available. You can release your captives someplace where they won't get into trouble.

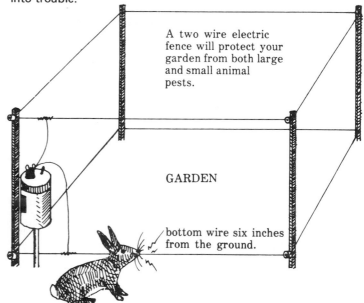

A two wire electric fence will protect your garden from both large and small animal pests.

GARDEN

bottom wire six inches from the ground.

SCARING 'COONS WITH A PUMPKIN FENCE

"Every year I plant pumpkins around my corn patch. I interlace the vines to make a row or "fence" without any gaps. The raccoons will not go through this network of vines. I've done this for ten years and never lost any corn to raccoons." — L.O.S.

76

Harvesting the fruits of your labor

Harvest time is one of the busiest times of the gardening season. Even with the best of planning, there is often an overabundance of vegetables to freeze, can and put on the table.

The home gardener has an advantage over the commercial vegetable grower; he does not have to harvest his crops before they are ripe. The commercial grower, of course, has to plan ahead so that his produce will ripen as it reaches the market. You can pick your vegetables just as they reach their prime.

Knowing when vegetables are perfect for picking is a skill that you will gain with experience. In general, though, it is best to bring things in from the garden just before you are going to eat them or prepare them for storage in the freezer, in a root cellar, or in canning jars. With every minute that passes from the time the produce is picked until the time it is eaten or processed, the vegetables lose quality and food value. Never leave fresh vegetables sitting around for a long time. If, for some reason, you have to pick vegetables a while before they are going to be used, keep them either in a refrigerator or in a cool, dark cellar. This will slow down the deterioration process.

Some vegetables can be picked before they are completely mature. Young onions, beets, carrots, cabbages, and the leaves from head-lettuce plants that have not had time to form heads are all delicious. I think you will find that most of the early crops in your garden will mature quite suddenly, and that there is an all-too-short period of time to harvest them before they go by. Later varieties and succession crops are not so frustrating because they ripen in the fall when the weather is cooler, and, because it is cooler, they are not apt to mature so quickly.

When harvesting leaf lettuce, cut the whole plant back to a height of one inch (as has been done in the row on the right). New leaves will soon grow to replace the cut ones.

Pole beans will continue to bear over a longer period if you keep them picked off.

Cauliflower heads should be blanched just as they start to form. To do so, tie the large outer leaves together over the top of each head.

If you want your plants to continue to bear vegetables, you must keep them harvested. Pick everything you can as soon as it is ready, even if you know that it is impossible for you to use it all. If you have to, throw your surplus in the compost pile. Putting unused vegetables back into the garden soil is not nearly so wasteful as throwing them away. Better still, make plans to preserve some of what you have left over, or share some with neighbors and needy folks. Giving fresh vegetables away is the friendliest gesture I know of.

The crops you harvest latest in the season are the easiest and best ones to store. Your root cellar—if you have one—will have cooled off by this time. Potatoes, cabbages, and turnips should be ready just in time to go into the root cellar. Eat your first plantings of beets and carrots throughout the summer months, and plan to use your later plantings for canning and freezing.

People often boast about having the biggest beets or carrots. This is fine for your ego, or if you want something to take to the fair, but eating these things is sometimes like chewing on a piece of old shoe leather. I like to grow vegetables which I call "table size." This means harvesting beets, for example, when they are slightly larger than a lemon. Carrots shouldn't be much bigger around than your thumb. Big, big vegetables have "gone by;" they have passed the point of being ripe, tender, and flavorful.

The more you harvest, the more you grow. It is very simple. If you don't pick your lettuce, it will go to seed. If you can't use all you have grown, give some to a friend. You will probably find that you can cut down the plants about three times before the lettuce gets bitter. Chard and other heat-tolerant greens can be cut continuously all summer long. If you keep cutting spinach, you can get as many as four harvests. Don't forget to cut little leaves, big leaves—the whole works.

Too often, when folks harvest leaf lettuce, they just pick at it. They take off one leaf at a time, picking only the biggest ones. What you should do is take a long knife or scissors and cut the whole row down to a height of about one inch. Don't cut down more than you can use at any one time. Keep moving down the row, cutting the lettuce as you need it. By the time you get to the end of the row, you can go back to the beginning and start all over again on the new lettuce that will have grown back.

This works just as well with chard. If you only pick the outer leaves, as many people do, you never get at the really good chard because you keep eating the older, tougher leaves. If you cut back the whole row, the little leaves will add to the tenderness and flavor of your crop, and the plants will continue to grow new leaves all season long.

People just pick at spinach in the same way. It's too bad that more folks don't cut it down. If you let spinach get three or four inches high and then cut down the whole row to a height of one inch, you can cut it several more times before it "bolts" and goes to seed. If you just pick away at it, one leaf at a time, you won't harvest much. A single 100-foot row of spinach will yield as little as two or three bags; by the time you cook it, you may wind up with only a quart or two. But if you plant a ten-inch row, or even a fourteen-inch row, which is 100 feet long, I guarantee that you are going to get lots and lots of spinach—more than enough to give away, believe me.

PROLONGING THE HARVEST IS IMPORTANT

I believe in planting early to extend the growing season as much as possible. Grow things as late as you can too. An old gentleman once told me that if I didn't lose at least some of my first or last crops, I wasn't planting early enough and wasn't trying to stretch out the season enough. Plant all of your hardiest crops as soon as the soil can be worked in the spring and again later in the summer for a fall crop.

There are two other ways to prolong your garden's productive period. One is to make several successive plantings of the same vegetable in different parts of the garden. The other method is to sow two or three varieties of the same crop—an early, a mid-season, and a late variety.

You might, for example, plant three different varieties of sweet corn. You will find growing times listed on seed packets or in your favorite catalog. If you choose the right combination of varieties, you can have a second crop ripening at just about the time you have finished harvesting the first. If you sow bush beans and pole beans at the same time, your bush beans will have stopped producing by the time the pole beans are ready.

Believe it or not, a program for a long harvest period begins sometime in the middle of winter, when you should be carefully reading and studying the maturation times of the vegetables you want to plant. If you know the number of days to maturity, you can accurately stagger the harvesting times by selecting the right varieties and by making successive plantings at strategic times.

Lettuce, cabbage, Brussels sprouts, beets, turnips, broccoli, carrots, chard, and rutabagas will continue to grow even after there has been a frost. But as fall approaches, get into the habit of listening closely to the weather forecasts on the radio and TV. Most tender plants can be protected from frost—at least for a while. It is a shame to let the very first frost of the season kill most of your garden. Many times, there will not be a second one until weeks later.

Protecting tender plants like tomatoes, eggplant, peppers, cucumbers, and beans can add several weeks to your gardening season. Cover them with whatever you can find—old sheets and towels, polyethylene, old burlap bags, and any number of other things. The idea is just to keep them from being nipped by the frost. There is no need to try to keep the soil from freezing. It will stay warm enough by itself.

Later, when there is frost nearly every morning, you can bring some plants inside to grow a little longer in a warm window. This is a good time to cut "slips" from your tomato plants. Cut off a small sucker and put it in a glass of water. It will start to root in a day or so, and when it does, you can plant it in a pot. Use the smaller varieties, such as Pixies and cherry tomatoes, unless you have lots of room inside.

Don't leave unripe tomatoes outside to freeze and rot. Bring them in to ripen while still green. Pull up the whole plant if you like. I have done this with peppers as well as tomatoes. I just hang the plant bottom-side-up in a dark room. Sooner or later, the fruit will ripen.

Soil building the foundation of your garden's health

If one gardening practice is more important than any other, it is building the structure and fertility of the soil.

by Rich Alther and Dick Raymond

Your soil is alive! And if you want it to be healthy, fertile, and continuously productive, it must be fed plenty of organic matter. By "alive," we specifically mean that each square inch of good garden soil contains teeming millions of microorganisms. Most forms of soil life are too small to see. Of course, we're all familiar with one of the largest soil organisms, the ordinary earthworm, which feeds entirely upon raw, undigested vegetable matter. In the gradual process of literally consuming and decomposing all dead plant and animal remains, the soil organisms cause the release of valuable minerals and trace elements in a form that plant roots can absorb.

You've heard the term, "humus," which is organic matter at its final stage of decomposition. Humus gives a good soil its important spongy texture. It allows the necessary circulation of air to plant roots and soil, and it enables the soil to absorb and retain just the right amount of moisture too.

Soil that is not regularly refueled with organic matter can truly become lifeless and unable to support plants. Earthworms, which are ravenous eaters, will go elsewhere in search of food. Minerals and other nutrients will stay "locked up" in soil particles, unavailable for plant growth without the intense activity of microorganisms (microbes, for short).

Decomposing organic matter produces weak carbonic acids which help to dissolve soil nutrients. This beneficial process is one of many that come to a halt when fresh supplies of organic material are unavailable. Chemical fertilizers can be poured on in huge quantities, but, unfortunately, they won't do a thing for the soil texture or for the soil-life population in the long run.

There are many ways to put organic matter into your soil. Following are the most common methods.

1. You can buy it in packaged form. Peat moss, dehydrated manures, even sewage sludge, can be hauled to your garden and worked in.

2. You can chop and till all garden residues and weeds into your soil.

3. You can also buy bales of hay or straw, use it for mulch, then chop and till it into the soil.

4. You can obtain wood shavings or wastes from canneries, cider mills, and other local processors, usually free for the taking.

5. You can use all kinds of animal manures, household garbage, leaves, and grass clippings.

6. You can collect any of the above materials, compost them, and then work the finished product into your garden.

7. You can grow various crops as "green manure" strictly for their soil-improving benefits, then chop and till them into the soil.

HERE'S HOW TO DO IT

If your soil has been neglected for many years, it will most likely take more than one year to restore it to a productive, fertile state. Nature does things gradually, but there are some things that the gardener can do to create ideal conditions and give nature a boost.

Growing green manures is an outstanding technique for improving soil texture by increasing its humus content and building up the available supply of topsoil plant nutrients. Plants grow by drawing nutrients from the soil, die, and then return to the earth those nutrients that were used in growing. Green manures are crops grown simply for the purpose of being chopped and mixed directly back into the soil.

SEVEN REASONS FOR GROWING GREEN MANURES

1. With green manuring, you can avoid the time and work of collecting and hauling organic matter to your garden.

2. Green manure is a very economical source of organic matter.

3. Once a green-manure crop has been turned under, it provides excellent food for earthworms.

4. The roots of many green-manure crops reach deep into the subsoil, absorbing valuable nutrients and bringing them up into the plant tissues. When the crop is turned under, the nutrients will revitalize the topsoil.

5. Certain crops, called legumes, have the ability to capture and fix large amounts of nitrogen from the air. Legumes actually add more of this important plant nutrient to the soil when tilled under than they consumed in growing.

6. Depending upon your specific soil profile, growing green manures can cut down on your need to purchase fertilizers and other soil additives and conditioners.

7. A green-manure garden becomes more and more weed-free every year because the crops choke out weeds.

NITROGEN CONTENT OF GREEN MANURES

Most impressive of all, perhaps, is the evidence which the experiment stations have turned up on the actual fertilizing qualities of various green manures. They produce a broad range of minerals for enrichment of the soil. They are a particularly good source of nitrogen, which is essential to plant growth. Here are some crops with approximate percentages of nitrogen (N) on a dry basis.

CROP	PERCENTAGE OF N
Alfalfa	3.0–4.0
Vetch, hairy	3.0–4.0
Austrian winter peas	3.0–3.8
Clover, crimson	3.0–3.3
Clover, red	2.8–3.2
Cowpeas	2.5–3.0
Lespedeza, common	2.2–2.5
Lespedeza Sericea	2.1–2.4
Lupine, blue	2.0–2.5
Oats	1.3–1.4
Rye	1.2–1.3
Rye grass	1.2–1.3

All but the last three crops in the above chart are legumes. Note their higher percentage of nitrogen.

Summarizing many experiments with corn, the USDA reports that a good growth of a winter legume turned under three to four weeks before planting corn will produce as much corn per acre as fifty to one-hundred pounds of commercial nitrogen. If you use nitrate of soda, a common nitrogenous fertilizer, a good green-manure crop can benefit your corn as much as 250 to 500 pounds of this fertilizer.

In a Maine experiment, green manure increased the yield of potatoes by an average of thirty-five bushels an acre. In Alabama, a study was made comparing the value of vetch with that of commercial nitrogen. During a six-year period, an average of only three bushels of snap beans per acre were harvested when neither green manure nor nitrogen was used. Snap beans following vetch produced 161 bushels. This was better than the results obtained with commercial nitrogen. Sixty pounds of chemical fertilizer per acre produced 144 bushels of beans.

Enriching the soil with plenty of organic matter (like the green-manure crop of buckwheat on the preceding page) establishes a firm basis for a successful gardening program.

An effective green-manuring program can reduce by about one-half the fertilizer needs of the average garden.

WHEN AND HOW TO SOW A GREEN-MANURE CROP

You can sow an appropriate green-manure crop at any time during the growing season, but if you want to raise green-manure and vegetable crops in the same spot during the same year, you should embark on a green-manure plan in late summer.

If you have plenty of land, perhaps you'll want to grow food crops in one part and begin improving another part with green manures. Each year, you could rotate your food crops and green manures. This would be ideal, but most gardeners don't have the luxury of so much land.

Here's how to proceed if you can't rotate your garden spots. All garden residues should go back into the soil before you sow a green-manure crop. Turn under those residues when they're still green—the sooner after harvest the better. They're more succulent to the earthworms and microbes, and they break down much faster. You can get a jump on green manuring by sowing seeds between the rows after your final fall cultivation. Later, you can turn under the crop residues and some green manure.

If you have a rear-end tiller, it's very easy to turn under all kinds of residues—tomato and pea vines, thick roots, even standing cornstalks. Cutting garden plants and weeds down with a rotary mower will make it possible to incorporate organic matter with any good tiller or garden tractor. If you are gardening by hand, without power equipment, then you may want to reduce your garden residues in a compost pile. The tough fibers will be at least partially broken down—enough so to make reasonable the work of spading under by hand.

PREPARING THE SEEDBED

After your garden is clear of crop residues, you are ready to prepare a fall seedbed. Most green-manure seeds are on the small side, so the seedbed should be groomed fine. This will speed germination and get the crop off to a fast start.

If you didn't get a chance to add some ground limestone last spring, now is a good opportunity. A soil test is one way to judge more accurately the amount needed. Lime will not interfere with the green-manure seeds you're about to plant. Lime can be lightly broadcast by hand, then tilled into the topsoil.

One of the disadvantages of using commercial fertilizer is that it sometimes overstimulates foliage and green growth in food crops at the expense of the fruit. You need not worry about this with green manures. Stimulating green growth is exactly what you want to do. Especially if you've had a very poor gardening season on neglected soil, you should apply a generous amount of 10-10-10 fertilizer before planting green

This fine seedbed was prepared with a tiller. After sowing the seeds of his green-manure crop (in this case, buckwheat), Dick will use his tiller to cover the seeds with a one-inch-deep layer of soil. (Small seeds, such as those of the clovers, should be covered with only ½ inch of soil.) Of course, he puts his tiller to good use again when it's time to turn under the lush crop of buckwheat.

manure. This will boost the growth of the crop and will assure an ample harvest of organic matter. You can spread and till the fertilizer in at the same time you apply the ground limestone.

SOWING THE SEED

The easiest way to sow the seeds of your green-manure crop is by hand, broadcast style. Just make sure you don't get heavy-handed and sow too thickly; your crop will grow fastest if the plants are spaced far enough apart.

Next, the seed should be lightly covered with fine soil. This can be done with a rear-mounted rotary tiller or you could do this essential step by hand with a rake, just as you would if you were planting a new lawn. Most grains, such as wheat, oats, and buck-wheat, should be covered to a depth of one inch. Smaller seeds, such as the clovers, need only be covered by one-half inch of soil. Firming the seed in by walking over the seedbed or by rolling will hasten germination, as will watering if conditions are dry.

UP AND GROWING

In a few weeks, a green-manure crop of rye grass will be a light green blanket of grass and roots, which will do much good for your garden, even if it only grows a few inches before winter sets in. The tight web of roots will hold the soil securely and stop erosion that could result from wind and rain. It will also prevent needless evaporation of moisture from uncovered soil.

The next spring, a thick matting of dead (annual) rye grass will be all ready to chop up and spade or till under once the soil has warmed up sufficiently. Already the dead and decomposing grass and roots are providing food for the earthworms.

If you had used a perennial crop, such as a rye which survives the winter, then you would allow it to grow up again in spring before tilling it under in order to get a double helping of organic matter. Since it's best to till under any kind of organic material ten days to two weeks before planting, the area in which a perennial green manure was grown will have to be reserved for a late-planted crop, such as sweet corn or tomatoes.

THE MOST POPULAR GREEN-MANURE CROPS FOR HOME USE

RYE GRASS. The hardy one with lush, rapid, green growth, rye grass is easy to grow and yields abundant organic matter. It will take hold in almost any soil any-where in the country. It also is easy to find in farm-supply stores. For most purposes, we recommend the annual type, which will survive only until the heavy freezes of winter. It's ideal for the early section of the garden; by the next spring, the grass and roots will be dead, partially decomposed, and easy to turn under.

If you plant the perennial or permanent variety of rye grass, called winter rye, it can survive the winter and yield another harvest of green growth in the spring. Till-ing it under will completely shred and bury

Rye

Buckwheat

the roots so they won't return to interfere with your next crop.

BUCKWHEAT. It's hard to beat buck-wheat as a green manure for really im-poverished soil. It will grow in sand, clay, and overly dry or wet areas. Of course, it will be scraggly and reflect the low soil quality, but at least you can get a cover crop going. Buckwheat can be broadcast by hand.

Like rye, the advantage of buckwheat as a green manure is that it produces a lot of organic material very quickly. It's es-pecially good for loosening up tough sod and killing weeds and lawn grasses when you're making a brand new garden.

Buckwheat is much hardier than most of the other grains, such as wheat, corn, and oats. It does particularly well in the north-east, but don't hesitate to try it in other sections of the country too.

Buckwheat is actually a summer green manure. It's best to sow it when the ground is thoroughly warmed in summertime, say in June or July, after you've harvested your peas and other early crops. It will reach the blossom stage in about six or eight weeks and will be ready for harvesting as a mulch, as chicken feed, or—a little later when seeds are fully mature—for your own buckwheat flour.

You'll usually find honeybees swarming through buckwheat blossoms. Pollen is often hard to find at that time of year, and the bees love it. It makes a wonderfully rich, dark honey.

In late summer, a rear-end rotary tiller can be used to chop up and turn under a hip-high growth of buckwheat. A better alternative to turning under your buckwheat crop is to simply mow it down and leave it. The seeds will settle in the loosened soil and replant the crop the following spring. This way, you can get two green-manure crops from a single sowing if your soil really needs improving and if you can wait that long before planting a food crop. To get rid of buckwheat permanently, be sure to till it under after blossoming but before the seeds develop.

LEGUMES. Legumes have a very special importance when used for soil improvement. They attract certain types of soil microbes to their roots; these microbes extract nitrogen from the air and convert it to a form usable by the plants. So a legume actually returns more nitrogen to the soil than it used in growing.

To make sure the nitrogen-fixing microbes are present, it's usually recommended that you "inoculate" legume seeds with a mixture of these tiny creatures before planting. The inoculant culture, which comes as a dark powder, can be purchased from most suppliers of legume seeds. Mix the inoculant with water according to the directions and evenly coat the seeds.

Clover is the best-known legume. There are many kinds of perennial clovers, so there is most likely one well suited to your climate. The blossoms are ideal for honeybees. With both vetch and clover, you should plan to allow the crop to grow at least one full season, perhaps two, to get the maximum benefit from nitrogen fixation and green growth. Alsike clover has

the benefit of growing on ground too wet for the red clovers. One disadvantage of vetch and clover, however, is that they're wiry and sometimes difficult to destroy completely if left for several years.

Hairy vetch, one of the many types of vetch, is perennial but relatively slow-growing. It's good to plant a fast-growing, annual "nurse crop" like rye or oats along with the inoculated vetch seed to provide shade and check competitive weed growth. Rye also gives support to the vine-like growth of vetch. If you do decide to plant two crops at once, plant the perennial more thinly than you would ordinarily. Otherwise, the annual nurse crop may be choked out.

Soybeans

Many common vegetables are legumes, so you can get both food and green manure from the same crop. All members of the bean and pea families are legumes. As you have probably found, it takes a large planting of garden peas to provide enough for your family. They're so delicious that they don't go far. Well, you can really stretch the garden-pea harvest and get many of the beneficial effects of a cover crop by broadcasting the seeds in very wide rows. This way, they'll choke out competitive weeds and keep the ground moist and cool too.

You can get away with thick plantings of peas in most soils because they're so hardy. And, as legumes, they produce helpful amounts of nitrogen.

Cowpeas are a fast-growing crop excellent for use as green manure because they produce so much foliage. Try sowing them in combination with oats to help support the vines.

Another good, edible legume is the common soybean, which is becoming increasingly important as a true meat substitute. Soybeans are the only vegetable which has the essential proteins of meat. A crop of soybeans can, of course, be grown strictly as green manure. They will greatly improve the soil in just one season.

ALFALFA, THE KING OF SOIL-IMPROVEMENT CROPS

Alfalfa

From all the research we've done, it seems that alfalfa is number one when it comes to green manures. American farmers and gardeners realize the value of this legume. It is estimated that over one-third of all the hay produced in our country is now alfalfa.

Alfalfa is right on top in terms of protein content, which breaks down into usable nitrate "fertilizer." It's one of the most palatable and nutritious foods for livestock, so it must be a delicacy for earthworms too!

If you'd like to take advantage of this fertile green manure, you can either plant alfalfa and let it grow for at least two seasons in a section of your garden, or you can grow it in a permanent spot nearby and harvest it as mulch. More than one season is needed for its roots to reach their full length—up to twenty feet.

Alfalfa's nitrogen content is considerably higher than that of most legumes. Its leaves and stalks store up many more nutrients than they use in growing. Alfalfa also contains calcium, magnesium, phosphorous, potassium, manganese, and zinc, which makes it a nearly complete natural fertilizer.

WEEDS. Weeds—a green-manure crop? Yes! These guardians of the soil must not be overlooked. They are Mother Nature's most common green manure. Weeds help to correct for nutrient and trace-mineral

Kale

Kale and soybeans serve as both green-manure and food-producing crops. You could even harvest a little of your alfalfa for making a pleasant herbal tea. All kinds of garden peas and beans can do double duty as food crops and green-manure crops.

imbalances in a soil. Most weeds are very deep-rooted and draw valuable elements up to the topsoil. We think of them as a nuisance because they compete with food crops, but in that idle section of your garden, they're busily at work, if only keeping the topsoil covered and intact. Just be sure to till them under before they go to seed, especially if you plan food crops there the next year.

KALE. A lot of people have never tasted freshly picked kale. It happens to be an amazing crop for a lot of reasons. It's very easy to grow; bugs don't bother it much; you can plant it anytime from early spring to late fall; and it can be sown as a green-manure crop. It does everything for your soil that a good, thick, nonleguminous green-manure crop should do. Frost helps to improve the flavor; you can actually dig it out of the snow in the dead of winter. Kale can be picked anytime to provide delicious greens for cooking like spinach or serving raw in salads. It's also extremely high in vitamin A.

Winter picking of kale is an unusual experience. The kale stays crisp and delicious even under snow. Quite often, the kale survives the winter and produces another crop of greens the following spring. Finally, the crop can be tilled back under.

PLANT GREEN MANURES ALL YEAR FOR MAXIMUM RESULTS

Once you see the improvement that comes from green manuring, you'll try not to let bare parts of your garden waste valuable growing time again. A few weeks after turning under the residues of your early crops, like peas and lettuce, you can start your green-manure program. Broad strips of annual rye grass can get a head start in midsummer, well before the onions and other nearby vegetables are harvested.

SPRING. If you'd like to plant a green manure in very early spring to improve soil that will be planted later in the season, try regular garden peas of an early variety. They produce rapid growth in great quantity and can be planted as soon as the soil can be worked in spring. After you harvest the peas and turn under the residues as green manure, wait a week or so, and plant your next food or green-manure crop.

SUMMER. For growing in midseason, we recommend buckwheat. It thrives in dry, hot, summer weather because its dense clusters of stems shade and cool the ground. As discussed earlier, buckwheat grows practically anywhere and does an excellent job of disrupting the weed cycle. Oats are good too, if moisture is sufficient, and they're always easy to buy.

FALL. Rye is the ideal fall crop because of its hardiness. You can even plant it in late October, if unseasonably mild, and still get a few inches of green growth. The perennial winter rye will survive and shoot up again in the spring, allowing gardeners in the warmer climates up to four full green-manure crops in one year.

FERTILIZER AND GREEN MANURES

An experienced Tennessee "pick your own" farmer believes Balboa rye is the best green-manure crop he can grow. He likes to let it get tall enough in the spring so just a few heads of rye show before tilling under.

Planting time in his area is as close to the first of September as he can plant. In the spring he likes to plow under the rye as late as possible. About ten to fourteen days before plowing under, he broadcasts about 1/3 of the total fertilizer he plans to use on his crop throughout the season, about 500 pounds per acre. He uses a balanced fertilizer like 5-10-10. The remainder of the fertilizer is broadcast over the entire field just before planting and worked in well.

If a rain comes before the rye is plowed under, it will pick up the fertilizer into its stalk and leaves. Then after the rye has been turned under and is beginning to decompose, it will gradually release these nutrients for the next crop to use over a long period of time.

If he doesn't get a rain, he cultivates the fertilizer in deep. He wants the roots of the vegetable crop to go down as deep into the soil as he can get them. He also cultivates deep — down to about twelve inches — the first time he cultivates, while the plants are still small. This encourages these roots to grow downward instead of staying near the surface.

He used to plant vetch and clovers for green manure crops, but found he was getting too much nitrogen for his main crop of beans.

No additional side dressing is used as long as the plant leaves have a rich green color. If they develop streaks or otherwise indicate a nutrient deficiency of some kind, he side dresses with a corrective fertilizers. JLG

OATS AS A COVER CROP

If you use oats for a cover crop, plant early in the spring to give the plants time to "stool," which means a cluster of stalks will grow up from one root clump. You will get more growth from a smaller amount of seed planted. RA

This lush crop of Sudan grass and soybeans is part of the owner's rotation program. Next year, he will plant a food crop here; the second year, he will plant sudan and soybeans again.

RYE GRASS ROOTS

One rye plant can grow an estimated three miles of roots — in one day. In one year, it will produce a total of 387 miles of roots. The plants are continually building underground compost piles. In a one-half-acre garden, a crop of rye will produce 400 to 800 pounds of root growth, all of which will decompose and add humus to the soil.

TRENCH COMPOSTING

"I dug deep ditches across my garden in the fall. During the winter, I put in all garbage, newspapers, and scraps of all kinds that would decay. Every time I threw in a load, I covered it over with a little dirt. In the spring, I tilled over this and planted. My, my, I had a good garden!" SR

CORN AND VETCH

"I've grown acres of sweet corn on the same land for ten — twelve years, and it gets better every year. I never rotate it. I sow a cover crop of vetch along with some rye as a nurse crop to hold the vetch up — around twenty pounds of vetch to three pecks of rye. After it makes some growth in the spring, about a foot or two, I plow it under. Vetch, I believe, is the best cover crop you can grow! About two weeks after the vetch is plowed under, I broadcast with 5-10-10 fertilizer. Vetch supplies plenty of nitrogen." HL

TILLING UNDER GARDEN RESIDUE

It's important that corn stalks or the residue of any other harvested crop be worked into the soil as soon after harvest as possible. The greener the material, the more nutrients are returned to the soil. When you're through picking a row, don't let it lie idle until next spring. Work that green material back into the soil, and plant another vegetable or a green-manure crop to till under in the spring. ES

GREEN MANURES

Common Name		Legume	Soil Preference	Lime Requirements (Low, Medium or High)	Adapted to Soils of Low Fertility	Relative Longevity of Seed	Seeding Rate (lbs. per acre)	Seeding Rate (lbs. per 1000 sq. ft.)	Depth to Cover Seed	N.E. and N.C. States	Southern and S.E. States	Gulf Coast and Florida	Northwestern States	Southwestern States	When to Sow	When to Turn Under	Comments
Barley		No	Loams	L		Long	100	2½	¾	•					Spring / Fall	Summer / Spring	Not good on sandy or acid soils. Sow spring varieties in north, winter varieties in milder climates.
Beans	Mung	Yes	Widely Adaptable	L	•	Short	70	2	1		•	•			Spring or Summer	Summer or Fall	Warm weather crops. Do not sow until ground is warm and weather is settled.
	Soy	Yes	Loams	M	•	Short	90	2½	1½		•	•			Spring or Summer	Summer or Fall	
	Velvet	Yes	Loams	L	•	Short	120	4	2		•	•			Spring or Summer	Summer or Fall	
Beggar Weed		Yes	Sandy Loams	L	•		15	½	½		•	•			Spring or Early Summer	Summer or Fall	Seeding rate is for scarified seed. Treble the amount if unhulled seed is used.
Brome Grass, Field		No	Widely Adaptable	L		Long	30	1	½	•			•		Fall / Spring	Spring / Fall	Good winter cover. Easy to establish. Hardier than rye. More heat tolerant.
Buckwheat		No	Widely Adaptable	L	•		50	1½	¾	•					Late Spring and Summer	Summer or Fall	Quick growing. Plant only after ground is warm.
Bur Clover		Yes	Heavy Loams	M		Long	30	1	½			•		•	Fall	Spring	Not winter hardy north. One of the best winter crops where mild winters prevail.
Chess or Cheat Grass		No	Loams	L		Long	40	1	¾	•					Fall	Spring	Less sensitive to soil acidity and poorly drained soils than most clovers.
Clover	Alsike	Yes	Heavy Loams	M		Long	8	¼	½	•			•		Spring / Fall	Fall / Spring	
	Crimson	Yes	Loams	M	•	Medium	30	1	½		•	•			Fall / Spring	Spring / Fall	Not winter hardy north. A good winter annual from New Jersey southward.
	Subterranean	Yes	Loams	M		Medium	30	1	½			•		•	Fall	Spring	
Corn		No	Widely Adaptable	L		Medium	90	2½	1	•	•	•	•	•	Spring or Summer	Summer or Fall	Do not sow until ground is warm.
Cow-Pea		Yes	Sandy Loams	L	•	Short	90	2½	1½		•	•			Late Spring or Early Summer	Summer or Fall	Withstands drought and moderate shade well. Do not sow until weather is warm and settled.
Crotalaria		Yes	Light Loams	L	•	Long	15	½	¾		•	•			Spring or Summer	Summer or Fall	Does well on acid soils. Resistant to root knot nematode. Sow scarified seed.
Fenugreek		Yes	Loams	L		Long	35	1	½					•	Fall	Spring	
Guar		Yes	Widely Adaptable	L	•	Long	40	1½	1		•			•	Spring or Early Summer	Summer or Fall	Thrives on warm soils. Do not plant too early.
Indigo, Hairy		Yes	Sandy Loams	L		Short	10	½	½		•	•			Spring or Early Summer	Summer or Fall	
Kale, Scotch		No	Widely Adaptable	H	•	Long	14	¼	½	•	•				Summer or Fall	Spring	Can be eaten after serving as winter cover. In Northern areas interplant with winter rye for protection. Except in deep south, plant in summer for good growth before frost.
Lespedeza	Common	Yes	Loams	L	•	Short	25	1	½		•	•			Early Spring	Summer or Fall	Good on acid soils of low fertility. Easy to establish on hard, badly eroded soils.
	Korean	Yes	Loams	L	•	Short	25	1	½		•	•			Early Spring	Summer or Fall	
	Sericea	Yes	Loams	L	•	Medium	25	1	½		•	•			Early Spring	Summer or Fall	

Lupine — **Blue**	Yes	Sandy Loams	L		Short	100	2½	1			●			Spring Fall	Summer Spring	
Lupine — **White**	Yes	Sandy Loams	L		Short	120	2½	1	●		●			Spring Fall	Summer Spring	Less popular than the yellow lupine and blue lupine. } Good on sour and acid soils.
Lupine — **Yellow**	Yes	Sandy Loams	L		Short	80	2	1	●		●			Spring Fall	Summer Spring	
Millet	No	Sandy Loams	L		Long	30	1	½	●					Late Spring or Summer	Summer or Fall	Sow only after ground is warm, a week or ten days after normal corn planting time. Fast growing.
Mustard, White	No	Loams				8	¼	¼	●					Spring	Summer	
Oats	No	Widely Adaptable	L		Long	100	2½	1	●	●	●	●	●	Spring Fall	Summer or Fall Spring	Winter oats (sown in fall) are suitable only where mild winters prevail.
Pea — **Field**	Yes	Heavy Loams	M		Short	90	2½	1½	●	●	●	●	●	Early Spring Fall	Summer Spring	Sow in fall only where winters are mild. Distinctly a cool weather crop.
Pea — **Rough**	Yes	Sandy Loams	L	●	Medium	60	1½	1		●				Fall	Spring	
Pea — **Tangier**	Yes		M		Medium	80	2½	1	●				●	Spring	Summer	
Rape	No	Loams	L			8	¼	¼	●			●		Spring or Summer	Summer or Fall	
Rescue Grass	No	Widely Adaptable	L		Long	35	1	¾		●			●			Adapted to mild winters and humid climates.
Rye, Spring	No	Widely Adaptable	L		Long	90	2	¾	●	●				Spring	Summer	
Rye, Winter	No	Widely Adaptable	L		Long	90	2	¾	●	●				Fall	Spring	One of the most important winter cover crops. Can be sown late.
Rye-Grass, Italian	No	Widely Adaptable	L		Long	35	1	¾	●	●	●	●	●	Fall Spring	Spring Summer	An important winter cover crop where winters are mild. In severe climates sow in spring or summer.
Sesbania	Yes	Widely Adaptable	L	●	Long	25	1	¾		●	●		●	Spring or Summer	Summer or Fall	Quick grower. Is better adapted to wet soils and will grow at higher altitudes than crotalaria.
Sorghum	No	Light Loams			Long	90	2½	¾	●	●			●	Late Spring or Summer	Summer or Fall	Do not sow until ground is warm and weather is settled. More drought resistant than corn.
Sudan Grass	No	Widely Adaptable	L		Long	35	1	¾	●	●	●	●	●	Late Spring or Summer	Summer or Fall	Rapid grower. Do not sow until ground is warm and weather is settled.
Sunflower	No	Widely Adaptable	L			20	¾	¾	●	●	●	●	●	Spring or Summer	Summer or Fall	Intolerant of acid soils.
Sweet-Clover — **Common White**	Yes	Heavy Loams	H		Long	15	½	½	●	●		●	●			Quite winter hardy. Best results are from fall sowing.
Sweet-Clover — **Annual (Hubam)**	Yes	Loams	H		Long	15	½	½	●			●				A true annual. Best results from spring sowings.
Sweet-Clover — **Yellow**	Yes	Loams	H		Long	15	½	½	●	●		●	●			Stands dry conditions better than common white sweet clover.
Sweet-Clover — **Yellow Annual**	Yes	Loams	H		Long	15	½	½	●	●	●	●	●			Most useful south of the cotton belt as winter cover. North not winter hardy. Makes short summer growth.
Vetch — **Common**	Yes	Widely Adaptable	L		Medium	60	1½	¾	●	●	●	●	●	Spring Fall	Fall Spring	Not winter hardy where severe cold is experienced. Needs reasonably fertile soil.
Vetch — **Hairy**	Yes	Widely Adaptable	L	●	Long	60	1½	¾	●	●	●	●	●	Spring Fall	Fall Spring	The most winter hardy vetch. Best sown in fall mixed with winter rye or winter wheat.
Vetch — **Hungarian**	Yes	Heavy Loams	L		Long	60	1½	¾	●	●		●	●	Spring Fall	Fall Spring	Next to hairy vetch the most winter hardy of the vetches. Not winter hardy where winters are severe. Needs fairly fertile soil.
Vetch — **Purple**	Yes	Loams	L		Long	60	1½	¾	●	●	●	●	●	Spring Fall	Fall Spring	Least hardy of the vetches. Suited for winter cover in mild climates only.
Vetch — **Woolly Pod**	Yes	Widely Adaptable	L		Long	60	1½	¾	●	●	●	●	●	Spring Fall	Fall Spring	
Wheat, Winter	No	Loams	L		Long	100	2½	¾	●			●		Fall	Spring	

DICK'S COMPOST ADVENTURES

The simple way to magically turn old leaves, hay, weeds, and garbage into compost.

THANKS, I NEEDED THAT.

1 Take a strip of wire mesh 2 or 3 feet wide by 9 feet long. Fasten the ends together to form a circular compost cage.

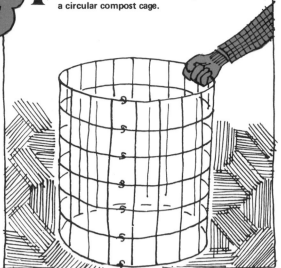

Compost organizers can be made of different materials and in various shapes.

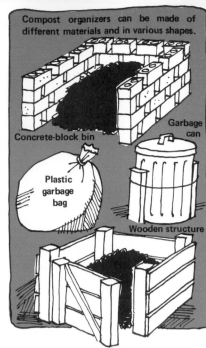

Concrete-block bin

Garbage can

Plastic garbage bag

Wooden structure

2 Place a 2- to 6-inch thick layer of coarse material, such as leaves, hay, or weeds, in the bottom.

MEAL

3 Sprinkle on a large handful of an activator, rich in nitrogen and protein, thoroughly covering the coarse material. You can use alfalfa meal, soybean meal, cottonseed meal, bone meal or other high-protein meal. Commercial fertilizer will not work.

4 Continue building the compost pile by alternating layers of coarse material and meal.

5 Moisten pile thoroughly. Don't oversoak. Most failures are due to the pile's being too dry or too wet.

6 Compact the outer edges of the pile.
IMPORTANT:
The center must remain loose to allow air to penetrate the pile. The composting process depends upon the meal, coarse material, moisture, and air all coming in contact with each other.
If the pile is made correctly, the temperature will reach 140° to 150° F. in several days.
In about one week, turn the pile, mixing the materials together. Fork outside dry material into the center of the pile. Moisten pile again if it's too dry. The heating process will start up again. Compost is ready to use when the pile stops heating in two to three weeks.

7 To turn pile, remove wire cage by placing your foot on pile and lifting off wire. Fork the material back into empty cage.

Compost, the do-it-yourself fertilizer

Practice good ecology. Take waste materials, like leaves and kitchen scraps, and turn them into a natural form of fertilizer that plants love.

Garden compost is a mixture of various kinds of decomposed organic matter. In a way, it is a "synthetic manure," every bit as rich and fertile as the real thing, and in some ways better.

There are probably as many ways to make compost as there are recipes for salad. Everyone does it a little differently. I won't try to tell you exactly how to do it; you should develop some of your own techniques. I will just make a few general suggestions and describe a composting method that I have helped to develop. My method is for people who don't generate a huge amount of garbage, who don't have enough land to have a lot of excess organic matter, and who like to keep their places looking neat and attractive.

You can make compost in an open pile, but some kind of a container keeps things better organized. The simplest compost containers are round, wire cages or boxes made out of slats of wood. The main purpose of a compost pile—in or out of a container—is to mix moisture, air, and organic matter in equal amounts so that the organic matter will become humus as quickly as possible. In other words, you are trying to get a mixture that is one-third air, one-third water, and one-third organic matter. No one expects these proportions to be perfect, naturally. This is just a rough formula.

Any compost system needs to be activated. In other words, you need to get the helpful bacteria and fungi working for you within the pile. My tests here in Vermont have proven to me that this should be done by adding some sort of protein-nitrogen substance. Commercial fertilizer does not work as an activator. The microorganisms you are trying to encourage do not seem to be interested in man-made nitrogen. It does not help the pile to decompose, and it does not help it to generate heat—an essential factor in successful composting.

Manure, rich soil, alfalfa meal, soybean meal, blood and bone meal, cottonseed meal, and dry dog food are all sources of protein and nitrogen. Animals, of course, take in protein in many different forms and excrete a good deal of it in their manure. Blood meal, bone meal, hoof and horn meal are types of animal matter, which always contains protein. Alfalfa meal and soybean meal come from legumes, so both contain much protein and a lot of nitrogen. Good soil is rich in protein and nitrogen, as is cottonseed meal. The higher the protein content in the activator, the more efficiently the pile will work and the richer your compost will be.

Begin by collecting whatever organic material you have. Next, build yourself a small wire cage or box large enough to hold all of this material and more. Put a few leaves in the container, throw on some garbage, and sprinkle in a handful of activator. Then add a little of some different kind of material, such as grass clippings, and add water—just enough so that the leaves and grass feel like a damp sponge. Don't soak it. Then add another two or three handfuls of activator, and sprinkle on more water. Keep building up layers of material this way until the container is full. If you can't fill the whole thing up right away, add more organic matter to the pile as you get it.

If you have so much organic matter, you don't know what to do with it all, and have access to a supply of manure, you can go into composting on a larger scale. You could build a five-foot pile in a container that is as large as four or five feet square. Begin layering your pile just as before. Throw in some old hay, leaves, or weeds. Then put in a thinner layer of manure and maybe a little soil, and add water. Keep building the pile until you run out of materials or until the container is filled.

Turning and mixing the materials every once in a while is a very important step. Don't forget that the pile needs oxygen.

Microbes at work in the material need to breathe if they are to function properly. Turning and mixing the materials with a pitchfork lets more air into the pile. If the pile suddenly starts to smell bad, the wrong type of bacteria and fungi have taken over inside. This is a sure sign that the pile needs to be turned. You shouldn't have to do this more often than once every several weeks.

Don't expect your compost pile to pro-

The purpose of a compost pile is to mix moisture, air, and organic matter in equal amounts so the organic matter will turn to humus as quickly as possible.

duce rich, black humus which is perfectly decomposed—unless, of course, you plan to let it sit for years. It takes a long time for things like leaves and cornstalks to break down completely. Don't worry if some of the ingredients are not completely rotted. The compost you have made is still good stuff to use in your garden, especially under transplants. The final decomposition will take place in the soil itself. In the meantime, your plants will be getting lots of nourishment. Partly decayed compost is good fertilizer because it releases its nutrients to the plants gradually, not all in one shot.

Lots of people like to add lime to their compost piles. I have always believed that lime slows down the bacterial action in the pile, but I have never seen this proven anywhere. I usually add lime after the compost is removed from the pile and before I use it in the garden. If you have used many different types of material, you don't have to worry about adding lime. Your compost should naturally develop a fairly neutral pH.

Many people believe that compost made out of oak leaves or pine needles will be acidic, and this is true. But experiments in Connecticut and Missouri have proven that tilling oak leaves and pine residues directly into the garden will not lower the soil's pH. It may be wise to have a sample of your compost analyzed. If it really is acidic, treat it with lime.

It is a good idea to grind extremely coarse material before you put it in the compost pile. This exposes more surface area to bacterial action and helps speed up the decomposition. But grinding things so fine that they tend to pack down may hinder air circulation within the pile. If everything is going to be chopped up, you'd better insert some sort of ventilation pipes to get air into the inner parts of the pile.

Are there any materials that you should not put in a compost pile? I am sure you know enough not to put in anything that will never decompose—nonbiodegradable things like plastic, glass, aluminum, and charcoal. Some people use meat scraps; these are fine if you have a very active pile that heats up to temperatures between 100 and 160 degrees F. On the other hand, meat scraps can attract dogs and other carnivorous animals, like raccoons. These creatures will tear up your pile and make a mess. Protect it from them by putting a strong wire screen over the top. Or leave out the meat scraps.

Everyone can compost garbage, even if they have no additional organic matter to add to it. You can do this in a small container that is only two or three feet in diameter. I have made garbage compost by adding peat moss, alfalfa meal, and water to ordinary garbage. I could have used soybean meal, blood or bone meal just as well, I'm sure. The final product of this mixture was a wonderfully rich compost which I added to my potting soil. The seedlings which grew in it turned out to be some of the best I have ever had.

A PERPETUAL-YIELD GARDEN

Can there be such a thing as a garden which yields forever without having any sort of artificial fertilizer added to it? The answer to this question is not clear, but it is something that we should be trying to find out. I have been so concerned about the possibility of a world-wide fertilizer shortage, that I have been doing a little experimenting in my own large garden.

I am trying to grow vegetables on individual test plots without ever applying chemical fertilizer, manure, or organic matter that was not grown right on the garden plot itself. I do this by rotating vegetables and various cover crops and by constantly tilling the residues from all crops right back into the soil. I have added to these plots only lime and some trace minerals which the soil was lacking to begin with.

I rotate the cover crops from one year to the next. I plant annual rye grass, soybeans, winter rye, and vegetable crops. I have been doing this with great success for several years now, but I am not sure how long it can be done. I have been able to grow tremendous cover crops and vegetable crops, apparently without depleting the soil.

The first year, I grow vegetables on a plot. As soon as they have been harvested and the residue tilled back into the soil, I plant annual rye and leave it in place until the spring of the following year. The second spring, I plant soybeans, a nitrogen-fixing legume. When the soybeans get to be around twelve to sixteen inches high—right in their prime, as far as the plants are concerned—I till them into the soil. This gives back all of the nutrients that the plants have gathered while they were growing. After the soybeans, I plant winter rye, which will grow well into the winter. The following spring, I plant vegetables again.

On other plots, I have vegetables one year, and then green-manure crops for the next two years. This technique obviously adds a great deal more organic matter to the soil, but I am not sure if it is better than the other method or not. You should try some similar experiments yourself. It will improve your soil. You will be killing weeds, adding organic matter, and encouraging a large population of earthworms.

Dick Raymond uses no fertilizer of any kind on these experimental plots. One year, he plants vegetables, harvests them, and sows annual rye. The next spring, he tills under the rye and plants soybeans, which he tills under when they are right in their prime. Then he plants winter rye, leaves it in place until spring, and plants vegetables again.

The owners of this charming, kitchen-door herb garden like to use their harvest to brew up healthful and delicious herb teas. If you'd like to try a few yourself, include chamomile, lemon balm, spearmint, peppermint, red clover, catnip, or rosemary in your herb garden. You can make teas out of individual herbs or experiment with blends. There are many other herbs you can try too.

The herb garden

It's easy to grow your own herbs, and they'll add zest to vegetable cookery.

Herbs are easy to grow—a few as easy as lettuce. Some of them should be started indoors and then planted outside, but most of them can be started from seed right in the garden. Plant just the herbs that you like.

Many herbs are annuals; some are biennials; and some perennials are treated as annuals. Some of them will winter over with a little protection. Check the herb chart on the next page to find out which are perennials and which are annuals or biennials. Because the perennials will be in the same spot for a long time, be sure to select a place that needs no tilling or cultivation.

A good mulch over the herbs in the fall will often prevent winter-kill, though a cold, wet winter may cause the mulch to rot the roots of some perennials. Normally, you can go out and harvest herbs from under the mulch in winter.

Plant only a small amount of each variety. A few, like mints, will spread because of their "wandering roots." Most will grow happily in a few square feet of space. You may wish to keep small paths or a gravel mulch between beds, or grow herbs in a border at the garden's edge.

Some herbs, like chives, can be transplanted to an indoor window box in the fall; others, like parsley, do not transplant well beyond the seedling stage. I usually dig up the two- to three-inch dill plants that germinate in the fall from my spring dill crop and bring them inside to pot.

For complete information on herbs, read Betty Jacob's *Profitable Herb-Growing at Home* ($5.95 from Garden Way Publishing).

HERBS

HERB	HEIGHT (INCHES)	DESCRIPTION	CULTURE	HARVEST	USE
ANNUALS AND BIENNIALS					
Annuals grow from seed and complete their life cycle in one year. They will be killed by frost and must be started from seed each year. Biennials will overwinter one season and produce seed the second season.					
ANISE (Annual)	20-24	Serrated leaves, small white flowers. Low spreading plant is a slow growing annual.	Moderately rich soil. Likes full sun. Space 6-8 in. in rows 12-14 in. apart.	When seeds turn brown or use leaves while green as needed.	SEED - pastries, candy, cookies, beverages, meat, soups. LEAVES - salad or garnish.
BASIL (Annual)	20-24	Leafy, light green foliage; flowers white or lavender. Fast growing annual.	Start seed indoors in early April or seed in early spring. Space 12 in. Prefers protected sunny location.	Harvest leaves when flowering begins. Cut plants 4-6 in. above ground.	LEAVES - soups, stews, omelets, salads, meats, sauces.
BORAGE (Annual)	20-24	Coarse, rough hairy leaves. Produces light blue flowers in drooping clusters.	Seed directly in early spring. Space 12 in. apart. Seeds may be slow to germinate.	Harvest the young leaves & dry or cook fresh like spinach.	LEAVES - salads, greens. Flowers and leaf tips - pickles, soups, stews.
CARAWAY (Biennial)	12-24	Carrot-like leaf with small creamy white flowers.	Seed directly in spring & locate in full sun. Space 6 in.	Harvest leaves when mature. Seeds will form midway through second season.	LEAVES - garnish. SEEDS - breads, cakes, soups, sauces, salads.
CHERVIL (Annual)	18	Similar to parsley, with its green lacy leaves. Flowers are small white clusters.	Sow seed in moist, partially shaded location. Space 6 in.	Harvest mature leaves & dry or use directly for garnishes.	LEAVES - salads, soup, meat, poultry, garnishes.
CORIANDER (Annual)	36	Large, coarse plant with white flowers.	Sow seeds directly. Use full sun area and thin to 10 in.	Harvest seeds when they begin to turn brown. Seeds are generally used crushed.	SEEDS - pastries, sauces, pickles, liquors.
DILL (Annual)	24-36	Tall plant with feathery green leaves. Open umbrella shaped flower heads.	Seed directly & thin to 12 in. If seeds mature & fall they will come up again next year.	Harvest mature seed heads before seeds drop. May use small leaves as well.	SPRIGS OF SEED HEAD - pickles, sauces, meats, salads, vinegar.
PARSLEY (Biennial)	5-6	Curled or plain dark green leaves.	May be slow to germinate. Seed in early spring. Space 6-8 inches.	Harvest mature leaves as needed.	LEAVES - garnishes, omelets, salads.
SWEET MARJORAM (Annual where there is frost)	12	Fine textured plant with white flowers.	Start seedlings in shade. Mature plants will grow in full sun. Space 8-10 inches.	Harvest mature leaves.	LEAVES - salads, soups, dressings.
SUMMER SAVORY (Annual)	18	Small gray-green leaves with purple and white flowers.	Plant after danger of frost. Space 6-9 in.	Harvest mature leaves.	LEAVES - salads, soups, dressings, poultry.
PERENNIALS					
Perennials will grow from seed the first year but will grow year after year. Some can be propagated by several other means as well. A straw or leaf mulch through the winter may protect them from winter damage.					
CHIVES	12	Onion-type leaves with mauve round flower head.	Can be grown in containers or outdoors in spring. Divide to increase. Space 8 in.	Clip leaves as needed.	LEAVES - Omelets, salads, soups, sauces, dips.
FENNEL	36	Fine, feathery leaves with broad bulb-like leaf base.	Sow in early spring and thin to 12 inches.	Harvest either young sprigs & leaves or seeds.	SPRIGS - soups LEAVES - garnishes SEEDS - soups, breads
GARLIC CHIVES	12-16	Similar to chives.	Same as chives.	Same as chives.	Substitute for garlic flavor.
PEPPERMINT	18	Vigorous plant with purple flowers.	Prefers rich, moist soil. Space 8-10 in.	Harvest young or mature leaves.	LEAVES - Sauces, tea, jelly. SPRIGS - tea, sauce, summer drinks.
SPEARMINT	18	Pointed, crinkled leaves.	Same as peppermint.	Same as peppermint.	LEAVES - summer drinks, tea, mint sauce.
LEMON BALM	24	Crinkled, dull green leaves with white blossoms. Vigorous grower.	Space 12 in. Prefers full sun.	Harvest mature leaves.	LEAVES - soups, meat, tea, summer drinks.
LOVAGE	24-60	Long stems with umbrella-shaped flower heads.	May start indoors & move to sunny location. Space 12-15 inches.	Harvest mature leaves.	Substitute for celery flavor.
OREGANO	24	Choose English strains. Produces pink flowers.	Plant in rich soil. Space 8-10 in. Start in protected location and move to full sun.	Harvest mature leaves.	LEAVES - soups, roasts, stews, salads.
ROSEMARY	36	Dark green foliage with small blue flowers.	Start cuttings in early spring from old growth. Space 24 in.	Harvest mature leaves.	LEAVES and SPRIGS - meats, sauces, soups. DRIED LEAVES - sachets to hang in closet with garments.
SAGE	18	Shrub-like plant with gray leaves & purple flowers.	Plant in well drained location. Space 30 in.	Harvest leaves before flowering.	LEAVES - meats, teas, fish, dressing, stews.
TARRAGON	24	Select French tarragon. Fine, dark green leaves.	Prefers well drained soils. Space 12 in.	Harvest mature leaves or sprigs.	LEAVES - salads, sauces, eggs, vegetables, salad vinegar.
THYME	8-12	Narrow, dark green leaves.	Start seeds indoors. Prefers full sun & well drained soils. Space 10-12 in.	Harvest leaves & flower clusters before first flowers open.	LEAVES - soups, salads, dressings, omelets, gravy, bread, vegetables.

Cooperative Extension Service of Kansas State University

The fall garden

The fall garden can supply fresh vegetables for your table well after the first frost.

What you do in your fall garden will greatly affect the success of your garden next year. So don't neglect putting your garden to bed, so to speak. If you have already started a cover-crop program, you know you should have some cover crops growing by the time fall rolls around. Be sure that you till in all crop residues. If you leave them in the garden over the winter, you will be creating a haven for insects, worms, and diseases. Once this material is tilled under, the microorganisms will take care of it. If at all possible, plant a cover crop. As an alternative, you might mulch some areas of your garden. It is not always possible to protect your garden through the winter with either a cover crop or mulch, but you should always strive to do so. This will really improve your garden for the next year and will also get rid of weeds and other unwanted garden pests and diseases.

With my late crops, such as broccoli and late cabbage, Brussels sprouts, celery, all lettuces, beets and carrots, I cultivate along in September, then I plant annual rye grass as a cover crop. I put it right between the rows so that when I harvest my late vegetables, I have a cover crop which is already three, four, or five inches tall. I put all the crop residues in the compost pile or till them back in so that I have only a few narrow spots not protected with a cover crop. I mulch these areas if I have some extra organic matter.

EXTEND YOUR TOMATO HARVEST

When you cut suckers off tomatoes in the summer, allow some to get as big as your little finger and to produce a bud. At this point, remove the sucker from the plant and cut all the leaves off up to the bud. Set it in a glass of water for about four hours, make a hole in the ground, set this slip in the hole, and firm the soil around it. Water it liberally for two or three days. In a few weeks, that sucker will produce wonderful fruit, just as a plant grown from seed would. Late in the fall, these late-started plants will be producing large, green tomatoes which you can put in your cellar to ripen long after frost has destroyed your garden plants. The ones you take downstairs will be of the best quality, unlike those from the plants that have been bearing all summer long. Harvest tomatoes for storage from plants that are just coming into the bearing stage. Be sure to leave your stored tomatoes in the dark so they'll ripen evenly.

You can cut suckers from a healthy tomato plant before frost and root them in a pot. Remove the large leaves and plant the sucker in some good potting soil. These will grow indoors and provide tomatoes in winter months. Pixie and patio varieties make good tomato houseplants.

PUTTING IT ALL TOGETHER

We've been paying a lot of attention to the details of gardening — so much so that we may have made gardening sound more complicated than it is. Actually, the basic principles are quite simple. Just to clarify things, we put together this brief summary to help you maintain a proper perspective.

1 PLAN AHEAD WHAT TO PLANT, WHERE, AND HOW MUCH

Here are the decisions you need to make — early, while the nights are still long and cold. (A) Size and kind of garden wanted. (b) How much to plant of each vegetable. Remember that overplanting can be disastrous! (C) Selection of vegetable varieties that you like and that are best for your area. (D) Map out on paper your garden plan to allow room for different vegetable growth habits and harvest times.

2 PREPARE THE SOIL FOR PLANTING AND INSURE FERTILITY

Roto-till or plow your garden deeply, breaking the dirt up smooth, into a fine seedbed. Work into the soil all organic matter — such as manure, compost, leaves, and vegetable waste — that you can. Broadcast a balanced fertilizer over the garden and work it in. Add lime if a soil test indicates a need for it.

3 PLANT AT THE RIGHT TIME — AND THE RIGHT WAY

Find out which vegetables like cold weather and which prefer hot, and plant accordingly. Remember to allow plenty of room for vine crops; to plant corn in a block for good pollination; to plant each type of seed at the proper depth; and to thin seedlings to allow room for growth. If you want to set out home-grown plants instead of seeding directly in the garden, study the charts and plant indoors or in a cold frame at the proper time.

4 CULTIVATE AND GIVE TENDER LOVING CARE TO GROWING PLANTS

Use the hoe often to skim over the soil surface and destroy grass and weeds just as they sprout. Cultivate to allow oxygen to get to the roots and to keep a hard surface from forming on the soil. Or put down a mulch to keep down weeds and conserve soil moisture.

5 PROTECT YOUR PLANTS FROM INSECT PESTS, ANIMALS, AND DISEASES.

Take a walk in the garden each day. Look for signs of pests and disease. Hand-pick insects, pull up and burn diseased plants, or use the best chemical control before a minor problem gets out of hand.

6 HARVEST AT THE PEAK OF GOODNESS AND KEEP THE PLANT PRODUCTIVE

Pick your vegetables as soon as they mature so the plant will keep producing. Know when to harvest for fresh eating, canning, freezing, or drying. Study various winter-storage methods for extending the garden season.

7 PLANT LATE CROPS FOR A FALL HARVEST

Sometime in July, or early August in the South, plant root crops, greens, peas, and other cold-hardy vegetables for a fall harvest. This planting is extremely important as it will provide most of the vegetables you'll store and eat fresh long into the winter.

8 BEGIN A SOIL-BUILDING PROGRAM FOR NEXT SEASON'S GARDEN

As soon as a crop is harvested, chop up and till in the spent plants, or remove them and add to a compost pile. Plant a green-manure crop or sow greens, like kale, or a root crop, like turnips. These will serve double duty, providing a winter harvest and a cover crop. Fall is a good time to add lime and natural rock fertilizers. Cover bare areas in the garden with leaves. Collect any organic waste available to mulch the soil through the winter, or use it for compost or for mulching next spring.

Keeping vegetables all winter

Before the days of supermarkets, keeping fresh vegetables on hand throughout the winter was a necessity. Here's how to get back to this healthy and practical habit.

When people think about root cellars, they usually picture a hole dug into the side of a bank, walled up with stone masonry, and covered with a high mound of soil. It is pretty hard to have a real, old-time root cellar like this these days. Fortunately, there is a much easier and more efficient way to make one.

If you have a basement in your home, you can partition off one corner and turn it into a storage area for vegetables. Don't insulate either the floor or the two outside walls along the foundation. The soil outside the foundation wall will remain at a fairly even temperature all year long—right around fifty-five degrees. This is just about right for a root cellar. Your storage area will be cooled in summer and warmed in winter without your having to put in any kind of artificial heating or cooling system.

Because the northeast corner of the cellar will stay coolest, it is the best place to put your storage area. The two inside partitions and the ceiling of your root cellar (the joists for the floor above) must be insulated. You can use regular 3½-inch fiberglass building insulation. A good, sound door, one that seals reasonably tight, is very important. It is not a bad idea to insulate the inside of the door.

In most cases, it is not necessary to have an outside window in the root cellar. I have none in mine and have never had any trouble. If your basement is particularly damp, though, it might be good to build your partitions in a corner where there is a window so that you will get extra ventilation, or you could add a vent.

I have a storage area like the one I've described in my own cellar, and I find it more than adequate. After a little bit of experimentation, I learned what fruits and vegetables I could store well and for how long. I learned, for example, that apples need to be stored in a much cooler place, and that I could only keep them for a couple of months.

Another thing I've realized is that the temperature varies a lot inside the storage room. It is much cooler near the floor than it is near the ceiling. This is not bad, though; it gives me a wide range of temperatures in which to store several different types of vegetables. Onions need to be somewhat warm, so they can be hung near the ceiling. Squash should be put on a rack of some sort, part way down the wall. Root crops can be stored down near the floor, where the temperature is coolest.

If you plan to put canned goods in your root cellar, remember that they should be at least three feet off the floor. If possible, place them nearer the ceiling than the floor. Don't forget that the temperature variation from the top to the bottom of the room may be as much as ten degrees.

Never put anything on the floor itself. The vegetables need to have air circulation on all sides. If you set them on the floor, they will become moist underneath and will start to rot much sooner. The best thing to do is to build shelves out of wooden slats.

It is a serious mistake to store any diseased vegetables or fruits. Also try to avoid anything bruised or not yet ripe. If you do put less-than-perfect vegetables in the root cellar, keep them separate from the ones that you are going to store all winter, and try to use them up first.

It is important to check vegetables like potatoes, root crops, and squash every once in a while. If you find some that are starting to deteriorate, throw them out onto the compost pile. Not every single vegetable you put in will keep well. Don't be dismayed by the few you lose.

When it is time to store root crops in the fall, pull your carrots, beets, and similar vegetables out of the soil, and let them lie on top of the ground for a few hours on a sunny day. The idea is to let the dirt dry and to kill the roots. Never wash them. Just brush the loose dirt off with your hands. As

Dick always plants a late tomato crop so he'll have plenty of top-quality (but unripe) fruit for winter storage.

Hubbard squash are excellent winter keepers because of their thick skins.

If you don't have a root cellar, you can pack carrots and other root crops in fresh sawdust and keep them all winter.

I said earlier, washing causes vegetables to store poorly.

When you are getting ready to store carrots, you can cut the tops off very close, but when you prepare beets, leave one-half to three-fourths of an inch of stem on each bulb. If you cut beet tops back too close, the bulb will bleed and rot very quickly. Never cut off the small roots on the bottom of a carrot or a beet.

If you do not have a root cellar, you can store root crops in sawdust. I have had good luck with this method. I try to get fresh sawdust—the kind that is still light colored and unweathered. Then I take a regular cardboard box; put two or three inches of sawdust in the bottom; add a layer of carrots, making sure that the carrots are at least two inches from the sides of the box; and cover them with a half-inch layer of sawdust. I keep adding layers of carrots and sawdust until the box is full.

Are you old enough to remember how people used to pack ice in sawdust to make it last? When I was a boy on the farm, this was the only way we could keep ice over the summer. Sawdust is just as good for storing vegetables. Some people like to use sand. I have tried it, and it works fine, except that it seems to leave the vegetables with a certain unpleasant taste. Sawdust doesn't seem to have this disagreeable side effect.

If I am going to keep my boxes of root crops and sawdust in an unheated area rather than in a warm spare room, I use a much larger box. I put in as much as four or five inches of sawdust, and lay in the beets and carrots. I leave four or five inches of space between the vegetables and the sides of the box. The extra sawdust acts as insulation. You can leave a large box like this in your garage, where the temperature might get down to zero or below during the winter months. The vegetables inside will never be spoiled by freezing. You can store turnips and apples this way too.

Success in keeping vegetables and fruits depends a lot on how you handle them between harvest time and storage time. You must always be very careful not to bruise them in any way. Again, do not wash them before you store them. Wait until you are about to use them. Washing destroys Mother Nature's special protective coating.

VEGETABLE STORAGE

Vegetable	Common Storage	Drying	Curing & Salting	Canning	Freezing
Artichokes					X
Asparagus		X		X	X
Beans (all kinds)		X	X	X	X
Beets	X	X	X	X	X
Broccoli		X		X	X
Brussels Sprouts				X	X
Cabbage	X	X	X	X	X
Carrots	X	X		X	X
Cauliflower			X	X	X
Celery	X	X		X (cooked)	X (cooked)
Corn		X		X	X
Endive	X				
Greens (all kinds)		X		X	X
Herbs		X			X
Kale		X	X	X	X
Mushrooms		X		X	X
Okra		X		X	X
Onions	X	X		X	
Parsnips	X	X	X	X	X
Peas		X (mature)		X	X
Peppers	X	X		X	X
Potatoes (white)	X			X	X
Potatoes (sweet)	X	X		X	X
Pumpkins	X	X		X	X
Rutabagas	X	X	X	X	X
Salsify	X				
Squash	X	X		X	X
Tomatoes	X	X (paste)	X (green)	X	X
Turnips	X	X	X	X	X

This well-stocked root cellar makes it obvious that Dick's gardening skills are perfectly complemented by his wife Jan's talent for canning, pickling, and preserving.

FREEZING POINTS, RECOMMENDED STORAGE CONDITIONS, AND LENGTH OF STORAGE PERIOD OF VEGETABLES AND FRUITS

Commodity	Freezing Point	Place to Store	Storage Conditions Temperature	Humidity	Length of Storage Period
	°F.		°F.		
Vegetables:					
Dry beans and peas		Any cool, dry place	32° to 40°	Dry	As long as desired.
Late cabbage	30.4	Pit, trench, or outdoor cellar	Near 32° as possible	Moderately moist.	Through late fall and winter.
Cauliflower	30.3	Storage cellar	Same as above.	Same as above.	6 to 8 weeks.
Late celery	31.6	Pit or trench; roots in soil in storage cellar.	Same as above.	Same as above.	Through late fall and winter.
Endive	31.9	Roots in soil in storage cellar	Same as above.	Same as above.	2 to 3 months.
Onions	30.6	Any cool, dry place	Same as above.	Dry	Through fall and winter.
Parsnips	30.4	Where they grew, or in storage cellar.	Same as above.	Moist	Same as above.
Peppers	30.7	Unheated basement or room	45° to 50°	Moderately moist.	2 to 3 weeks.
Potatoes	30.9	Pit or in storage cellar	35° to 40°	Same as above.	Through fall and winter.
Pumpkins and squashes	30.5	Home cellar or basement	55°	Moderately dry.	Same as above.
Root crops (miscellaneous).		Pit or in storage cellar	Near 32° as possible	Moist	Same as above.
Sweet potatoes	29.7	Home cellar or basement	55° to 60°	Moderately dry.	Same as above.
Tomatoes (mature green).	31.0	Same as above. Same as above. Same as above.	55° to 70°	Same as above.	4 to 6 weeks.
Fruits:					
Apples	29.0	Fruit storage cellar	Near 32° as possible	Moderately moist.	Through fall and winter.
Grapefruit	29.8	Same as above.	Same as above.	Same as above.	4 to 6 weeks.
Grapes	28.1	Same as above.	Same as above.	Same as above.	1 to 2 months.
Oranges	30.5	Same as above.	Same as above.	Same as above.	4 to 6 weeks.
Pears	29.2	Same as above.	Same as above.	Same as above.	4 to 6 weeks.

FOOD STORAGE TECHNIQUES

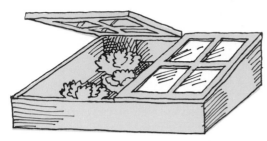

WINTER VEGETABLES IN HOT BEDS

Even in cold Connecticut weather, a properly constructed hotbed can grow salad greens and cool-weather vegetables throughout the winter. Walter Fair says that his "super-rich soil" along with a heating coil produces huge vegetables. Nailed together, two wooden storm windows, which can be bought secondhand for very little money, make a nice insulated sash.

POTATO CELLAR-LOCKER

John Zircke has a simple way to keep potatoes at earth temperature throughout the winter. He buried a metal wall locker in the dirt floor of an old shed. The door faces upward to give easy access. An old rug or some straw is thrown over the top. Any cabinet or box would do as well. His potatoes keep fine this way.

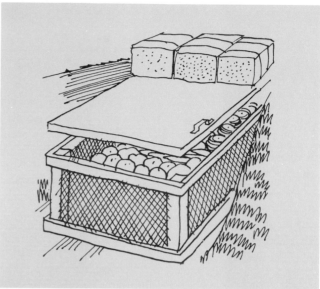

STORAGE BIN

A two-feet-deep storage bin, preferably built on sloping ground for good drainage. A covering of hardware cloth will keep out rodents, and a styrofoam lining will provide excellent insulation. Cover the top with boards and hay bales for easy access. Place sand between layers of vegetables.

KEG-OF-THE-MONTH PLAN

Ruth Harmon, a practical Kentucky gardener, harvests a keg full of assorted fresh vegetables every month throughout the winter. In the fall, she places a layer of straw in the bottom of a nail keg, then lays the keg on its side. She adds more straw, then half-fills it with white potatoes. Next come carrots, more straw, beets, and still more straw. Finally, she adds a layer of lettuce or another favorite vegetable — except any member of the cabbage family — and packs straw around it. She fills ten of these kegs, sets them all in a deep trench, and covers them with dirt.

LEATHER BRITCHES

"Leather britches" is a down-home name for dried green beans. String fresh green beans on white crochet thread, using a large-eyed needle. Hang on a clothes line in full sun for two or three days, taking them in at night. Once they're dry, slide them off the strings onto a cookie sheet. Warm up the oven, turn it off, and set the cookie sheet inside for five minutes. Store in glass jars. To cook, break beans, wash, and soak overnight in plenty of water. Pour off soaking water, add more, bring to a boil, and simmer ALL DAY.

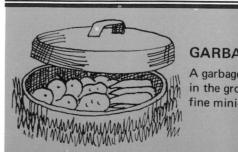

GARBAGE CAN

A garbage can sunk in the ground makes a fine mini-root-cellar.

CARDBOARD BOX FOOD DRYER

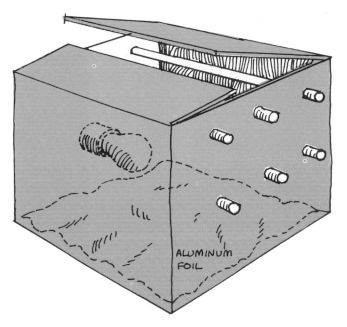

You can convert a cardboard box, a handful of dowels, and a 200-watt light bulb into a small, indoor drier for fruit, pumpkins, squash, tomatoes, beans, and herbs. You'll need a heavy-duty box; the ones in which small TV sets are packed work well. Make sure all the top flaps are intact, so you can close the box up tight. From standard ¾-inch dowels, cut six pieces, each 2 inches longer than the width of the box. On one side of the box, mark a line two inches down from the top. Punch three holes along this line. Repeat on the opposite side and insert three dowels through the three pairs of holes. Insert the other three dowels about halfway down the box to make a "shelf" for drying pans or aluminum foil. When installing the light bulb, try to keep it at least six inches away from the cardboard; if it is closer place a plate or pie tin in between.

Rings of peeled pumpkin and winter squash can be hung on the top row of dowels to dry. Close the top flaps; you may have to lay a book on top to hold them down firmly. Turn on the light. After about ten hours of drying, move the shriveled rings to the foil-covered bottom of the box, let them finish drying there.

Fruit and green beans can be dried on cheesecloth lined trays. Set the trays on the middle shelf. Store dried foods in clean, tight glass jars. They will keep up to two years.

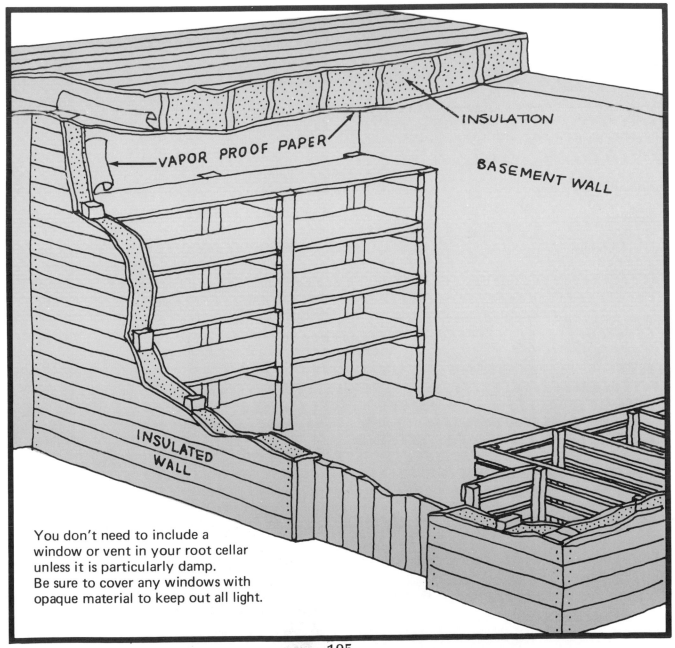

You don't need to include a window or vent in your root cellar unless it is particularly damp. Be sure to cover any windows with opaque material to keep out all light.

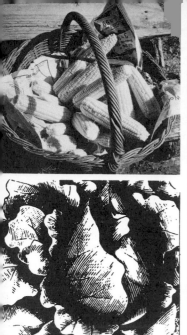

Culture
for each
vegetable

Each vegetable has its own personality and its own likes and dislikes. This alphabetical listing of individual vegetables will guide you to success and satisfaction.

ASPARAGUS

Asparagus is a perennial, which means that it will come back year after year. Remember that a perennial bed must stay in the same place for a long time, so you should give careful thought to its location. Once an asparagus patch is established, it is very difficult to work the soil there very thoroughly. Be sure to add all the humus, manure, and organic matter you can when you prepare the bed, because the plants may be there for twenty years or more.

I'm sure you know that asparagus is only harvested in the spring when the young shoots come up. In the summer and fall, the ferns must be allowed to grow very tall as they go to seed. The seeds come in lovely, bright red berries, and the feathery ferns make a fine hedge. But be careful not to put the bed in a spot where the ferns will shade shorter garden plants.

You can raise asparagus from seed, but it is better to buy roots that are one or two years old. You will get asparagus much more quickly this way. Asparagus grows in most types of soil, but it does best in sandy loam. Drainage is important; asparagus cannot survive in water-logged earth. An annual application of fertilizer will keep the bed in good condition. I recommend about ten pounds of 10-10-10 for every 200 square feet.

If you live in the North, set out asparagus roots in the early spring. In the South, they should be set out in the fall. Plants should be set about one foot apart, with four feet between rows. A 100-foot row is enough to feed a family of four.

Planting asparagus takes a bit of work, but it is worth doing right. You won't have to do it again for twenty or thirty years if you take care of the bed properly. Dig a trench about a foot deep and about a foot and a half wide. In the bottom of this trench, make little mounds of earth combined with compost, manure, or fertilizer. Space them about one foot apart. Make the mounds tall enough to place the "crown" of the plant, the point where the roots converge, about three inches below the top of the trench. Drape the roots, like a skirt, over the mound. Once all the crowns are positioned properly, fill in the trench and firm the soil. Each crown should be covered with about three inches of gently compacted soil.

A week or so after planting, rake the top of the bed to destroy whatever weeds may be growing there. Be careful not to cut or disturb the asparagus

crowns. Some people like to mulch young asparagus with hay, leaves, or some other kind of organic matter. This is not a bad idea, but don't mulch until the asparagus is up.

Expect no harvest at all the first year. Leave the plants alone throughout the summer and fall; do not cut the ferns until the dead of winter. Better still, don't cut them down at all. Wait until spring. The ferns are very important to next year's crop of asparagus.

You can harvest very sparingly the second spring. Pick or cut shoots for a week or so, then allow the ferns to grow freely again. Harvest only those that are as big around as your thumb. The shoots are at their prime when they are six to eight inches tall. If they are small and skinny, about the size of a pencil, leave them alone and let them grow. They will produce a crop for the following year. During the third spring, you can harvest liberally for four to six weeks. Normally, you can plan to harvest asparagus for five to ten

ASPARAGUS PLANTING INSTRUCTIONS

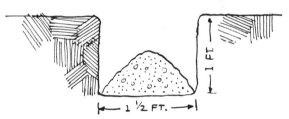

Mound up a mix of soil and compost, manure, or fertilizer in bottom of planting trench. Space mounds 1 foot apart.

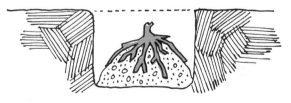

Drape asparagus roots over mound, leaving crown 3 inches below top of trench. Fill trench and firm soil.

To extend the harvest, plant crowns at 3 different depths. The deepest plants will send up shoots last.

weeks in an established bed, depending on your location.

I've discovered a few tricks that allow me to extend my harvesting time. I plant my asparagus at different levels. In one-third of my asparagus bed, I dig a deep, deep trench. Here I plant the crowns six or seven inches below the surface. In the next third of the patch, I come up a couple of inches so that the crowns are about four or five inches beneath the surface. In the last third, I plant the crowns two or three inches deep.

In the spring, the plants that are closest to the surface send up shoots first. I get a very early harvest from these. Those that are a little deeper come along a little later, and those that have been planted six or seven inches below the surface come up later still. I find that I can prolong the harvest for an extra three weeks this way.

You can do the same thing with mulch. Lay about four inches of fairly heavy mulch over your entire bed. Leaves will work fine, especially if they are chopped. Early in the spring, pull the mulch away from about half of your patch. The asparagus will come up much more quickly where the soil has been laid bare. The mulched soil in the rest of the bed will stay cool longer, and this will hold back the growth of the asparagus. As soon as shoots begin to poke through the mulch, carefully rake it away. If you don't, the asparagus is apt to come up and then curl over.

Early in the spring, as soon as the ground starts to thaw, I go over the surface of the soil with a roto-tiller, being careful not to till more than an inch or so deep. This gets rid of a good share of the weeds, grinds up the old ferns, and adds organic matter to the soil. I find that this is one of the best times to fertilize because I can really see what I am doing. If fertilizer is added in the fall, the nitrogen in the 10-10-10 seems to disappear into the soil and lasts no longer than about a month. Fertilizing in the spring helps to assure a bountiful harvest.

BEANS, POLE

The nicest thing about pole beans is that you can easily raise a lot of them in very little space. All you have to do is cut some poles about eight feet long, stick them in the ground about three feet apart, and plant five or six seeds in a circle around the base of each pole. The seeds should be six to eight inches away from the pole itself.

As the plants begin to grow, they will send out tendrils which will wind themselves counterclockwise around the pole as they climb to the top. Be sure that poles are set firmly in the ground so they won't blow over in windy weather. Sometimes you will have to direct the bean tendrils toward the pole. They have been known to grow in the wrong direction—away from the pole.

Pole beans live up to their name. They will not interweave themselves through horizontal wires;

Pole-bean vines like to wrap themselves around vertical supports like the pole above. If planted near horizontal objects like wire fence or the strings below, the vines will twist tightly around one another for support, as you can see in the photograph.

STAKING POLE BEANS

A good way to stake beans is to place a pole where you will plant every other hill, then run a string, or binders' twine, along the bottoms and tops of the poles down the entire length of the row. Between the poles, tie a vertical string to the ground string. Plant a hill of beans at every pole and every vertical string. You'll find that a bean plant will climb up the string quicker than up the pole. JLG

Fasten three bean stakes together at the top to form a tripod. Anchor tripods firmly so they don't blow over.

they will only grow up poles or similar vertical objects. If you try to support the vines with horizontal strings or wires, they are likely to wind around each other and choke themselves out. You can put a pole at either end of a row, run a wire from the top of one to the top of the other, and then run strings from this wire directly to the ground. Pole beans will grow on these, but they will not grow well on chicken wire or snow fence. Some folks hitch the tops of three poles together and spread out the bottoms so that they make a sort of tripod or tepee. Then they make plantings around the base of each pole. This is more than just an efficient way to use space; these tepees stand up well in the wind. I have also seen pole beans planted in with corn. The tendrils grow right up the cornstalks. Just plant one bean seed for every three kernels of corn.

The most popular variety of pole bean is Kentucky Wonder. Romano, a slightly wider, Italian pole bean, is good too. They both have a slightly nutty taste—excellent flavor!

BEANS, BUSH

Beans are one of the easiest vegetables to grow. Every garden should include at least a few because they return a lot of vegetable protein for very little effort. Beans will be ready for harvest eight to twelve weeks after they are planted, depending on the variety. Unfortunately, you must not plant them until after all danger of frost has passed. They are not at all hardy.

Beans require very little fertilizer. As a matter of fact, they are what we call a nitrogen-fixing legume. This means that they contribute more nitrogen to the soil than they take from it.

When you plant bush beans, be sure to leave plenty of room between rows because the plants will grow quite wide. If you plant in a single row, the row will become at least a foot wide as the plants mature. Leave yourself enough room to walk, harvest, and cultivate between rows.

If you plant in wide rows, you will be able to grow about four times as many beans in the same garden space. Bean seeds should be planted 2½ to 3 inches apart, so if you lay out rows ten to fourteen inches wide, you should sprinkle three to five seeds across the row. With a little practice, you will be able to space the seeds evenly. You should have ripe beans ten days to two weeks after the first blossoms appear.

There are two basic types of bush beans—green-podded snap beans and yellow-podded wax beans. Two excellent varieties of snap beans are Bountiful and Tendergreen. To get a continuous harvest of beans, you should make at least two plantings at two- to three-week intervals. Harvest them when they are just about the size of a pencil. Do not wait until large seeds start forming inside the pod, making the whole bean look lumpy. The most flavorful and nutritious beans are the young and tender ones. After your first picking, you can pick again in about three days. Beans grow very

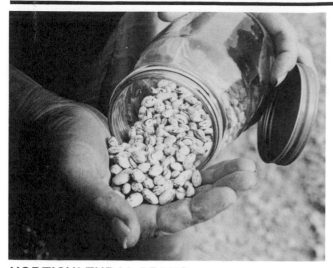

HORTICULTURAL BEANS

"Horticultural beans" is the standard catalog name for a colorful, popular bean known by a number of aliases. The Moores of Joelton, Tennessee call them October beans, not because they mature in the fall, but because they become streaked with shades of red and orange at maturity. The Moores say the plump, attractive beans are best if shelled after the pods begin to turn slightly dry. (Southerners call beans used at this stage "shucky.") In other parts of the country, horticultural beans are called speckled cranberry beans or birds egg beans.

fast, and you can get several harvests from one planting as long as you keep them picked.

Once your bushes have finally stopped bearing, they should be tilled into the garden or pulled up and thrown on the compost pile. The bean-growing area can immediately be replanted with a fall crop, like beets or carrots. You must never weed, cultivate, handle, or harvest beans either when the weather is wet or right after a heavy dew. If you touch the leaves when they are damp, you may transmit disease organisms which will cause a rust or blight that can ruin the quality of the beans and even destroy the plant.

BEANS, LIMA

Lima-bean plants are very bushy. They need even more distance between rows than regular bush beans—at least three feet. The seeds should be planted about four inches apart with about an inch and a half of firmed soil over them. They too can be planted in single rows or in wide bands. I personally like wide rows because the plants hold each other up and keep the pods off the ground.

It takes eleven to twelve weeks for lima beans to reach maturity. Remember these dates when you plan your garden, and be sure that you have a long-enough growing season. In many northern areas, lima beans must be planted very early to produce any crop at all. You can gain a week or so by sprouting them inside in paper towels.

Lima beans like warm, well-drained soil and need little fertilizer. As is the case with most bean patches, stay out of the lima beans when it is wet. Lima beans are ready to be harvested when beans have formed inside the pods. The pods will look fat when the limas are ripe. You will find anywhere from two to five beans in each one, depending on the year and on how well they have grown. If your season is long enough, you can let them mature and then dry in the sun.

POLE LIMA BEANS

When grown in wet weather, bush lima beans pick up an unpleasant, earthy taste where the pods touch the ground. This is an advantage pole limas have over bush limas. Pole limas also have a better over-all flavor and yield much better and longer than bush limas.

BUTTER BEANS

Lima beans, picked when the bean is small and green and cooked in milk and butter, are called "butter beans" in the South. Of course, many southerners use the popular name, butter beans, for all lima beans.

LIMA BEAN HONEY

The nectar which bees collect from lima bean blossoms makes one of the lightest colored honeys — and one of the most delectable. Be careful not to spray with toxic insecticides when the beans are in bloom. If you need to spray, do so very late in the day when the bees are not working. JLG

PICKING LIMA BEANS

Pick pole lima beans heavily. If you keep enough moisture and fertilizer in the ground, the more you pick, the more they produce. They produce to make seed, as do all plants, so if you leave a few beans on the plant, it is satisfied and quits bearing.

Be sure lima beans are filled out completely before picking. You should get 1 pound of shelled limas for every 2 pounds of beans in the pod. JLG

BEETS

Beets are very hardy and will grow in most kinds of soil. They can be planted in the spring as soon as the soil can be tilled; frost will injure neither the seed nor the young plants. Later in the year, other sowings can be made to provide beets for fall eating and storage.

Again, you can plant beets in single rows or in wide rows. Wide rows will yield a lot more for a lot less work. You should plant beet seeds about an inch deep and about two inches apart. Because they are slow to come up, I like to plant radishes in with beets to mark the rows. Every beet seed you plant may produce as many as six seedlings. When the tiny beet leaves poke through the soil, there may be four or five plants in a cluster. These must be thinned.

Cultivation is important too. One of the first things I do is take a regular garden rake and drag it gently across the row. This seems to make an awful mess, but it is an easy way to get the first thinning done.

When the beets start to form little bulbs about the size of marbles, I pull out the largest ones and use both the green tops and the small beets for eating. This leaves room for the other bulbs to expand. I keep harvesting beet greens throughout the summer. I pick few greens from the beets I have earmarked for winter storage because I want to grow a strong, nutritious root beneath each plant.

I try to keep the soil around beets as loose as possible. This is pretty easy for me because the soil in my garden is quite sandy. Raising beets and other root crops in heavy clay soil is another matter. But there are ways to solve the clay problem. The simplest answer is to dig a shallow trench or furrow and throw in a liberal amount of organic matter; leaves, manure, or compost will do just fine. Cover the organic matter with a small amount of soil and plant your seeds on top of it. The loose organic matter will not only provide lots of nutrients, it will also give the root crops some room to expand. Don't forget about using icicle radishes as a natural cultivator in clay soil.

The Detroit Dark Red beet is a wonderful winter keeper. For delicious greens and early eating, try the Early Wonder variety. Plant plenty of beets. You may want to make pickles or beet relish from the extras. Starting beets inside for later transplanting is a good way to have a crop before anyone else in the neighborhood.

Fortunately, insects don't trouble them very much. They take care of themselves for the most part. You shouldn't have to worry about dusting or spraying.

BROCCOLI

Broccoli, along with cauliflower and Brussels sprouts, is a member of the cabbage family. All of these vegetables should be treated in pretty much the same way. They can be started inside in late April or early May. They can stand some frost, but not too much.

I like to have broccoli early in the year, so I start some seed indoors and transplant them outdoors when the seedlings have become small, healthy plants. Unfortunately, broccoli that is set out this way does not seem to be as good as broccoli grown from seed in the garden.

When I set out transplants, I space them at the recommended interval—eighteen inches apart. At the same time, I plant two broccoli seeds between each plant. Weeks later, when the transplanted broccoli starts to head, the new seedlings will be coming along quite well and will soon be forming heads of their own. This will be delicious late broccoli.

Broccoli plants grow fairly large, so they require quite a bit of room. The normal spacing is eighteen inches between plants and three feet between rows. They like a little fertilizer, so do them a favor and put a handful of manure or compost under each plant. If you prefer, you can mix a bit of 5-10-10 with the soil surrounding the roots.

Worms seem to think that broccoli is particularly tasty. When you transplant, be sure to wrap a collar of newspaper around the stem to keep cutworms away. Then keep the plants dusted with rotenone, Sevin, or some other insecticide. This should keep out the cabbage maggot, which lays eggs on or near the roots of broccoli plants. If given a chance, the larvae will eventually kill the plant. Green cabbage worms may find their way into broccoli heads if you don't dust them once every three or four days.

A broccoli head is actually a cluster of many flower buds. This cluster should be harvested before the tiny, yellow flowers begin to open. The first head may be as small as an apple or as large as six or eight inches across. A few days after you have cut out the central cluster, smaller lateral heads will start to form on different parts of the stem. These will not be nearly as large, but they are just as good to eat.

As I have said before, keep your crops harvested! The more you pick, the more heads your broccoli plants will produce. As soon as you allow them to blossom, they will stop trying to make those little flower buds which eventually produce seed. Harvest as often as every three days, and keep harvesting as long as there is something to pick.

For a fall crop of broccoli, you might start plants from seed right in the garden in early May. The seeds should be planted three or four inches apart. By mid-June, they should be about right for transplanting at eighteen-inch intervals. The best thing about late broccoli—aside from its great taste and its ability to withstand some frost—is that it is relatively worm-free. The natural worm cycles seem to occur in the spring and throughout the warm summer months. Somehow, the worms miss you if you make a late planting.

It is always a good idea to rotate your crops. If you plant broccoli in one spot this year, don't plant broccoli—or any member of the cabbage family, for that matter—in the same spot next year. Plant beans or spinach or something else.

BRUSSELS SPROUTS

Some people like to start Brussels sprouts early to get a midsummer crop, but I see them as basically a fall vegetable. They sure taste better if you harvest them then. They will stand many, many freezes during September, October, and November. Here in Vermont, I have picked Brussels sprouts as late as January. I had to dig in the snow for them.

Space your transplants just as you would space broccoli—eighteen inches apart. The edible portion is the marble- to golf-ball-size head that grows right on the stem. A sprout will form just above the point where a leaf grows out of the thick stalk. If you break off some of the lowest leaves, you can encourage early heads to form higher on the plant. I like to remove all the leaves on the bottom six inches of stalk. I do it in the morning when the dew is still on them, and they snap off very easily.

Once I start harvesting, I take off another two or three layers of leaves, stripping the stalk three or four inches higher. I find that this stimulates very tall growth. The plants will grow three feet high if you fertilize them well and keep breaking off the lower leaves.

Bugs will bother Brussels sprouts in the same way that they bother cabbage. It is a good practice to keep the plants dusted with rotenone or Sevin.

The sprouts can be picked as soon as they are a little bigger than the end of your thumb. Some-

times two or three new sprouts will grow to replace each one you pick, as long as you don't cut them too close to the stem. Brussels sprouts are fun. Don't be afraid to experiment with them a little.

CABBAGE

Cabbages will thrive in nearly any kind of soil. I have discovered that early cabbage does well in light soil, and that fall cabbages do best in heavy, damp soil.

Start your seedlings three to four weeks before you plan to set them out. You will see that they grow very fast. Harden them off, but don't worry too much about a late spring frost killing them. They are quite hardy and will survive a light freeze or two. Keep in mind that a handful of manure or compost under each plant will be a real asset to it. Cutworms can be a problem, so don't forget the newspaper-collar trick. Spacing is not so critical with cabbage plants. Leave from fifteen to eighteen inches between them, and they should do fine.

When you harvest early cabbage, cut off the head and leave the stem. If you are lucky, three or four smaller heads will grow to replace the first one. These small heads will be useful in recipes calling for small amounts of cabbage.

Your fall crop can be planted from seed in the middle of May. When these seedlings get to be about three inches tall, transplant them a little farther apart than you did your first crop. Leave eighteen inches to two feet between plants. For some reason, late cabbage tends to get larger than early cabbage.

Cabbage requires some fertilizer, but not much. If you feed it too much, the heads may burst. I used to be alarmed by this until I discovered a cure. Cabbage heads, like all vegetable heads, grow from the inside out. If you notice that yours are starting to crack, this probably means that the cabbages are growing so fast in the center that the outside growth cannot keep up. If you let this continue, the whole thing will break wide open. Whenever you see a crack starting to form, take hold of the head and give the whole plant a half turn. What this does is break off some of the roots, which slows the growth of the plant and gives it time to catch up with itself. Give the plant another half turn in a week or so if the cracking continues.

All members of the cabbage family are very shallow-rooted plants. When you transplant them, be sure that you dig a whole deep enough to give the roots a chance to grow down. I know this sounds ridiculous, but if you don't give them a good, deep hole, the roots will actually grow back up toward the surface. Because most of the roots are no more than an inch below the surface, you should be very careful when you cultivate these plants.

Cabbages, unfortunately, attract quite a few bugs. There is the cabbage maggot, which gets into the roots of the plant. This insect can be discouraged with tobacco dust and various poisons. There is also the green cabbage worm which is the larva of the yellow and white butterflies you may have seen flying around your garden. Cabbage worms will eat tremendous holes in the leaves and will ruin the heads if they are allowed to burrow into them. Once again, rotenone and Sevin should take care of them.

SAUERKRAUT IN THE JAR

Here's a good method of making sauerkraut right in the jar. There is no smelly crock of fermenting cabbage, and it doesn't take weeks to prepare.

Use good, mature heads of cabbage. For every five pounds of cabbage, measure out 3½ tablespoons of plain salt. (One pound of cabbage will fill a one-pint glass jar). Slice the cabbage in thin slices as you would for any sauerkraut, mix in the salt, and pack solidly into clean jars. Fill the jars with cold water, and screw the jar lids down tight. The kraut will ferment for three or four days and will be ready to eat in four to six weeks. Store the jars in a cool place. MR

You can also try using salt. Take a salt shaker, go out each morning when the dew is still on the plants, and sprinkle each one. In fact, early morning is the time of day when you should be doing all your dusting. The dew will help the dust stick to the plants.

Growing very large heads is a challenge, but I have to admit that I prefer to eat the smaller ones. Besides, my family and I can't possibly eat one of those large heads all at one time. We have to cut it in half and save the second part for later in the week. I am sure we get more nourishment when we eat all of a smaller head at one sitting. To grow smaller heads, I sometimes squeeze the plants a little closer together in the row, planting them ten inches apart instead of eighteen. This way, I can grow three heads where I would normally grow two. I use a little more fertilizer this way, but the heads are not so apt to crack.

CARROTS

Carrots are like any other root crop. They will do best in loose, sandy soil. But that doesn't mean you can't grow them if the soil in your garden is not sandy. You can make almost any soil loose by tilling it often and by working humus, compost, or leaf mold into it.

You should plant carrots very early in the spring. The seeds are very fine, so it is hard to keep from planting them too thick. One trick is to mix fine soil with the seed. Carrot seed is slow to germinate, so you might mix in a few fast-sprouting radish seeds to mark the rows.

It is very important to thin carrots. If you don't, you won't get many that are large enough to eat. I thin them first the same way I thin beets, by drawing a steel rake across the row. The rake's teeth will do all the thinning that is necessary. This procedure can be a little frightening at first. In fact, you may think that you have ruined your whole crop. Don't worry; most of the plants will recover and look fine in a day or two. Thinning is always a painful process, but it helps to produce healthier crops in the long run.

Carrots like fertilizer, so give them an ample supply of compost or some commercial fertilizer.

Chemical fertilizer can burn tiny carrot seeds, so don't get it too close to them. Be careful about planting carrot seeds too deep. Remember the formula: four times the diameter of the seed.

I find that Half Longs are the best variety for most people. Regular carrots that grow very long and thin have to be grown in sandy loam. If you want tender, young roots all summer long, plant carrots once every three weeks, right into August. The reason for planting late in the season is to have carrots coming to maturity just in time to store them in a root cellar in the fall. An early-August planting will be ready right around the first of October.

The largest carrots, as I already mentioned, are beneath the darkest, greenest tops. This is one way you can tell if a carrot is ripe without having to pull it up and see. Finger-sized carrots are delicious. Don't try to grow the monstrous, prize-winning ones. They are much too tough. Carrots are prime when they have about the same diameter as a quarter. Let them get much bigger and they become "woody"—fibrous and pulpy.

Carrots are almost trouble-free as far as insects are concerned. Plant them, cultivate them once in a while, harvest them, and enjoy them.

CAULIFLOWER

Cauliflower seems to suffer in very hot weather. It should be grown either early in the gardening season or in the fall. In other words, you should try to avoid having the heads come to maturity in late July or August.

Don't be afraid to start cauliflower indoors quite early. If you harden off the plants properly, there is little chance that they will be killed or injured by an unexpected cold snap. Transplant them during the last week of April or the first of May, even in northern states. When you set them out, firm the soil very tightly around the roots. The idea is to keep excessive air from getting to the root hairs and drying them out.

As cauliflower heads start to form, they should be "blanched." This simply means that you prevent sunlight from reaching the head for a while. Normal blanching time is four to eight days, but it may take a little longer in the fall. Blanching will make the cauliflower white and tender. To accomplish this, take the large outer leaves, pull them up over the top of the head, and tie them there with twine or fasten them with a rubber band. Or you can take a leaf, break it partially, lay it over the top of the cauliflower, and tuck it in on the other side of the head. Break leaves on all four sides, and fold each one over the top. This will let air in but keep sunlight out. I like this method better than tying the leaves together.

Late cauliflower can be started from seed outdoors around the middle of June. When seedlings are two to three inches tall, they should be transplanted in rows two to three feet apart, with two feet between each plant. Cauliflower will do poorly in soil that is acidic. It will be quite happy if the pH in your garden is right around 7. This means that the soil is neither acidic nor alkaline. Acidity encourages a disease in cauliflower called "whip tail."

CELERY

Celery seems to require reasonably good, loamy soil. If yours is heavy clay or extremely sandy, it would be best to add organic matter in the form of leaf mold, compost, or manure; otherwise, you are not likely to have good luck with this particular vegetable. Celery likes fertilizer, so be sure that you keep it well fed.

I start seeds inside in February. The seeds are very fine, so you must take care not to plant them too deep. Just sprinkle them in the flat and firm the soil with a board. When the celery plants get to be two inches high, I transplant them. When I transplant most things, either inside or outside, I remove some of the leaves. By doing this, I am intentionally throwing the plant out of balance. I am making the roots stronger in relation to the top of the plant. Eliminating all the extra foliage makes the plant less apt to wilt, and it will eventually grow stronger. When I transplant celery, I pinch off all but the center sprays. Sometimes after it has been transplanted the first time, I begin to harden celery off. It can be transplanted into my garden sometime between the first and the tenth of May if I have been conscientious about getting the young plants accustomed to the outdoors. If a plant is tall and strong, I put a rubber band around its top to pull it all together for transplanting.

I dig a trench or a furrow—the furrowing attachment on the back of the rotary tiller works just about perfectly—and plant the celery in the bottom. As the plants continue to grow, I keep pulling soil up around them. This is called "hilling." The only part of the plant that shows above the dirt is the topmost tuft of leaves. Keeping the main part of the plant growing below ground will blanch the stalks.

For a late crop of celery, you can plant your seed outside at the end of April or during the first part of May. Celery plants should be spaced no closer than a foot apart after the final transplanting. The spacing between rows is not all that critical.

If hilling celery seems like too much of a job, you can use boards to blanch it. When the plants get to be about ten inches high, prop a 1-by-10-inch board up against either side of the row. Fasten the tops of the planks together with a small wooden cleat or with wire so they won't blow over on a windy day. After two or three weeks of being shaded like this, the plants should be white and succulent.

There are certain self-blanching varieties of celery. You can try some of these if you want, but the easiest thing is not to blanch celery at all. I think that green celery is a real delicacy. You may also find that the crop you grow at home tastes a little stronger than the celery you buy at the store.

Celery will appreciate lots of cultivation, but the roots are near the surface. Don't scratch too deep

with your cultivating tool.

Celery and warm weather do not mix well. Plan to have an early crop and a late crop, and avoid trying to produce good stalks during the hottest summer months. If you begin blanching in September, using the hilling technique, you will be insulating the stalks against cold at the same time. The crop should last until long after frost has set in. In fact, you can store it right in the ground until well into winter if you put a good, thick mulch over it.

Not many insects are attracted to celery, so there is no need to plan on using insecticides. You can start harvesting as soon as the stalks are as big around as a pencil. These are delicious. Larger, outside stalks which come along later can be used in soups or as garnish.

CELERIAC

Celeriac can be grown like celery except that it does not have to be blanched. Its thick roots are delicious in soups, in salads, or just by themselves. The seed can be sown very early, so there is no reason to start plants inside. Plant the seeds about an inch apart. When the plants are three inches high, more or less, transplant them into rows which are a foot to a foot and a half apart. Leave six inches between plants.

If you're going to transplant celeriac, soak the ground with water beforehand. It seems to enjoy muddiness—for a while at least. Try to keep as much of the original soil as possible around the roots when you move the plant. Dig in under the roots with your hand and squeeze the plant with your fingers to keep the soil in contact with the roots. If you expose them to too much oxygen

during transplanting, they will dry out very quickly and the plant will die.

I recommend the Snowball variety of celeriac. This will grow round, smooth roots about three inches across.

CHICORY

Chicory is a green that grows wild in most sections of the country. You can recognize it by its little, blue flowers. You have probably seen it growing in fields and along the roadside. It is a very tough plant, mainly because its deep root system permits it to grow in any kind of soil, even very dry hardpan. The young tops can be eaten very much the same way that you eat endive.

Chicory can be planted in the late spring or early summer. The plants should be at least six inches apart in rows at least two feet apart. They will

grow to be two to four feet high without much further assistance from you. Cut the tops off within an inch or two of the crown when you want greens.

The roots can be harvested after there has been a killing frost. Cut back whatever tops remain, and trim off some of the root—which by this time will be very long. Store these roots in a box of sand or fresh sawdust. In the middle of winter, you can "force" them simply by starting to water them. In about three weeks, they will start to send out tender, white shoots, which are a very tasty salad item. A good time to dig wild chicory roots is in the fall. Force them if you like, or store them and plant them in your garden in the spring.

CABBAGE, CHINESE

Chinese cabbage has a long and compact head. When you take off the outer leaves, it looks a little like a tight bunch of celery. The light green leaves have a crisp, nutty flavor. I understand that the Chinese use this vegetable in practically all their cooking, but our family uses it mainly for salads.

Chinese cabbage does best in cool weather. It can be started indoors, but should stay in seed flats

no longer than about four weeks before it is transplanted outside. Most of the outer leaves should be stripped off when you do transplant. The cabbages should be about twelve inches apart with two feet between rows.

Your fall crop can be planted the last week of July or the first week of August. Plant the seeds right where you want the plants to be so you won't have to transplant. They will grow very rapidly because there will be no transplanting shock to set them back. Your late crop may turn out better than your first. Bugs and worms do not seem to bother them so much in the fall as they do during the summer. In fact, my suggestion to someone trying Chinese cabbage for the first time would be to plant only a fall crop directly from seed. A spring crop takes a lot more care. If you don't look after them and dust almost daily, the outer leaves will be riddled with insect holes. This looks unattractive, but the inner leaves are usually untouched.

CHIVES

Every garden should have some chives. They are a perennial, so once you plant them, you can have them year after year. Chives, as you probably know, are a member of the onion family. It would be impossible to list all the good uses that chives can be put to. They add a zesty flavor to almost any dish.

Plant chives where they can stay undisturbed for several years. You can start them inside, but wait until the soil warms up in the spring before transplanting them outside. They are attractive enough to be planted in borders along with flowers.

Chives are almost completely disease-free. After they have been growing for a couple of years, you can separate the plant clusters and expand your bed by moving some of the plants elsewhere. In the fall, you can take up part of a cluster, plant it in a pot indoors, and have fresh chives all winter. Clip off the tops whenever you need them. It is impossible, I think, to cut them so much that they can't recover and grow more. Nicest of all, they will put out lovely blossoms sometime in the middle of summer.

COLLARDS

Collards are members of the cabbage family. They like the same soil as cabbages, and they are susceptible to cabbage diseases and may be attacked by the same insects. They too need to be dusted with rotenone, treated with Sevin, or sprayed with some other insecticide.

Collards can stand hot weather as well as or better than any other vegetable in the garden. This is one reason why they do very well in the South. They can be grown directly from seed. They form no heads; we are interested in the leaves themselves. These can be blanched either by tying the leaves together or by putting a rubber band around them. Blanching is, of course, not necessary.

No member of the cabbage family should be planted in the same spot two years in a row. This rule applies to collards.

CORN

Sweet corn will grow in almost any kind of soil, but it will do best in light, sandy loam. The reason for this is simple if you think about it. Sandy soil dries out quickly in the spring. It also tends to warm up faster than heavy clay, for example. You can usually plant corn many days—even weeks—earlier in lighter soil.

Everybody likes early sweet corn, and there is no reason you can't have it. Here in Vermont, I have been able to have sweet corn as early as two weeks before anyone else, even before the commercial growers. My method is quite simple—although I should admit that it took me nearly ten years to figure it out.

I try to have corn planted by my birthday, April 13, which is very early for Vermont. Most people here don't plan on planting corn much before May 15 or 20. You must decide the previous fall where you are going to grow your extra-early corn. Choose a place where there is no sod, little fresh organic matter in the soil, and no cover crop. (Annual rye grass might be all right in this spot, because it will be dead and gone by the time spring arrives.)

If you have an area in your garden that slopes slightly to the south or west, great! This is the perfect spot for early crops, because the soil will be much warmer there. Till this area as soon as you can work the soil, but put nothing on it—no manures, no fertilizers whatsoever. Plant your corn in rows, but plant it a trifle deeper than you would ordinarily—slightly more than four times the diameter of the seed. Normal planting depth for corn is about one inch. Plant early corn about 1½ inches deep.

Remember: use absolutely no fertilizer or organic matter. (If you do, the seed may rot! Be patient. It may take six weeks or so for your corn to come up. Eventually, it will sprout and put out a root system, but it might just hover there until the temperature gets right. Then it will suddenly put in an appearance. I have found that it can stand two or three frosts once it has come up. I have seen my early sweet corn lying frozen right on the ground and completely brown. To my surprise, it came right back up. If you put fertilizer near the seed, the seedling will grow so fast and so tender that a good freeze or frost will kill it for sure. Organic matter or manure in the soil will encourage microorganisms to start working there. This will cause the early corn to have very, very tender roots. The microbes may even start to decompose the roots themselves. Obviously, it makes sense to plant an early variety if you want early corn. Span Cross, Butter and Sugar, or Sugar and Gold all work very well. I have also had good luck with early plantings of some mid-season varieties.

That's my patented way to become the first in your neighborhood to have sweet corn. Following are some thoughts on growing corn the conventional way.

Corn likes two things—hot weather and lots of fertilizer. It should be, as the old farmers say, "knee high by the fourth of July." You can plant corn either in hills or in rows. If you choose the hill method, you should plant four or five seeds in each hill. When the plants come up, thin to four seedlings per hill.

I like to plant corn in rows rather than in hills. I find that if you plant a seed once every eight to ten inches in a straight row, the plants are better nourished. Hills force the root systems of the plants to compete with each other for nutrients and moisture. By the time corn is knee-high, its roots will extend about fifteen inches in all directions.

Don't forget that corn requires a large investment of garden space for a relatively small return, and it ties up the space for a long time. One of the advantages of growing early corn is that after harvesting it, you still have time to plant and harvest a crop of beets, lettuce, chard, or late beans. Corn, as you know, is very tall when it reaches its full growth. If you can, plant it on the north or east side of your garden so that it will not shade your other crops.

Always try to plant more than one variety of corn if you have the space—an early, a mid-season, and a late variety. Late corn, of course, tastes the best. Silver Queen is one of the best varieties of late corn I know of, but unfortunately it has a ninety-day growing time. Here in Vermont, it doesn't mature until September, but it is well worth waiting for.

Cultivation is essential, but keep in mind that the roots of cornstalks grow fairly close to the surface of the ground. Don't go deeper than an inch or an inch and a half at the most. Keep the weeds down in your cornfield. It is too easy to neglect them. Because corn grows high, it seems hard to believe that weeds sometimes get the upper hand. Don't let them compete with the corn for fertilizer and moisture; they will steal a lot of it and corn needs all the nutrients it can get!

I do not recommend that you pick the suckers off the sides of cornstalks as some people do.

For maximum flavor, pick sweet corn as close to cooking time as possible; otherwise, the natural sugars will turn to starch.

118

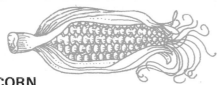

SWEET CORN

I like to plant sweet corn in furrows. I use the furrower behind my Troy-bilt, which makes a furrow about four or five inches deep. I plant my corn in the bottom of these furrows, covering it with the usual amount of soil. Do not fill the furrow to the top. Because we have bird problems, I purchased some twelve-inch-wide chicken wire with 1½-inch mesh. I lay this right over the top of each furrow so the birds cannot get at the corn until it is well established. Once the corn gets up to the chicken wire, I roll it up and take it off the field.

Planting in deep furrows has another advantage. When it rains, water will collect in these furrows. The extra moisture encourages the corn to germinate very fast. Once you start to cultivate with the tiller, dirt tumbles down into the furrow in which you planted your corn and your corn is automatically hilled. The dirt also covers up a good share of the weeds and saves you a lot of weeding. After a couple of cultivations, the furrow will be filled up level, and your corn will stand up much better in the wind.

Another way to keep the birds from getting your corn is to take two strings and run them parallel, about two inches apart, right over the top of each row of corn. (Fishing line will work well.) When a bird reaches in to pull out a kernel of corn, the back of his head bumps these strings. This usually scares him so badly that he forgets all about the corn. You can also take chicken wire and make a long "pyramid" down the length of each row. Just unroll your chicken wire and bend it in half lengthwise. This works very well. Of course, chicken wire lasts for many, many years, so it is well worth the initial investment.

Some varieties put out several suckers, each of which will bear an ear of corn if the plants are well side dressed with fertilizer. Corn should first be side dressed when it is eight or ten inches high. You can side dress a second time when the corn silk first appears. This second side dressing will encourage the plant to produce nice, full ears.

Ear worms are a problem to corn growers everywhere in the country. The ear worm works his way through the outer husk and feeds on the kernels inside. If you find one, or evidence of one, in an ear of corn, this doesn't mean that you have to throw the whole thing away. Cut out the bad part and enjoy the rest. Rotenone and Sevin discourage ear worms. So does a drop of mineral oil placed in the corn silk just as it begins to form. You may also have an invasion of European corn borers from time to time. I am sorry to admit that I know of no spray that really discourages them.

It is nice to be able to pick fresh corn over a long period of time. This is the best reason for planting both early and late varieties. A packet of seeds will tell you how long the corn inside will take to mature. Early varieties are usually ready about ten weeks after sowing; later ones normally need about ten to twelve weeks.

Harvest corn when the kernels are at the "milky" stage. Make a little slit in the husk while it is still on the stalk. If the kernels look full and yellow, give one of them the thumbnail test. If white liquid squirts out, the corn is of excellent quality and is ready to eat.

Whether you are going to eat it fresh, can it, or freeze it, you should have everything ready to cook or process it immediately. The old maxim that says you should "have the water boiling before you pick the corn is true." As soon as the ears are off the stalk, the sugars in the kernels begin turning to starch, and the flavor begins to decline. There is nothing like fresh corn picked from the garden just before supper.

As soon as your corn crop is harvested, you should dispose of the residue. Don't leave the stalks standing in the field or you will encourage disease, ear worms, and borers in future crops. The best way to dispose of cornstalks is to till them directly into the soil. This provides good nourishment for your friends, the earthworms and microorganisms. If you don't have any way to till your corn wastes under efficiently, compost them, either in an active compost pile or by throwing them in a trench and covering with three or four inches of soil. Don't burn or throw away cornstalks. Use them to build up the humus content in your soil.

Corn that you plan to freeze should mature in September or later, when it will be at its sweetest. There is not much point in freezing corn that ripens in July. By the time you eat it in the winter, it will have been in the freezer too long to taste really good.

CORN, roastin' ears

In the South, roastin' ears are a long-time favorite crop. This is usually an extra-tall, white corn which bears several ten-to-twelve-inch ears on each stalk. Sometimes the kernels are cut off the cob and fried. Popular varieties recommended by many experienced home gardeners are Neal's Paymaster, Silvermine, Truckers' Favorite, and Hickory King. RAM

FREEZING CORN

Mr. and Mrs. James E. Speight of Whites Creek, Tennessee use a large-eared, white variety of corn called Silver Mine for freezing. This variety is used only for cutting off the cob. A smaller, yellow corn like Golden Bantam is used for freezing on the cob.

The Speights' recipe for freezing corn attracts happy comments from all who are lucky enough to taste it. Cut the corn off and scrape all the milk from the cob. Then prepare the corn as if you're fixing it for the table. Season it with a little sugar, salt, and flour, add a little vegetable oil, then cook just until the mixture starts to thicken. Take it from the stove, allow it to cool thoroughly, bag it, and place in the freezer. When preparing the corn to eat, add some butter and cook for a short time in a skillet.

When the Speights take this to a covered-dish social at the church, everybody wants to know the secret of freezing such great tasting corn. JES

CRESS

Cress is a plant with sharp-flavored leaves that add a tangy taste to salads. The mature plant is practically inedible, so we are interested only in the small, first leaves. It is best to plant cress early and let it grow during cool weather. If it is planted when the weather is hot, it will grow too quickly and go right to seed before you have a chance to harvest any of it.

Sow cress seeds very thickly in rows about one foot apart, cover them with about one-fourth inch of soil, and keep them well watered. There is no reason to thin; you don't want the plants to get too large. Pick only what you need for the table at any one time.

Cress will be ready six to eight weeks after it is planted. Plant successive crops every couple of weeks if you like. I think you will see that the plants deteriorate very rapidly. Some folks don't even bother to plant it in the garden. You can grow plenty indoors in a seed flat. All you need is a sunny window.

CUCUMBERS

Cucumbers are a very tender crop. Normally, you should not plant them without some sort of protection until all danger of frost has passed. This means late May where I live, but I have a plan that lets me get started a little earlier than this. I sprout cucumber seeds in wet paper towels, plant the seedlings under hot caps about two weeks before the average date of the last killing frost, and leave the hot caps on until I am pretty sure there will be no more freezing temperatures. This is one way to get cukes before most other people do.

You can also start them inside, but not until about three or four weeks before you are going to set them out. If you start them too early, they will get too big too fast. It is a good idea to plant seeds in a cube of sod, as I told you earlier, or

you can use peat or "jiffy" pots. These containers can be transplanted right into the garden soil without disturbing the tender cucumber roots.

Under normal conditions, around the first of June, cucumber seeds can be planted in hills, in mounds, or in rows. I can hear you asking, "What is the difference between a hill and a mound?" A hill is an area a few inches in diameter where you plant six, eight, or ten seeds in a circle. A mound is a place where you have built up the soil, added manure, and planted seeds on top of the hump. If your soil is wet and heavy, a mound would be more advantageous than just a hill. A mound gives your plants drier feet. Heavy soil will grow larger cucumbers than sandy soil, by the way.

I have light soil, so I personally like to plant cucumbers in rows. If you grow them in hills, your plants tend to be concentrated in one area. As soon as the seedlings come up, tiny black flies and other insects may invade them. They may eat the tender leaves of the plants as soon as they appear aboveground. These bugs congregate for food, yes, but they are also there to mate. If one stops by your cucumber patch, another will stop, and before you know it, you have a whole troop of them. If you happen to be away for a day or two, or if you don't catch them in time, they will devour the whole hill. If your cucumbers are planted in a row and the bugs attack, they might destroy a chunk of the row, but they probably won't wipe out the entire planting. The surviving plants will fill in that area again.

I plant cucumber seeds six to eight inches apart in the row. I lay the seeds in good compost or manure, and I usually plant radishes among them. Radishes help a lot because that troublesome, little black fly will eat the radish leaves before he gets interested in the cucumber plants.

If you use the mound or the hill method, build

CLIMBING CUCUMBERS

Here is our way of growing cucumbers: We build an oblong frame 18 by 6 feet. This is placed in the ground and filled with good composted soil. We then place 2 posts with wire stretched between, inside the frame. The wire mesh is 3 by 5 inches. When the cucumbers come up, we gently train the plants to climb the wire. We give the plants tender loving care by giving them a side dressing of bone meal and cotton seed meal (equal amounts) when we plant the seeds and again at the height of the growing season.

It's such a thrill to watch them grow and so easy to pick the cucumbers. There is no worry of stepping on the vines. KB

your mounds every four feet in rows about six feet apart so that you will have room later to walk between the rows. If you plant eight or ten seeds in a hill, let them grow four or five leaves apiece; then pull up the weaker plants, leaving only five. These five seedlings will have plenty of room to grow.

Cucumbers seem to consume lots of fertilizer. If you do nothing else to prepare your soil, you should at least mix in an ample amount of fertilizer before you plant. But don't do this immediately before you sow or the fertilizer will burn the seed. Give yourself a couple of days' leeway to allow the chemicals to dissolve in the soil.

A side dressing is great for cucumbers. The best time to do this is just before the vines have really started to crawl along the ground. The plant will stand up and grow about a foot tall before it lies down and starts to spread out in all directions. Take a hoe and make a very shallow trench on either side of your rows or in a circle around the mounds or hills. Don't make this indentation any closer than four inches from the centers of the plants.

Sprinkle compost, manure, or a commercial fertilizer like 10-10-10 in the trench, and be sure to cover it up with soil again. If the leaves or stems make contact with the fertilizer, they will be burned. The fertilizer should take effect just as the plants blossom—the time when they need nutrients the most if they are going to produce an abundant crop.

Plant two or three varieties of cukes. Some will do better in a given year than others, depending on the weather. I always plant picklers because they bear very early. If you are smart enough to plant dill just as soon as the ground can be worked in the spring, your dill should be ready about the time the early cukes are ready for pickling. I think

a lot of people are afraid to pick little cucumbers because they are afraid they won't get any more. Actually, if you keep picking the baby cucumbers, the plant will never get a chance to produce good, big seeds, and it will continue to blossom and bear. Harvest all the small cucumbers you want during the summer, and I can assure you that you will have bushels more by fall.

You should try to control the growth of cucumber vines. When they have grown about three feet to either side of the row, I like to stop them. I am not looking for record-breaking vines, after all; I am looking for lots of good vegetables. You will find a little fuzzy tuft at the end of each vine. It looks like a little cottontail about the size of your little finger. If you pinch this off with your fingers, the vine won't grow any farther. Every time I pick cucumbers, I also try to make a point of pinching off a bunch of these little fuzzy ends. Of course, the plant may send out a new vine once you do this; wait until another fuzzy end appears and pick it off. This does less damage to the plant than actually cutting the vines themselves.

You can do the same with squash and pumpkins. Picking off the fuzzy end allows the plant to put more strength into the vegetables. If you grow cucumbers on a trellis or on a fence, stop their growth when they reach the top. There is no point in letting them grow back down the other side.

DANDELIONS

Wild dandelions grow all over the place, and the greens are good eating. People who work hard at getting them out of their lawns are sometimes amazed to see packets of dandelion seed for sale in a garden store. These "tame" dandelions are larger, juicier, and much less bitter than the wild varieties.

Plant seeds outdoors just as soon as the ground can be worked. They should be spaced about three inches apart and thinned later to approximately six inches apart. They are usually ready in eight or nine weeks, and you can harvest them continuously. Dandelions will replenish themselves as you pick the greens. Don't bother to till them under in the fall. If you leave them in the ground, you can have an early crop in the spring.

DILL

Dill is used primarily in making pickles, but it will add a little extra flavor to all of your cooking and salad-making. Plant dill very early in the spring so that the heads will ripen just as your cucumber plants start to produce their first, small cucumbers. This is the time when you should be making your first batches of pickles.

It may take one to two weeks for dill seed to germinate and come up. It is another of the crops that should be marked with radish seeds. I like to plant dill in wide rows. Three feet of ten-inch-wide row gives me all I need for pickles, salads, sauces, and seeds for next year's crop. Dill can be grown successfully in a pot inside the house.

Dill leaves can be harvested anytime. If you want to save the seed heads, cut them just before they turn dark brown. If you wait much longer, the seeds will start falling off. Hang the heads up to dry, and you can use them throughout the winter. Fresh-cut heads, harvested just before they are ripe, have the most dill flavor. These are ideal for pickling if the timing is right.

EGGPLANT

Eggplant will do fine in well-drained, sandy soil, but it is extremely tender and can stand no frost. In fact, it likes heat almost as much as it likes fertilizer.

Eggplants should be planted 2½ to 3 feet apart in rows about two feet apart. It is best to use plants that are anywhere from four to eight weeks old. Wrap a piece of newspaper around each plant for cutworm protection. Eggplants need to be watched very closely. Bugs, especially aphids and potato

bugs, like them, so they will have to be sprayed from time to time. Cultivate them gently and not too deep; their roots are very close to the surface of the soil, as are the roots of most other heat-loving plants. They are finicky about moisture and will suffer if the water supply is not regular.

You can start to eat eggplant when they have reached about one-third of their full growth, and you can continue to eat them long after they have matured. There is no need to pick them as soon as they ripen.

ENDIVE

Endive can be treated and cared for very much like lettuce. You can plant it in wide or single rows. Harvest it just the way you would harvest leaf lettuce—by cutting down the whole plant.

Endive can be planted very early because it is quite frost-resistant. I find that in warmer weather it has a tendency to become quite bitter. The best times to sow endive seed are around the first of May and then again around the first of August. I think that fall endive is better than the early crop, but this may have something to do with our cool Vermont autumns.

You can blanch endive and reduce its bitterness by gathering up the leaves and putting a rubber band around the top of the plant. It takes two to three weeks to blanch it properly. Moisture can gather in the inner leaves and cause rotting during this time, so it is important to harvest the plant as soon as the blanching is finished.

GARLIC

Garlic is closely related to the onion family, but instead of producing one bulb, it produces a group of small bulbs called cloves. The cultural recommendations for garlic are very similar to those for onions. You should plant them in the spring. Break the bulb up into individual cloves. You may get as many as fifteen from one bulb. You can plant them in a row, but I personally prefer to plant them in a wide row so they will take up less room in the garden. They do like fertilizer, so add either a complete fertilizer or some organic fertilizer—compost, manure, blood meal, or bone meal. When the tops fall over or die in the fall, pull up the bulbs and let them dry in the sun for a few days, just as you would do with onions. Then put them in a mesh bag and hang it in an airy place for a week or two before storing them in the cellar. Planting garlic in the spring produces an average garlic bulb, but if you really want to get large garlic, plant the cloves in the fall. Set fall-planted garlic about 3 inches deep; spring garlic should be planted very shallow. Garlic very rarely goes to seed, so you don't have to worry about removing the seed pods. Garlic is widely used for flavoring foods, but it is also used to make a brew to spray on plants to repel insects. Ground or crushed garlic is soaked in water, which is then used as a spray. Organic gardeners use this simple brew successfully on a lot of plants, but you do have to spray on a daily basis.

HORSERADISH

I love horseradish. People are amazed to see so much of it growing in my garden. What they don't understand is that I eat horseradish each and every morning with eggs! This breakfast diet probably won't appeal to you so much as it appeals to me, so you probably won't want to grow quite as much as I do.

Horseradish is one of the easiest crops to raise because it spreads so rapidly. The simplest way to get started is to send away by mail for some root cuttings. The root cuttings will arrive with the small end cut on a slant. These should be planted about two inches below the surface of the soil with the small end down. Give them a little fertilizer, and they will grow like mad. Before you know it, you will have huge plants. Horseradish tends to take over, so you should give some thought to the location of your planting. It can spread to other parts of the garden, and once it gets there, it will be hard to get rid of. You only need to buy half a dozen roots to start with. This will give you and several of your neighbors more than enough to eat.

The roots can be dug in the fall and stored like carrots or beets, but you can dig them and use them any time of year. Store them right in the garden if you like.

A kitchen blender is a great device for making horseradish sauce. Put sliced horseradish roots, water, and a few drops of distilled white vinegar in the blender, and grind the mixture to whatever texture you want. Ground horseradish keeps very well when canned.

JERUSALEM ARTICHOKES

The nicest thing about Jerusalem artichokes is that they are almost completely free of diseases and pests. Believe it or not, they are related to the sunflower. They are very prolific—so prolific that if you do not watch them closely, they will try to take over your whole garden.

Jerusalem artichokes are grown for their underground tubers, which are both delicious and low in calories. (They are very good for diabetics, incidentally.) They will grow just about anywhere in the United States. They can be planted either in the fall or in the spring as soon as the ground can be worked. The easiest way to start them is by planting roots, which you can buy. You will need about two quarts of roots for a twenty-five-foot row. Bury the chunky roots about four inches deep and space them two feet apart. It is best to leave at least three feet between rows. Four feet is even better. When it is mature, a Jerusalem artichoke plant will be six or eight feet tall, so be sure to plant them where they will not shade other plants in the garden.

Jerusalem artichokes need a very long growing season—about 125 days. Harvest them after the frost has killed the tops. They can be dug anytime during the fall and winter months.

There are a number of good ways to eat them. Cook them or eat them raw in salads. I like them boiled. They are also good cut into small pieces and cooked in a cream sauce.

KALE

Kale is one of the garden's freaks. It is probably the hardiest green of all. You can actually harvest kale from under the snow in the dead of winter. It will grow twelve months of the year.

Kale seems to do even better in cool weather than it does in the heat of summer. And I think it tastes best after the weather has been cold for a while. You might plant some early, some in mid-season, and some late. It will do well in any kind of soil, but it should be well fertilized.

Rows of kale should be two feet apart, and the plants should have anywhere from six inches to a foot of space between them. The same insects that like cabbage also like kale. This is another reason why the crop that comes along in September, October, or November is the best one; there are fewer bugs to infest it.

Too many people pull up or till under kale plants in the fall. I am upset when I see this. Let your kale keep growing right into winter. Fresh kale greens will be a real delicacy in February when you are beginning to get tired of canned and frozen vegetables. The deeper the snow, the better it tastes!

You can cook kale the same way you cook spinach; you can use it in soups; you can eat it raw in salads; or you can use it as a garnish for other dishes. Two good varieties are Blue Curled Scotch and Siberian. I think I prefer the former.

KOHLRABI

Kohlrabi is another member of the cabbage family. Instead of eating the leaves, you eat the large base of the stem, which looks something like a turnip that has formed aboveground. The best ones are those that have grown quickly; those that grow slowly are usually tough and woody. A side dressing of fertilizer will help to speed up growth.

Try to use kohlrabi before it has a chance to mature completely. It should be ready ten to twelve weeks after the seeds are planted. The seeds are hardy, which means that they can be sown early—either outside in the garden or in a cold frame. The plants should be five to six inches apart in rows. Cultivate them regularly. Once the bottom of the stem has reached two or three inches in diameter, it is ready to eat.

LETTUCE

No one ever argues with me when I say that lettuce is the world's most popular salad plant. One of the reasons for this may be that it grows well almost anywhere.

If you have ever pulled up a lettuce plant of any kind, I am sure you were surprised to see how small and shallow the root system was. This explains why lettuce needs well-fertilized soil. The roots do not go deep enough to bring up nutrients that have drained out of the upper layers of soil.

Plant lettuce when you plant peas, as soon as the ground can be worked in the spring. It will do well in late March, April, and May, and it can stand a number of freezes. It does not do very well in the heat of summer, but you can sow it again in late July, early August, or September and have an excellent late crop.

I am convinced that planting lettuce seed in wide rows is the best way, but it will do well in single rows too. If you do choose a wide row, you will discover that you need only about three to five feet of any one variety. This should leave you room to experiment with several varieties at once. In a single row, you will need about twenty feet of each variety to have enough for a family of four.

There are many, many kinds of lettuce, as I am sure you know. There is loose-head lettuce, tight-head lettuce, and several types of leaf lettuce. Here in Vermont, at least, tight-head lettuce almost has to be started inside and later transplanted outside if it is to be a success. The plants can be set out when they are about three inches tall. They should be spaced about eighteen inches apart if you are interested in growing very large heads. I personally prefer smaller heads, so I plant them eight to ten inches apart in wide rows. This way I get more heads, and most are just the right size to eat at one sitting.

When transplanting, all of the outer leaves should be stripped off the plant. After all, it is the center of the plant, the head, that we want to grow. All heading plants grow from the center out. Removing the outer leaves makes the top of the

There are four types of lettuce. (1) Head (or Iceberg) lettuce is the kind you probably see most often in your local grocery store. (It may be the only kind you see there.) Great Lakes, Ithaca, Imperial, and Pennlake are all good head-lettuce varieties. (2) The leaves of Butterhead lettuce are more loosely folded than head-lettuce leaves. Some good Butterhead varieties are Bibb, Buttercrunch, Deer Tongue, Big Boston, and Dark Green Boston. (3) There are many different kinds of leaf lettuce; all have a comparatively loose, open growth habits. Salad Bowl, Black Seeded Simpson, and Grand Rapids all produce dense clumps of crinkled, light green leaves. The leaves of Oakleaf, Prizehead, and Ruby range from bronze to red in color. (4) Cos or Romaine lettuce grows eight to nine inches tall; its upright leaves are tightly folded. Dark Green Cos and Paris Island Cos are widely popular varieties.

plant smaller in comparison to the root structure. This way, the roots will have time to gain the strength they need to produce good, strong tops later on. Lots of people who plant head lettuce think they must wait until it heads up before eating it. Actually, the leaves of all varieties of head lettuce can be eaten long before the head appears.

Some people I know grow loose-head lettuce and eat it like leaf lettuce. This is not a bad idea. As long as you keep it cut, it will never form a head. Loose-head-lettuce leaves are tastier and crunchier than some leaf varieties.

There are some diseases, blights, and insects that bother lettuce, but they do not seem to show up too often. You should not have to worry about dusting and spraying. Once in a while, a cutworm will get into your lettuce and do a little harm, but cutworms will rarely damage your whole crop. Trying to keep them out is hardly worth the effort.

Make several succession plantings of lettuce, using a number of different varieties. If you do, you should have fresh lettuce from May to October. Late in the fall, after frost has really set in, you can take up a few plants from the garden, put them in flats, and bring them inside to continue growing throughout the winter in a sunny window. And you can grow lettuce in an outdoor cold frame for a very early spring harvest. It is possible never to have to buy lettuce from a grocery store.

MELONS

Because of the climate here in Vermont, we are severely limited when it comes to growing decent melons. There is no way to get ahead of Mother Nature. But there are a few things you can do to gain a week or so.

The ideal soil for muskmelons is well-drained, sandy loam in a sunny spot. In northern states, it helps to have a garden spot that slopes slightly to the south or the southeast. Generally, melons like a lot of sun, dry feet, and lots of fertilizer. They do best when planted in hills with four plants to each hill. If you have compost, put some under each hill. If you have no compost or manure, mix a little extra fertilizer into the soil. I like to plant a few radishes around each hill to give the insects something to munch on besides the tiny melon leaves.

About the fifteenth of May, I take four paper towels from a roll, wet them, and fold them back on each other so that they are the size of one. I sprinkle my melon seeds on this wet towel and roll it up like a cinnamon twirl. Then I get a terrycloth face towel and soak it with all the water it will hold. I wrap the rolled paper towels inside this and put the whole thing inside a plastic bag. Then I put the plastic bag somewhere where the temperature stays around seventy degrees.

In four or five days, the seeds will have sprouted. On the twentieth of May, I prepare the melon hills and buy some hot caps, the waxed-

GOOD TASTIN' CANTALOUPES

One happy gardener, Fred Tucker, takes great pride in growing the largest, best tastin' cantaloupes in the town of Big Pool, Maryland. Here's how he does it.

"Around the middle of April I spread a twenty-by-fifty-foot area with old horse manure that doesn't contain much straw. I roto-till this in with my Troy-Bilt tiller. At this time, I plant Heart of Gold seed in peat pots. These begin growing in my cold frame, or you could use a window sill.

"In three to four weeks, I roto-till the plot again, adding another bushel or two of horse manure. Then I wait until at least June to set my plants out. There is a saying here in Maryland, 'Plant cantaloupes in May — you'll throw them away. Plant them in June, and they'll come just as soon.'

"Cantaloupes love water, so if I don't get rain, I water often. I roto-till again before the plants send out long runners. That's my method, and I have plenty to eat and give away many, many more."

Tins cans are ideal containers for starting melon plants early. Or you can sprout the seeds in damp paper towels and plant the sprouts (as described in the text).

paper kind, to protect the young plants from frost. I take the wet towels out into the garden and very carefully unwrap them. I usually find that most of the seeds have sprouted. Those few that haven't probably would not have germinated in the soil either. I plant these sprouts just as though I were planting seeds. If I want five plants to a hill, I plant six or seven seeds, just in case one or two don't make it. I make a hole with my finger, drop a sprouted seed into it, and cover it with enough soil to equal four times the diameter of the seed. Then I cover it with a hot cap.

I don't have to worry about the melons again until the first of June. The hot caps will protect the tiny plants from frost and insects and will hold heat in the soil beneath them. Hot caps can help you gain a week or more.

Melon seeds tend to be poor germinators. If they are planted without sprouting first, and then are not warmed and protected by hotcaps, only one or two seeds might come up in each hill. I use this sprouting technique with many different crops that I think need a head start. I have made it work with cucumbers, beans, onions, corn, beets, and squash. Years ago, when I sold vegetables from a stand in front of my house, I could get a week's jump on some of my competition by sprouting seeds this way. Sprouting eliminates guesswork.

To get ripe melons at least a week early, carefully place young fruits on upside-down tin cans. The cans will keep the melons warmer than those on the cool ground.

Wherever you plant a sprouted seed, you can be sure a plant will grow.

Melons are heat-loving plants. While the young plants are growing, I try to remember to save tin cans of all kinds. After the vines start to bear and the melons get a little bigger than a baseball, I will use the cans to hold the fruit off the ground. To do so, I carefully lift each small melon, then I push an upside-down can into the soil under it so that only two or three inches of the can shows above-ground. Then I place the melon on top of the can. Sometimes I punch a hole in the top of the can so that rain water will run out of it. Melons, as I said, like heat, but they don't normally get enough here in Vermont when they lie directly on the cool ground. The bottom of a melon placed on a can is warmed, so it will ripen at least a week sooner than those grown the normal way. Melons grown on tin cans are much sweeter than others because they are much riper. I have seen some people use aluminum pie plates for this; I have tried it myself, but I think the cans work better.

The same bugs that like cucumbers also like muskmelons, but they can be discouraged by rotenone and Sevin. Watch out for cutworms. A newspaper collar will protect transplants against them.

About the first week of August, I pick off the ends of all my melon vines. The melons are still growing or are just starting to ripen at this point. During the last week of August, I pick off the smaller, green melons, leaving only the ones that I think will ripen before frost. This allows all of the plant's strength to go into the fruit left on the vine. I keep controlling the growth of the melon plants by continuing to pick off the fuzzy ends of the vines.

How do you know when a melon is ripe? Try smelling it. If you know what a muskmelon smells like and you get a strong muskmelon smell, it is probably ripe. In any case, the stem will break off a ripe melon easily.

MUSTARD

Mustard is a cool-weather crop that can be used either as a salad ingredient or as a cooked green. If you plant it carefully, mustard should never need to be thinned. If you do have to thin it, just pull up the whole plant and eat it. Mustard is as easy to grow inside the house as it is outside. You can raise plenty of it in a window box. Mustard grows quite fast. It is ready to eat just four or five weeks after it is planted, and it is loaded with vitamin A.

ONIONS

I sometimes tell people that you have to use a hammer if you want to kill an onion. They seem to stand all kinds of abuse. They will grow in practically any kind of soil, and if you fertilize them well, they will give you a tremendous yield.

Most vegetables like humus-rich soil, and onions are no exception. They won't mind it a bit if you add some manure or compost to the plot where they will be planted. If you are going to plant onions in rows, put some of this rich organic matter right in the furrows.

There are several ways to plant onions. You can grow them from plants, from "sets"—little onions that grow up to be big onions—or you can grow them directly from seed. Start onions very early, regardless of which method you use. Frost will not hurt them. You can put them in just as soon as the frost is out of the ground and you can walk in the garden.

I like to use the wide-row method with onions. I plant radishes with them, as I do with so many other things. I do the first thinning of onions planted from seed by dragging a rake across the row. (I don't do this with onion sets.) Then I wait for the tops to grow a little bit before I thin again. I pull up some to use as scallions. After the final thinning, the remaining onions should stand about three inches apart. Large Bermuda onions are an exception. These should have at least four inches of space in all directions.

Onions, if they are going to be good ones, demand lots of cultivation. They are also very intolerant of weeds. If you want to grow very large onions, you will have to move some of the dirt away from the bulb. The onion should look as if it is hardly in the ground at all, with only the bottom third or so underground. This gives the onion lots of room to expand. Moving the dirt away takes lots of careful, patient work on your part, but, like so many other things in the garden, it is worth the effort.

Onions started from sets seem to want to go to seed quite quickly. You will have to see that they don't. A small seed pod, which looks exactly like the domes on the towers of the Kremlin in Moscow, will start to form on the onion top. (The domes were designed to look like onion seed pods.) This seed pod must be removed; otherwise, the bulb on the bottom will become small and tough. You can snap it off very easily with your fingers as soon as it appears.

The nicest time to have onions ripen is in the late fall—just in time for storage. I eat the ones that were started early from sets during the summer. Then in August and September, I go out and break over the green tops with a rake. The idea is to stop them from growing any more and to make the bulbs grow bigger. Once the tops are dead, which won't be right away, it is time to think about harvesting them. If you leave them in the ground

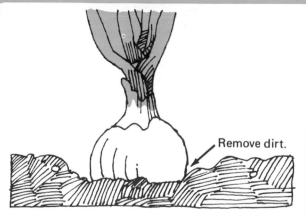

Move dirt away from the bulb so that only 1/3 is underground. In August or September, break over green tops with a rake.

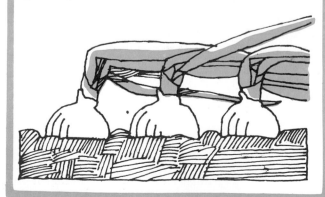

too long after the tops have turned brown, the onions will start to rot. Sometimes they will start to grow entirely new tops. Don't let this happen. Once it does, the onion is ruined for storage.

After you pull up your onions, let them sit in the sun to dry out. The point of drying is to kill the little root system at the bottom of each bulb. Each root should look like a very fine wire and be dry and brittle. When the roots are thoroughly dry, you can easily break them off with a wipe of your hand. Drying may take as long as several weeks.

I usually dig up my onions and put them along the side of the driveway to dry. Then I grade them according to size, put them in onion bags, hang them in the garage, and leave them there for three or four weeks. Later, in November, when the temperature is getting down around twenty-five degrees at night pretty consistently, I move them into the cellar. I find that the more I dry the onions, the better they store.

Most onion sets that you grow yourself keep very well. So will Yellow Globe onions, but I don't have such good luck with the Bermuda and Utah varieties. They will be all right until about February, but they will not last all winter. If you can, hang your onion bags from the ceiling of the root cellar. It is a little warmer there than down near the floor. But don't hang the bags too close together. Leave room for plenty of air circulation. This way, your onions will keep their garden-fresh flavor for months.

It is ridiculous to buy onion sets year after year if you have enough room to grow your own. I try to plant some onion seeds sometime in July. I plant them very thick, in bands about a foot wide. I fertilize them and let them grow, without ever bothering to thin them. Near the end of September, I break over the tops. I don't pull them then; I wait until the second week in October. Then I pull them up, dry them just the way I would dry larger onions, and let them hang from the ceiling of the root cellar until spring, when they will be planted again.

I have found that I can plant onions from seed in August, or even as late as the first part of September. I plant these in bands too—sometimes four feet wide. I rake the seeds into the ground and leave them there to grow as long as they will. Around the first of November, I break down the tops and mulch the onions with no more than three inches of leaves or hay. In the spring, after the snow is gone, I remove the mulch, and in a very short time, I have small onions growing green tops. Some of these can be used as onion plants in another part of the garden. It is amazing how many things you can do with onions if you take the time to play around with them.

There are few diseases, here in the North at least, that affect onions. I don't have to worry too much about spraying or dusting mine, although I understand that gardeners in the southern states are sometimes troubled by onion maggots.

PARSLEY

Parsley is an herb that almost everybody knows and likes. There's no need ever to buy any, because it is so easy to grow. I usually start mine in a cold frame or inside on a window sill. It can stand quite a lot of freezing weather, so it can be transplanted outside very early in the gardening season.

Curled Leaf parsley seems to be the best. This is the type of parsley you would find on your steak in a good restaurant. You don't need to try to grow an awful lot of this; two or three plants will go a long way.

In the fall, you can dig it up, pot it, and bring it inside. Use a good, big pot, as the taproot can be quite long. I have kept parsley plants for as long as a year or two, planting it outside in the spring and bringing it back in again in the autumn.

If you plant onions from seed you will have to thin them — probably several times. After the last thinning, the young onions should stand about three inches apart. If you plant onion sets, spacing them correctly as you go, you won't have to thin.

PARSNIPS

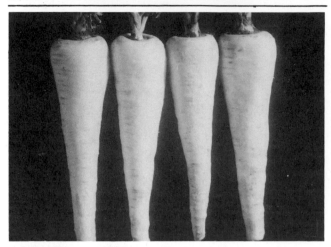

Parsnips are grown only for their roots because the tops are not worth eating. They will grow in practically any soil, but they prefer loose, deep earth. Parsnip seeds are slow to germinate, so don't be discouraged if they don't show up for a while. I like to plant radishes as a companion plant to parsnips. As I pull the radishes, I am cultivating the soil around the parsnips at the same time. Parsnips should be thinned so that they are spaced two or three inches apart.

The quality of parsnips is better after there has been frost. Leave them in the ground until late fall or early winter. They are at their very best after the ground has been frozen for a while. In fact, one of the best places to store parsnips is right in the garden. Leave some of them all winter and dig them up in the spring when you have more space to store them in your root cellar.

I like parsnips and think they are something everyone should consider planting.

PEANUTS

Peanuts are easy enough to grow, but they do better in the southern states than here in the North because of our shorter growing season. They need about five months of growing time, so take this into consideration when you lay out your garden. You may not have a long-enough season where you live. Spanish peanuts can be grown in about 110 days. They bear heavily and take up less garden space than some of the other varieties.

Peanuts thrive in slightly acidic, sandy soil which contains lots of organic matter. A peanut "seed" consists of a hull filled with nuts. These hulls should be planted one to two inches deep and anywhere from three to six inches apart. The rows need to be approximately two and a half feet apart.

A peanut plant will produce blossoms and flowers before the stem bends over toward the ground. When it touches the soil, it will root, and a cluster of peanuts will grow there. A mature plant will be a foot to a foot and a half tall. When it reaches about two-thirds of its full height, it should be hilled, by pulling dirt up around the stem, or mulched.

Harvest peanuts in the fall, and hang them in an airy shed to dry for a few weeks. Before they are eaten, they should be roasted in an oven at 300 degrees for about twenty minutes.

PEAS

I suppose there are a few people in the world who don't like peas, but I have never met too many of them. Peas are easy enough to grow, but you have to plant a lot of them to get a big harvest. Wide-row planting is about the only way to have enough peas, as far as I am concerned. Peas in wide rows tend to hold each other up as they lean one way or the other. The only plants that hit the ground are those on the outside of each row, and because they are so thickly matted, even they tend to hold themselves up. Most of the peas will be in the air, dry, and easy to get at when harvest time comes around.

Some years, I have planted peas in patches that were as large as twelve feet square. I am often asked, "How do you get in to harvest them in a patch so large?" Easy. I take a stool, go out in the patch, sit down, reach out for the peas around me, and pick a peck. Then I move the stool and do it again. You may raise so many peas you can't stay ahead of them!

Peas are a wonderful nitrogen-fixing, green-manure crop. After harvest, till the plant residues back into the garden whenever you can. This will help improve the soil. If you have no way to till them in, put them in your compost pile, or save the vines to use as mulch on other plants.

You can sow peas as soon as you can walk in the garden in the spring. They can stand many freezes. In fact, I've had some success planting them in the fall and covering them with mulch. This is a gamble that doesn't always work, but some years I have removed the mulch in the spring and had the peas start to grow as soon as the ground thawed. If you are lucky, you can have an incredibly early crop this way.

Always try to plant two or three varieties of peas. Plant some early ones, some mid-season ones, and some late ones. You could also try some Sugar Peas. They are so sweet you can eat pods and all. They are sometimes called Snow Peas, and they are delicious in salads, soups, and stews.

There are two basic types of peas—the dwarf pea, which will normally grow to be about twenty-six inches high, and the telephone pea, which will grow taller than three feet. The Alderman variety is a good example of a climbing pea. It grows so high that it needs to have some sort of support—like a wire fence.

There are not too many diseases that affect peas, mainly because they are growing at a time when the weather is quite cool. They should be planted fairly thick—about two inches apart. You can be eating early peas nine to ten weeks after you plant them.

Most peas do poorly once the weather has warmed up. It is a standard rule that the earlier you get them in, the better they will be. But there is one variety you can plant during the hot months;

Unlike pole beans, climbing peas will grow up chicken wire or other types of fencing.

it is called Wando. I like to plant these sometime after my earliest lettuce is done. I also plant them in July to get a late crop in September. This is right at the height of the weed season, but I almost never have to weed them. I just broadcast the peas in a (one- to four-foot) band and let them grow as I would any cover crop. When the time comes, I harvest the peas and till the plants back under. Planting peas in wide rows helps to keep the soil cool and moist, something peas need if they are to produce in hot weather.

For a big harvest of peas, plant them in wide rows. No staking is necessary.

131

PEPPERS

Peppers seem to grow much like eggplant. They like a sunny area and soil that is warm, dry, fertile, and slightly acidic. Don't plant them where you have used a lot of lime. There are two types—hot peppers and sweet peppers.

People sometimes ask, "How do I grow red peppers?" The answer to that is simple enough. Any pepper will turn red if it is left on the plant long enough. This is true with hot peppers, Hungarian Wax peppers, and even California Wonders.

An old-timer taught me a trick that seems to work pretty well. After the plants have been indoors for six to eight weeks, I set them out in the garden. Before I transplant, I rip the matches out of a couple of matchbooks and put them in the bottom of the hole where the plant will be set. The peppers seem to enjoy the sulfur in the matches, perhaps because the sulfur lowers the pH of the soil around the roots.

Place book matches under pepper plants; the sulfur makes the soil slightly acidic.

Peppers need fertilizer, but they don't seem to appreciate getting it in large doses. It is a good idea to put compost or manure under them when they are transplanted. Side dress them with some sort of rich, organic commercial fertilizer when they blossom. Keep insects off with rotenone or Sevin.

I use one other trick. When the plants start to blossom, I take an empty Windex bottle and put in a spoonful of epsom salts—a form of magnesium. I fill the bottle with lukewarm water, shake it, and then spray the mixture right on the leaves of the plants. The leaves turn dark green, and soon I have an abundance of peppers.

POTATOES

Potatoes will grow almost anywhere, but they are happiest in rich, sandy soil. Always try to plant more than one variety. Plant some in April or early May, and some more around the end of May. The second planting should be ready right around the end of September—just in time to put the crop in the root cellar. Your first planting will mature a little earlier. It should supply you with small, young potatoes during the summer, but you should not plan to store these.

Potatoes do not like soil that has a high pH. This means you should try to avoid planting them in ground where a lot of lime or wood ashes have been added.

Choose your seed potatoes carefully. Try to get good ones; you only get one chance at growing them. If you buy large seed potatoes, they should be cut into pieces. There should be two or three eyes in each piece. I like to cut up my seed potatoes at least one day before they are going to be planted. This gives the cut surface time to heal over and dry out a little. When I plant them, I put the cut side down. One of the easiest ways to plant potatoes is in trenches about four inches deep. Space them at least a foot apart. I put a handful of superphosphate fertilizer and a handful of good rich compost in each space between the potatoes. Superphosphate seems a little safer than a complete fertilizer like 10-10-10. If you do use something like 10-10-10, be sure that none of it touches the seed potatoes themselves. Later on, you can side dress with a complete fertilizer, as I do. By then there will be no danger of burning the seeds.

When the green tops of the potatoes come up, they should be covered with soil again—leaves and all. (A hoe works best for this.) This is called hilling. New potatoes form above the seed you plant, not below it. By building up a hill, you are giving the new potatoes plenty of loose, soft soil into which they can expand. After you have hilled a couple of times, you should have a long mound, about eight to ten inches high, over the row of potatoes. Pay attention to your earliest crop. If you hill it as soon as the green tops show, you will keep the plants protected from frost.

Leave 2 or 3 eyes in each piece of seed potato.

Hill potatoes as soon as the leaves appear so they'll have loose, soft soil in which to expand.

Seed potatoes can be broadcast over a plot of tilled ground, then covered with 12 to 18 inches of seed-free mulch. Harvesting will be easy, and your potatoes will be large and clean.

There is an even easier way to plant potatoes—under mulch. This technique is sometimes called broadcast planting. Till up an area of soil, say ten or twelve feet square, and prepare your potato seed just as though you were going to plant them in a furrow. Spread these cut-up seed potatoes right on top of the ground, about ten inches apart in all directions. You don't have to plant them; just lay them on the surface.

These should be covered with a foot or a foot and a half of mulch—seed-free mulch, if you have it. That's all! Just forget about them for a while. The tops will grow right up through the hay, and new potatoes will form right on top of the ground beneath the mulch. As the summer goes on, you should reach under the mulch from time to time; if you feel a potato that is big enough to eat, about the size of a golf ball, you can pick it. The first potatoes should be ready just about the time your beans are. Picking early potatoes this way does no harm to the plant.

There are still other advantages to planting potatoes under a mulch. Potato bugs do not seem to venture too far into a mulched potato patch. They will eat some of the plants around the perimeter, but you will see very few of them near the middle. You can walk around the edges and pick off any bugs you see. In the fall, you won't have to dig potatoes; you just rake back the mulch and harvest a whole crop of potatoes just sitting there waiting to be picked.

There are two diseases that seem to bother potatoes the most. The first is "late blight" and the second is "common scab." It is a good practice to spray your potatoes at least once a year with a complete spray specifically for potatoes. Common scab is encouraged by lime and by ordinary stable manure, so try to keep these out of the potato patch.

When can you harvest potatoes? Pick them whenever they are big enough to eat, as I have already said, but take a little extra care with potatoes that you are going to store. Don't pick them until the tops are completely dead. There is an easy way to tell a completely ripe potato from a green one. As soon as you dig it out of the ground, rub the skin with your hand. If the skin rubs off easily, the potato is still green. It is perfectly good to cook and eat this way; it just won't store as well or as long as one that has a tougher skin.

PUMPKINS

If you fertilize pumpkins well, they can get very big, and they take up a lot of room. It might be best not to plant them unless you have lots of garden space.

If you do decide to grow pumpkins, try to keep them well away from your winter-squash patch. The two plants will cross-pollinate. The seeds produced by the cross-pollinated blossoms may produce some unique and interesting vegetables the next year, but they will not produce "true" varieties.

Plant pumpkin seeds in hills that are at least eight to ten feet apart. Once the seedlings come up, the plants should be thinned to four or five per hill. I usually dig a hole beneath the spot where a hill will be and put in a shovelful of manure or compost. Then I sprinkle a little dirt over the top of it and plant the seed. I also plant some radishes to keep the bugs off the pumpkin leaves.

Pumpkins should be harvested when they are fully ripe. They should not be exposed to frost or they will not keep well. When you pick them, be careful not to break off the stem. If you do break one off, try to use this pumpkin first because it will be a poor keeper.

You can control the growth of a pumpkin vine if it seems to be getting out of hand or in the way of something else. All you have to do is pick off the fuzzy end of the vine and it will stop growing. This will also help the pumpkins already on the vine to grow larger.

For eating and cooking, we prefer the Baby Sugar pumpkins. One is just right for a pie or mashed for dinner.

NECK PUMPKIN

An unusual vegetable he enjoys growing is the Neck Pumpkin. It has all the qualities and uses of a regular pumpkin; the only difference is that the Neck Pumpkin has a small seed cavity, and the long, bent neck is solid flesh. OM

PUMPKIN SEEDS

The Lady Godiva pumpkin is a great treat for people who enjoy eating pumpkin seeds. The seeds have no shell so they can simply be toasted and eaten without the tedious task of shelling. The pumpkin itself is yellowish, generally has green stripes or markings, and averages about six pounds. The flesh is not table quality. RA

I am sure you know or have heard about people who grow pumpkins that weigh 125 to 150 pounds. This is not as hard a job as you might think. I have done it many times, even though these huge pumpkins are nearly worthless as far as eating is concerned. To grow a mammoth jack-o'-lantern, dig a big hole and put in about a bushel of aged cow manure mixed with fertilizer. Put a layer of dirt over the manure, and plant three seeds. When the seedlings have two or three leaves on them, choose the one that looks the healthiest and pull the other two up. As soon as the vine has grown three small pumpkins, break off its fuzzy end so that it won't grow any farther. Keep an eye on this vine. If new blossoms or small pumpkins start to form, pick them off. Let the plant concentrate on the original three.

When the pumpkins get to be about the size of a man's fist, select the best-shaped one and pick the other two. Let all the strength of the manure go into this single pumpkin. Roll it slightly every once in a while, but not so much that you twist or break the stem. It may have a tendency to flatten out on one side if you don't change its position from time to time.

This is a great project for kids. Before long, they'll be competing to see who can grow the pumpkin that weighs the most. A child will be astonished to find he can grow something that weighs far more than he does in just a few weeks.

RADISHES

Radishes will grow anywhere. They don't do quite so well in heavy clay as they do in light sandy soil because they are a root crop. Radishes can be planted as soon as the ground can be worked in the spring, and a second planting will continue to grow late into the fall, even after frost. They will not do especially well in hot weather, so it is best to plant them either early or late. Radishes have a very short maturation time, which means you can plant them many times during the growing season.

To get a really good radish, you should provide fertile soil and encourage quick growth. Those that grow slowly tend to be tough and woody tasting.

Radishes are a fine companion plant for just about anything else. They will not harm any other crop. Let the bugs chew on the radish tops. This does not seem to have much effect on the quality of the bottoms. Harvest them before they get too large or root maggots may get into them.

RASPBERRIES

There are two basic kinds of raspberries, just as there are two kinds of strawberries—early and everbearing. Raspberries are so easy to grow it seems to me that every garden should have some. Remember that they are perennials and that they will be in the same place year after year. If you prepare the soil with extra care to begin with, it will pay off in the years to come. Raspberries make an edible hedge, but they do grow quite high and can shade much of the rest of the garden if they are not carefully placed.

Raspberry plants should be set out about two feet apart in rows that are six feet apart. Planting should be done in the spring. I like to "root prune" the canes before I put them in the ground; I just cut off the ends of the roots to encourage the growth of newer, stronger ones.

Dig a trench or a series of holes, add organic matter and fertilizer, and make your plantings. The short canes that you buy will have been grown somewhere else. If you look carefully, you will see where the hard stem once came through the surface of the soil. Replant the cane slightly deeper this time. Soon the roots will begin to grow again under the ground, then they will send up new shoots nearby. For every plant you set out, you will get several back.

You won't get much of a harvest from your raspberries the first year, mostly because the plants will be too busy putting out new growth. They should require very little care during their first season. You might want to cultivate between the rows, but if you do, be careful not to cut off the new shoots that are coming up. A rake or an in-row weeder are better for hand cultivating than a hoe. Better still, you can mulch. This should eliminate any need for cultivating. Use a seed-free mulch so you don't invite rodents.

Let's discuss how to care for spring raspberries first. You set out the plants and get a minimal harvest the first year. The second year, you fertilize the patch in the spring. As soon as the canes have borne fruit, they should be cut back to within an inch or two of the ground and removed to the compost pile. By this time, you should see many new, green shoots coming up. Select the largest and best-looking ones, and cut off the others. After you do this, you should have one fresh shoot about every six or eight inches.

Raspberries need some sort of artificial support. The easiest thing is to drive two stakes in the ground about three feet apart on either end of each row and run two parallel wires between these stakes. The canes will be held up by the wires. The top wire should be three or four feet high. New shoots, the ones that will bear fruit the next year, can be cut back a little sometime in August if you want more lateral growth toward the wires. Don't cut back all the canes; prune selectively. The canes you do not cut will have the earliest fruit.

Everbearing raspberries, if they are treated well, should produce a heavy crop in the fall. Everbearing varieties will bear in the spring as well as in the fall, but it is best, I think, to discourage the spring crop so that the fall crop will be stronger. You do this by cutting back the canes, either as soon as they have been harvested in the fall or in the early spring. Don't cut them all the way back to the ground; leave about three feet. Cut the canes that do bear fruit in the spring as soon as they have finished producing.

If you help the fall crop this way, you will get much bigger and sweeter raspberries from your everbearing plants. Some good raspberry varieties include Sunrise, Taylor, Latham, Blackcap, Logan, and Teutonic.

PRUNING INSTRUCTIONS

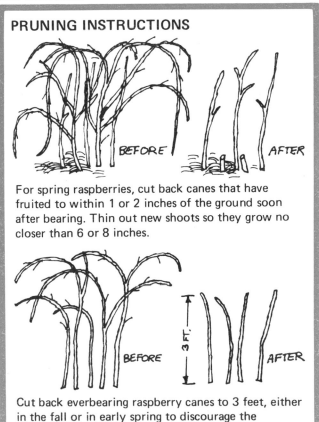

For spring raspberries, cut back canes that have fruited to within 1 or 2 inches of the ground soon after bearing. Thin out new shoots so they grow no closer than 6 or 8 inches.

Cut back everbearing raspberry canes to 3 feet, either in the fall or in early spring to discourage the production of a spring crop. The plants will produce an abundant crop of large, sweet berries in the fall.

RHUBARB

Rhubarb is a very hardy perennial. It does well even in northern states, and it will live for many years. It is best to plant rhubarb roots. You can buy these in a store or send away for them, but the easiest thing is to get some from a neighbor. Plant rhubarb somewhere out of the way. It will be in place for a long time, so choose a spot where it will not be disturbed. Three or four roots will give you all you can eat.

In the spring, dig a hole and put in some manure or decomposed organic matter. Plant the root in the hole, covering it with about one inch of soil. You will get no harvest from rhubarb the first year, but during this time, you should give it lots of fertilizer.

The second year, the rhubarb plants will start to put out seed pods. If you keep these cut, the roots will continue to produce tasty stalks all season long. The more leaves and stalks you harvest, the more the plant will produce.

A rhubarb plant will last ten years or so, but it will demand occasional attention. Every four or five years, in the fall, I take a shovel and drive it right down through the middle of the plant. Then I actually dig up half of the root. I fill in the hole with manure or compost. This assures a tender and juicy crop the following year. The half of the plant that I dug up can be saved and planted somewhere else—perhaps in somebody else's garden.

I have stored some of these dug-up rhubarb plants in my root cellar. They will do amazing things! One year, I kept some in a box filled with sand and some in a box filled with sawdust. In January, I soaked the sand and the sawdust with water just to see what would happen. When I did, the rhubarb roots sent out little stalks. These looked just like the rhubarb shoots that come up out of the ground in the spring, except that they had no leaves. They looked a little like asparagus shoots. We ate these, and they were a real treat in the dead of winter.

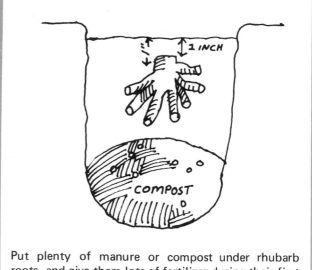

Put plenty of manure or compost under rhubarb roots, and give them lots of fertilizer during their first year.

RUTABAGAS

Rutabagas require exactly the same type of care as turnips, which I will get to shortly, except that they grow bigger than turnips and take about a month longer to mature. My favorite rutabaga is the Purple Top variety.

SPINACH

Spinach, although it will grow almost anywhere, likes cool weather best. It should be planted very early—as soon as you can work the soil in the spring. Late March or early April is a good time to sow seed here in Vermont.

Spinach seeds germinate very slowly. Spinach and any other crop that is slow to come up should be marked with radish seeds so that you don't forget the planting and walk on the area by mis-

take. Once they do appear, spinach plants should be thinned to two or three inches apart. The faster spinach grows, the more tender it will be and the better it will taste. Fertilizing the soil will help your crop grow faster. To get the most out of your space, plant spinach in wide rows.

There are a number of different kinds of spinach. Some varieties are meant to be planted early, and some have been developed for late planting. Take a look at the seed package to learn which is which. My own favorite varieties are Summer Savory, Bloomsdale, and New Viking.

The one bug that bothers spinach the most is a specialist called the spinach aphid. This is a tiny, yellow-green louse that is easy to discourage with a dusting of rotenone.

Let me remind you again that it is particularly important to keep leaf crops like spinach harvested. Start picking or cutting it for the table when there are just four or five leaves on each plant. It is best to cut the whole plant down close to the ground, somewhere below the lowest leaf. If you cut it off clean without destroying the stem, it will take the plant much longer to go to seed. If you wait too long before harvesting, hoping that the leaves will get nice and big, you will end up with less spinach in the long run because the plant will bolt and go to seed very quickly. Once it has done this, it will no longer produce. As soon as three or four new leaves appear after the first cutting, cut the plant back again.

There is also a green called New Zealand spinach. This is not a true spinach, although the leaves look the same and can be eaten in the same ways. New Zealand spinach will survive a lot of hot weather, which is a definite advantage. It grows much larger than regular spinach, sometimes getting two feet high. It should be planted in rows three feet apart with the plants spaced ten inches to a foot apart after thinning. After five or six weeks, it can be harvested, but you should do it a little differently. Leave the center shoot and pick only the side leaves. If you don't injure the center of the plant, it will continue to produce for a long time.

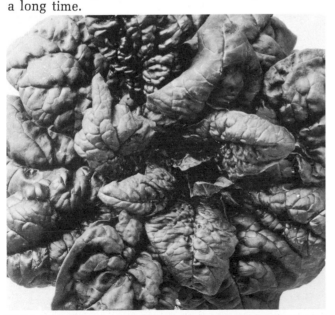

POTATOES, SWEET

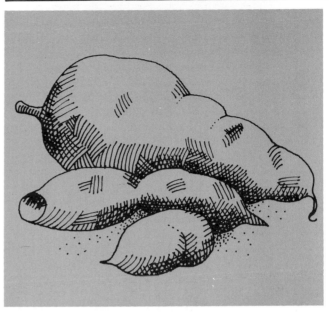

Sweet potatoes have to be started from plants. This is easy to do and kind of fun. Take a ripe sweet potato and put it in a glass of water. After a few days it will start to sprout, sending out a number of small shoots. When these get to be about six inches long, pick them off, and put each in another container of water. Leave them until tiny roots begin to form. Once they have roots, you can plant them in the garden.

Sweet potatoes are extremely tender. Be sure that you wait until there is no longer any danger of frost before you transplant them. They also need plenty of room. It's best to plant them in long ridges, about three feet apart. They like light soil and will require some fertilizer. Sweet potatoes are not bothered by insects very much, so there should be no need to spray or dust.

You can dig sweet potatoes as soon as there is anything big enough to eat. Storing them well is something of a problem—for me at least. To keep really well, they should be put in a very warm and humid place for eight to ten days before they go into the root cellar. I find it easier to can or freeze them.

SWEET POTATOES

Throw up a nice high ridge to plant your sweet potatoes on, advises one successful Kentucky gardener. He claims the sweet potato grows down until it hits hard dirt and then stops. He doesn't use any fertilizer when he sets out the slips. Later, he spreads fertilizer between the ridges and cultivates it in. When he hoes, he pulls fertilized soil up around the plants.

A neighboring gardener planted the same variety of sweet potatoes at the same time — but on a small ridge. When dug, the neighbor's potatoes were as small and round as baseballs. On the high ridge, the sweet potatoes grew large and long — up to twenty-nine inches in length.

SQUASH

Yellow crookneck

Squash is not a hardy crop, so don't plant it too early. Winter squash, such as the Blue Hubbard, Butternut, Butter Cup, and Table Queen varieties, should be planted in hills at least eight to ten feet apart. Put four or five seeds in each hill and later thin to three or four plants.

Here in Vermont, at least, we seldom plant winter squash until the first of June, at the earliest. If you wait this long, or even as late as the tenth of June, there will still be enough time to grow plenty of squash and also avoid a lot of bug problems. Planting radishes in each hill is almost a must. They will satisfy a good share of the hungry bugs. Thanks to radishes, I have not had to spray my winter squash at all for several years.

You should try not to plant pumpkins or any other orange squash near winter squash. If you do, you are likely to ruin the quality of the squash because the two plants are apt to cross-pollinate. Oddly enough, the squash does not seem to ruin the pumpkins. If you are forced to plant these two crops close to each other, plant the pumpkins at least three weeks after you plant the squash. This way, some of the squash blossoms will have started to turn into fruit by the time the pumpkin blossoms appear.

Summer squash, zucchini, scallop, and cockleshell squash can be planted somewhat closer together. You can plant them in hills three or four feet apart or in rows, laying seeds eight inches apart. I prefer to plant these types of squash in single rows because they take up less room this way. You don't need to plant much summer squash or zucchini to get a big yield. If you go overboard

with it, you won't know what to do with it all and will end up wasting a lot.

Too few people know about harvesting squash buds and blossoms. They are a real delicacy. Take the buds just before they are about to open into blossoms. Pick them just the way you would pick strawberries, wash them off, and saute them in butter. They are delicious in soups, with meat, or in stews. Squash plants will continue to produce new buds as long as you keep the fruit harvested. It is easy to gather dozens of squash and many quarts of buds at the same time; it's a little like having your cake and eating it too.

Squash will attract aphids and squash bugs, but you already know how to cope with these. Keeping the patch weeded will help prevent insect problems. If you discover that a squash-vine borer has attacked the main stem of a plant, you can cut out the insect with a knife. If you then quickly cover the injured part of stem with soil, it will heal and grow new roots.

Some folks don't seem to know when to harvest squash or what a harvestable squash looks like. I like to use the thumbnail test. When you are selecting a winter squash that you are going to store, for example, push your thumbnail against it as hard as you can. If the outer skin doesn't cut easily, you can be sure that that squash will keep for a long time. If it does cut, it probably won't keep so long, but that doesn't mean you can't eat it! It just means

Zucchini

White bush squash

SUMMER SQUASH

WINTER SQUASH

Butternut Acorn

There are many different kinds of squash. Be sure you know the difference between summer and winter types; the former cannot be kept over the winter (except by canning or freezing). Winter-squash vines spread rapidly; don't let them choke out other crops.

FRENCH FRIED SQUASH

If you'd like to try a new twist with squash, simply slice them in then strips and eat them raw in salads or along with an attractive plate of other colorful raw vegetables. Or you can slice yellow squash and fry just like french fried potatoes. Children love this different treat. RAM, JLG

---

that it won't be a good winter keeper. It should be placed near the front of your storage pile, used first, or shared with friends quite soon.

Be sure you leave the stems on your winter squash. If you pull the stem off, the whole squash will rot from that end. If a stem breaks off by accident, use that squash first. Don't wash any vegetables that you plan to store. In fact, handle them as little as possible. The more you handle them, the more likely you are to bruise them. Any blemish at all on the skin of a squash will cause it to rot more quickly.

STRAWBERRIES

Spring is the best time to plant any kind of berry plant because that is the time when the most moisture is available. As you plan your strawberry bed, remember that it is going to be there for some time, and that it is going to require more care than a plot of annual vegetables. After a certain point, it will be difficult to get in there with any sort of machinery; this will make weeding and cultivating difficult. Spend a little extra time tilling organic matter into the soil before you transplant. Then give the strawberry bed some fertilizer, and work it in really well.

Be careful when you buy strawberry plants. Do your best to get good, disease-free stock. Check with the people at your local gardening store, with neighbors who have success with strawberries, or with the seed catalogs. Strawberry plants you buy will have some leaves when you get them. I pick these off, leaving only one leaf in the center of the plant.

Ideally, your plants should arrive right at planting time so they won't sit around too long before they are set out in the garden. They can stand some freezing weather, so don't worry about waiting until after the frost-free date. Space the plants at twelve- to eighteen-inch intervals in rows at least three or four feet apart.

I like to put strawberry plants in a trench or a hole. After I have prepared the hole or trench, I build a little cone of soil in the bottom. I drape the roots over this pointed mound just as if the plant were a wig. This technique gives the roots access to more moisture and nutrients in the soils. Then I fill up the rest of the trench with soil, being careful not to cover the crown of the plant. Do not transplant a strawberry plant any deeper than

it was growing before. Finally, I firm the soil around the plant.

Do not expect any crop the first year. Plant in the spring, fertilize the plants well, and pick off any blossoms that appear. It is a mistake to let them bear any fruit this first season. You are trying to encourage them to put out long runners rather than berries. If you let the runners grow, each "mother" plant will produce ten to twenty "daughter" plants. If you plant 100 plants the first year, you could easily have as many as one or two thousand the next year.

Soon after a long runner grows out from the mother plant, it will root in the ground and grow leaves. Then it may establish still another daughter. Don't be afraid to go into the strawberry patch and move some of the runners around before they have a chance to take root. Try to get them well spaced in the area between rows. If you don't, the daughter plants may get too thick in one place.

After a heavy fall freeze, you should mulch your strawberry plants. My personal recommendation is that you use leaves or salt marsh hay because they have no weed seeds. If you use hay, you may be planting weeds as you mulch. Don't forget that you won't be able to get in there with a lot of fancy tools to weed and cultivate next year. As soon as there is a thaw in the spring, uncover the plants so they can begin to grow again.

Strawberries are biennials, which means that

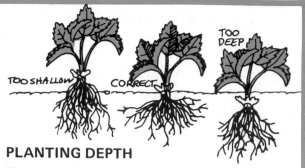

PLANTING DEPTH

The depth of the planting hole and the height of the soil mound in the bottom should be adjusted to allow the crown of the plant to sit exactly at soil level. The crown and upper roots will dry out if they sit above the soil surface. If the crown is below the surface, it will rot.

12-18 IN.

3 OR 4 FT. BETWEEN ROWS

RUNNER PLANTS

PLANTING INSTRUCTIONS

Strawberry plants should be set twelve to eighteen inches apart in rows at least three or four feet apart. Just before planting, remove all but two or three of the largest, healthiest leaves and cut off about one-third of the root system. To prevent the roots from drying out during planting, place the plants in a bucket containing enough water to cover the roots. Or you can dip the roots in then mid just prior to setting out the plant.

they grow one year and bear fruit the next. A bed can be harvested for two or three years, but after that, the berries start to deteriorate, and the strawberry plot may become choked with weeds.

But there is a way to keep a patch going strong for many years without having to replant it. I like to plant strawberries in short rows. After I have harvested the second year, I take the tiller and run it down the middle of the original rows, turning under the mother plants. This leaves a tilled area about two feet wide. I wait four or five days and then till these strips again. I also mix manure, compost, or fertilizer into the soil. Now the daughter plants, which have grown strong on either side of this newly tilled area, will become mother plants. They will send out runners and establish new plants where the original ones were. I encourage the runners to go in this direction by gently guiding them with a rake or with my hands. These new plants will be the ones to bear fruit the next year. I have kept a patch going for as long as ten years by shifting the rows back and forth this way. Each year, I just till under the old rows and let them grow back again from the runners of the other plants.

You may have to spray strawberries from time to time for various reasons. Treatment for straw-

berry diseases and insects can be a little tricky, so get advice from your Extension Service agent before you go too far with poisons.

Catskill and Fairfax are two of the best strawberry varieties that bear in the spring. There are also everbearing varieties that will keep producing all season; Mastodon and Gem are two good examples. I think these produce better fruit in the fall than they do the rest of the time. If you plant half your patch to regular strawberries and half to everbearing, you can have strawberries to freeze in the spring and fresh strawberries to eat all summer.

SUNFLOWERS

Growing giant sunflowers is a thrill that every gardener should enjoy. As you know, they will grow very, very tall—sometimes as high as twelve feet or more. If you apply plenty of fertilizer and organic matter when you plant the seed, your sunflowers will grow tall and sturdy. If you want to have early sunflowers, you can start them inside. They are very easy to transplant and can be put right in your corn rows. Sunflowers are one of the few beautiful flowers that produce an edible crop too. Just remember to plan carefully so that they do not shade other sun-loving crops.

People like sunflower seeds almost as much as birds do. Keeping the birds away can be a problem. As the seeds start to ripen, the heads of the flowers will begin to bend downward. This is the time to take a piece of plastic mesh (the material of which orange bags are made), tie it around the stem, and wrap it around the seed head. Birds will

not put their heads through the mesh to get at the seeds; they will only eat those few seeds that are exposed around the edges.

Harvest sunflower seeds late in the fall. Cut off the head, leaving about two feet of stem attached to it. Hang these in some dry place where birds and rodents will not find them. A well-ventilated attic is a nearly perfect place for drying sunflowers. Once the heads are good and dry, you can remove the seeds by rubbing them off with a stiff brush. You may find that the ends of the seeds are still a little damp. If they are, they should be spread out on newspaper to dry further.

SWISS CHARD

Swiss chard is closely related to the beet, but with chard, we are not interested so much in the bottom. We eat only the leaves. In fact, it does not grow an edible root at all.

Swiss chard will produce all summer long. It will stand several freezes, both in the spring and in the fall. Broadcast it in wide rows for best results.

Chard comes in a variety of colors. You can take your choice. The most common type is green. But there is also red chard, called rhubarb chard and white chard, which is not really pure white. Many gardeners like the taste of rhubarb chard best, and I can't say that I disagree.

Whichever color you choose, harvest it like spinach; cut off the entire plant about one inch above the ground. Many people make the mistake of picking off only the biggest leaves. These are always the toughest ones. The smaller ones near the center of the plant have the best flavor. Cut down the whole plant and mix the big leaves and the little leaves together. There may be times when your chard will get ahead of you and grow a foot tall. When this happens, it is best to mow down the whole row and let the chard start growing all over again.

TOMATOES

Let me tell you about my own method for planting tomatoes. Because our northern growing season is so short, and because this particular crop takes such a long time to mature, I have to start my tomatoes indoors about six to eight weeks before the last killing frost. The seeds are planted in shallow pans called flats.

When the seedlings are about three inches tall, it is time to transplant them into another flat. I always transplant them deeper than they were growing in the original flat. I leave only the top leaves showing above the soil. All but these uppermost leaves are picked off before transplanting. The buried section of stem begins to grow tiny root hairs. Before long, the stem will have become a tangle of healthy roots capable of supporting a rugged plant. A second transplanting takes place when the plant is about ten inches tall. Again, I take off all except the very top leaves and set the plant in a two-quart milk carton, putting the ends of the roots right at the very bottom of the carton. By the time these plants are ready to be set out in the garden, they have a stem the size of my little finger and a root structure as deep as the milk carton is tall.

When I get ready to transplant tomatoes into the garden, I dig a trench or furrow and put compost or manure in the bottom, filling it to within three inches of the ground surface. Then I very carefully take the tomato plant out of the milk carton or flat and lay it down in the trench. Again, all of the leaves except the topmost cluster are removed, even if there are blossoms and small green tomatoes. I cover the entire length of the stem with about 2½ inches of soil and firm it down with my hands. When I get to the leafy end, I support it with one hand and bring soil up underneath it with the other to prop it in a more upright position. Mother Nature will take over the job from there. In no time at all, the plant will have grown straight and tall, and will have developed an extensive and healthy root system.

Because the roots and stem are only 2½ inches below the soil surface, the heat-loving tomato plants get extra warmth early in the season. When the sun comes out and warms the soil, it also warms the roots. A tomato planted this way will grow much faster than one planted with its roots deep in the cold earth. Tomatoes should never be mulched until they have been in the ground for about four or five weeks. Mulch insulates the soil and shades it from the sun, so the ground stays cold longer, and this hinders the growth of the plant. Once the soil has warmed up, mulching does have certain advantages. For one thing, it will help prevent blossom-end rot by keeping an even moisture content in the soil.

TRANSPLANTING TOMATOES

When transplanting tomatoes, remove all but the topmost leaves.

When transplanting tomatoes, always plant them deeper than they were growing before. Only the top leaves should show.

When transplanting a tomato plant to the garden, lay it on its side in the furrow so it will root all along the stem.

What about staking? The best time to stake is right after you have transplanted into the garden so you will be able to remember where the underground stem is located. If you wait until later, you might cut the buried stem in half as you push the stake into the earth. Whenever you stake a tomato—or trellis cucumbers or peas, for that matter—always put the support on the downwind side of the plant, so that when the prevailing wind blows, the plant will be blown against the stake or trellis. Otherwise, it will blow against the tie, sometimes hard enough to sever the stem.

When you attach the plant to the stake, be sure to use a soft, wide tie. A strip of cloth is better than string, cord, or wire. Whatever you use, tie it tightly around the stake, but loosely and gently around the stem. If you decide to stake your tomato plants, keep all of the suckers picked off. Suckers are tiny stems and leaves that grow in the crotches of the larger stems and steal nourishment from the plant. If you decide to let the plants run free along the ground, removing suckers is not quite so important, but you should try to keep at least half of them pinched off.

Always try to plant at least two or three varieties of tomatoes; it is risky to rely on just one. What would happen, for instance, if there happened to be a very early fall frost or an extended drought? One of the various types of tomatoes will probably survive and provide a crop.

In the fall, as frost approaches, you can harvest the tomatoes that have not ripened yet. The very green ones may never ripen inside, but the whitish ones and the ones that have changed color slightly will. Bring them in and set them on a shelf or board. Lay some newspaper over them and check every once in a while to see how they are doing. Turn them over every two or three days so that they don't stay in the same position. You may find that you can keep them for a month or more after the first frost. You can also bring in the whole plant and hang it upside-down while the green

STAKING AND TRAINING TOMATOES

The most common method of supporting a tomato plant simply involves tying it to a wooden stake as it grows taller. But there are many other ways to train them; some of the best are explained below.

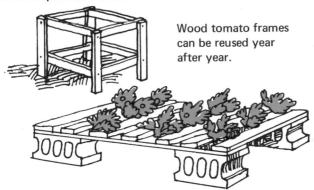

Wood tomato frames can be reused year after year.

A platform made of concrete blocks and planks will support many tomato plants.

Tomato plants can be tied to vertical strings for support.

The "Florida weave" system requires no tying. Run 2 strings between 2 (or more) posts and weave the tomato plants in and out the strings.

CAP

PIPE

A short piece of capped pipe should be placed over the top of tomato stakes before driving them in the ground. This keeps the wood from splitting. Remove cap and use to drive next stake.

Use concrete reinforcing mesh to make tomato cages. Snip out bottom rung and push vertical wires 6 inches into ground. Wire together loosely so cages can be unhooked for easy storage.

fruit ripens. Tomatoes should be stored where it is cool and dark.

One of the best varieties is the Pixie tomato. In December, you can plant a Pixie inside the house and by February be harvesting tomatoes from your window sill. Pixie plants stay quite small and do not grow leggy like other small tomato varieties. If you take good care of your indoor plants, you can grow fruit about the size of golf balls. When spring comes, you can gradually harden the plant off and set it right out in the garden. It will seem dormant for a while, but don't be discouraged. Soon you will have some early tomatoes. Pixies, unlike most other tomatoes, will bear fruit throughout the summer. The tomatoes grown outside will be somewhat larger than the ones grown indoors.

There are a lot of things you can do with tomato plants—Pixies or any other type. If you cut two or three suckers from a healthy plant before frost in the fall, stick them in a pot filled with fertile soil, and water them liberally, they will root just

COMPOST BIN TOMATOES

In the summer, the Greers camouflage their compost bin with tomato plants. They throw all their leaves, grass clippings, kitchen scraps, and whatever else will rot into the bin, which is made of wire fencing. In the spring, they set tomato plants close to the wire all around the bin. As the tomato plants get larger, they are tied to the wire "trellis." The roots grow up into the rich compost and provide the plants with the nutrients they need.

PRUNING

REMOVE SUCKERS

Single-stem method — Remove all suckers to prevent growth of side branches.

GROWING EARLY TOMATOES

For extra-early tomatoes, one gardener selects a few tomato plants after he's set them out and they've got a good start; then he digs them up and transplants them to another spot in the garden. In about two weeks, he transplants them again, being careful to keep some soil around the roots. He finds that these plants bear ripe tomatoes a week to ten days earlier.

PRUNING TOMATOES

Prune the young tomato plant to form a Y fork low to the ground. Train these two stalks up a trellis made of string. Tie by looping the cord around the stalk. Don't prune off any more suckers. Keep the vine growing vigorously so the leaves will shade the tomatoes and protect from sunburn. JLG

PIXIE TOMATO

This compact, sturdy tomato is ideal for growing in a flowerpot or in the garden.

If you've been harvesting from a Pixie all summer, you can extend the season by cutting off a slip or sucker and rooting it in a good potting-soil mixture. Do this around the first of September. When frost threatens, bring it inside and set it in a sunny window. You'll get tomatoes on Thanksgiving. ST

FROZEN RAW TOMATOES

Just slice peeled raw tomatoes into a plastic container and freeze. You can't eat them like fresh tomatoes, but they're fine cooked in meat loaves, spaghetti, soups and other tomato dishes. JES

like a geranium. You can harvest tomatoes again in December. If you plan carefully, you can grow fresh tomatoes the year 'round. A four-quart pot is large enough for most tomato plants. The potting soil should be fertilized with compost, dried manure, or some sort of commercial fertilizer.

I have already mentioned staking, but you can also encourage tomatoes to grow on wire or on trellises. If you use tomato stakes, you have to keep tying up the stalk as it grows taller and taller. When it reaches the top of the stake, you have to pick the end off so that the plant will not grow any higher.

A trellis is something that you construct from slats of wood or from wire-mesh fencing. This may seem like a silly thing to say, but if you decide to build a trellis, be sure there is enough room for your hands to get in between the slats or through the wire mesh. The tomatoes may ripen on the inside of the trellis, and there is nothing more aggravating or embarrassing than not being able to get at them when they are ready to pick!

If you use wire, first drive a row of five-foot stakes firmly into the ground. Between the stakes, string three strands of wire spaced one foot apart. The lowest strand should be about one foot off the ground. As the tomatoes start to grow, allow them to interweave their branches around and through the wires. Let two or three stems grow, and keep the suckers picked off. You may need to tie a stem to one of the wires now and then. Try to encourage them to grow on one side of the first wire, then on the other side of the second, and so on. When the tallest branch grows beyond the top wire, pick it off. This will stop the plant from growing any higher. If it grows too far over the upper wire, it will break off anyway. If you don't control its growth, the plant may expend all its energy and use up all its nutrients getting taller and growing new shoots. When this happens, the quality and size of the fruit suffers. Try to get your plants to concentrate more on producing fruit than on growing larger and leafier.

TURNIPS

Turnips are another of the crops that should be planted very early in the spring. They refuse to do well in hot weather, and they will be happiest in light, fertile soil. An average gardening season should give you two crops—one that matures just as the weather is getting really hot and a fall crop that was planted in midsummer. I usually plant turnips in May and again around the end of July.

Turnip seedlings should be thinned to about four to six inches apart. They may be threatened by the same diseases and insects that bother members of the cabbage family. You should harvest them like beets and store them the same way too—in a box of dry sawdust or sand. You will find a lot of insect holes in the leaves sometimes, but these will not affect the quality of the bottoms.

WATERCRESS

Watercress is simple to grow if you always remember its name. If you forget to give it lots of water, it will be a flop. It will grow almost indefinitely—from either seeds or cuttings—if you don't pick it too much. The best places to plant it are in the bottom of a trench which is watered regularly; on the side of a small stream, right in the water; or in a window box that gets watered liberally each day.

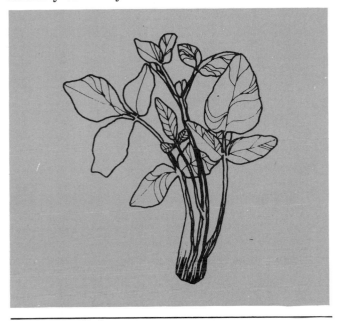

WATERMELONS

Watermelons are a lot of fun to grow, but they take a long time and need lots of sun and dry feet. An ideal spot for growing watermelons would slant to the south or west.

Sprout seeds in towels and plant watermelons under hotcaps, just as you would plant any melon. You can use the tin-can trick once a baby watermelon has gotten to be as big as your fist. This will help them to ripen earlier. Pick off excess blossoms and any fruit that is not going to have time to mature.

Watermelons are usually planted in hills no closer than six to eight feet apart. Don't cheat them out of the fertilizer they need. Use lots of compost and manure, and give them a good side dressing of fertilizer just before the vines are about to run out and away from the center of the plant. Keep checking for shriveled or decayed fruit. You will find some once in a while, but this is no reason to panic. Pick them off immediately, and you will reduce the danger of a disease called "stem-end rot." Watermelons are a little like beans; they can pick up diseases very easily. Try to stay out of the melon patch when it is wet.

Check the underside of a watermelon to see if it is ripe. If it is still white where it sits on the ground, it is not ready yet. If the underside has begun to turn bright yellow, the melon is ready to be eaten. Toward the end of August, select only those watermelons which you think have a chance of ripening and pick off all the less mature ones. You will get bigger, sweeter melons this way.

Dick Raymond sets his midget watermelons on cans, just as he does with cantaloupes. He says this makes the melons ripen faster and taste sweeter.

Icebox watermelons are good for growing in limited space. The vines are fairly compact, but they produce a generous yield of round, sweet melons 6 to 8 inches across. Good varieties are New Hampshire Midget, Sugar Baby, and You Sweet Thing.

HOW LARGE IS YOUR GARDEN IN ACRES

Often you see a formula calling for so much of something to be applied to an acre. But what size is your garden in acres? There's an easy way to find out by using this simple chart.

Measure the length and width of your garden, lawn, or whatever property you want to measure. Lay one end of a straight edge on the figure in line A that represents the longest dimension, and the other end on the figure in line C that represents the short dimension, or width. The point at which the straight edge crosses line B will show the approximate number of acres in the land you are measuring.

In the example shown, a piece of land 400 ft. long by 100 ft. wide contains a little over 0.9 acres.

The chart will measure areas from .002 acres to 40 acres. By adding or subtracting zeros to or from the figures in the columns, it can be made to apply to any size rectangular plot.

The chart might be used in this way. If you wanted to apply fertilizer at the rate of half a ton per acre on a plot of ground 10 ft. x 6 0 ft., you would figure:

1000 lbs.   x   .015 acres   = 15 lbs. fertilizer
(half a ton)   (area from chart)

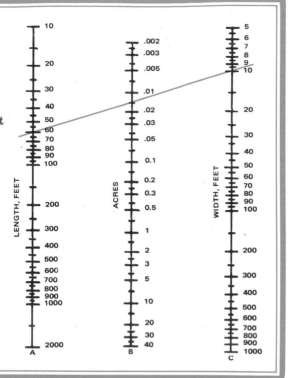

PLANTING VEGETABLES ACCORDING TO GROWING TIME

GROUP 1	GROUP 2	GROUP 3	GROUP 4
Crops that will occupy the ground for a year or more.	Crops planted early that occupy the ground only first part of the season.	Crops that occupy the ground the major portion of the season.	Crops to be planted in July and later for fall and winter gardens.
Asparagus	Early beets	Bush & Pole Beans	Bush beans
Rhubarb	Early cabbage	Lima Beans	Beets
Chives	Lettuce	Cabbage	Broccoli
Horseradish	Onion sets	Celery	Chinese Cabbage
Winter onions	Peas	Sweet Corn	Carrots
Herbs	Radishes	Cucumbers	Cauliflower
Raspberries	Early spinach	Eggplants	Endive
Strawberries	Mustard	Muskmelons	Kale
Blackberries	Turnips	Okra	Kohlrabi
		Peppers	Radishes
		Potatoes	Spinach
		Pumpkins	Turnips
		Squash	Collards
		Tomatoes	Lettuce
		Watermelons	
		Swiss Chard	

Regardless of the shape of your garden, decide in what section you will want to plant each group. Then, as the planting dates arrive, plant each in its respective area. Group 2 will all be planted before time to plant crops in Group 3. Group 1 should always be planted so that it will not interfere too much with normal cultivation-preferably at one side of the garden. Group 4 will be planted in the area formerly occupied by Group 2 as the early crops are harvested.

GARDEN WAY SURE CROP RECOMMENDATION CHART

Early Corn	Early Sunglow
Late Corn	Honey & Cream
	Silver Queen
Broccoli	De Cicco
Cucumber	Marketmore
Zucchini	Hybrid
Yellow Squash	Early Prolific Straightneck
Tomato	Big Boy
	Better Boy
Small Tomato	Pixie
Pepper	California Wonder
Cabbage	Copenhagen Market
Beans	Tenderpod
Beans (Yellow)	Brittlewax
Peas	Mammoth Melting Sugar
	Progress No. 9
	Wando
Carrot	Nantes Half Long
Onions	Southport Yellow
	Globe
Onion Seeds	Ebenezer
Beet	Detroit Dark Red
Swiss Chard	Fordhook Giant
Lettuce	Dark Green Boston
Radish	Cherry Belle

GARDEN PLANNING CHARTS

The beginning gardener should try these easy to grow vegetables.

Bush Beans	Kale
Beets	Leaf Lettuce
Carrots	Pumpkin
Collards	Radish
Corn	Rutabaga
Cucumber	Squash
Curlycress	Swiss Chard
Dill	Turnip

VEGETABLES THAT CAN BE HARVESTED ALL OR MOST OF THE WINTER

ROOT CROPS	GREENS
Parsnips	Kale
Root Parsley	Collards*
Salsify	Mustard*
Horseradish	Spinach*
Jerusalem Artichoke	
Turnips*	
Rutabagas*	
Brussels Sprouts*	
	*In Southern gardens

Root crops can be covered with straw to protect from hard freezes.

Early maturing vegetables for a quick harvest.

Cress — 10 days
Radish — 22 days
Mustard greens — 35 days
Scallions — 40 days
Loosehead lettuce — 40 days
Spinach — 42 days
Turnip — 45 days
Bush Snap Beans — 48 days
Summer Squash — 50 days
Early Peas — 55 days
Kale — 55 days
Kohlrabi — 55 days
Swiss Chard — 60 days

HOME VEGETABLE GARDEN COMPANION CROPS

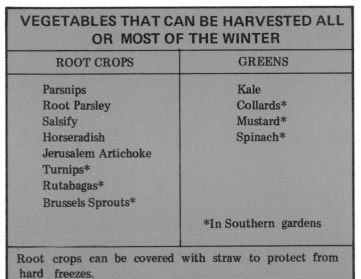

Some vegetables mature faster than others. If interplanted, one vegetable can be harvested and out of the way while the other continues to grow. Here's a list of vegetables that make good companions when planted together. If both vegetables are not planted at the same time, the crop listed first should be planted first.

peas and carrots	corn and spinach
cabbage and lettuce	corn and lettuce
carrots and radishes	tomatoes and spinach
onions and radishes	tomatoes and radishes
parsnips and radishes	tomatoes and lettuce
cabbage and radishes	swiss chard and peppers
cabbage and onion sets	onion seed and radishes

Plant in summer for a late crop to store through winter.

Beets	Pumpkins
Cabbage	Rutabaga
Carrots	Winter Radish
Celery	Winter Squash
Onions	Turnips
Parsnips	

Greatest yield for space and effort.

Tomatoes	Squash
Bush Snap Beans	Carrots
Lettuce	Beets

YIELDS FOR PROCESSING

Vegetables	Average Yield 100-foot Row		Amount Fresh Needed for One Quart	Number Quarts Processed from One Bushel
	12-inch Wide Row	Single-Row Planting		
Snap beans	5 bu.	2 bushels (60 lbs.)	2 pounds	12-15 quarts
Lima beans	4 bu.	2 bushels (64 lbs.) (in hull)	4 pounds	8-10 quarts
Beets	4 bu.	2 bushels (104 lbs.)	2½ pounds	16-20 quarts
Carrots	5 bu.	2 bushels (100 lbs.)	2½ pounds	16-20 quarts
Tomatoes	—	3 bushels (160 lbs.)	3 pounds	15-18 quarts
Greens	8 bu.	3 bushels (54 lbs.)	3 pounds	4- 8 quarts
Corn	—	6 doz. ears	6-10 ears	6- 8 quarts
Okra	—	1,000 pods	2 pounds	15-18 quarts
Peas	4 bu.	2 bu. in pods (60 lbs.)	4 pounds	8-10 quarts
Squash	—	135 squash	4 pounds	10-12 quarts

Cool weather crops for spring and fall planting.

Broccoli	Radish
Endive	Spinach
Kale	Turnips
Head Lettuce	Peas

Ideal for growing in pots or window boxes.

Pixie Tomatoes	Rosemary
Parsley	Curleycress
Chives	Leaf Lettuce

GARDEN PLANS

FLOWER FENCES

To protect her melons from hungry boys, Mable Lauhall an 81 year old gardener of Waynesboro, Pennsylvania, grows a fence of snow on the mountain flowers. Her beautiful garden borders on the highway and keeping the melons out of sight also keeps them out of mind!

lettuce, followed by carrots

carrots with radishes

onions

spinach, followed by Swiss chard

beets

cabbage

tomatoes

pole beans

12½ feet

8 feet

GARDEN WAY'S SURE CROP 25' x 30' GARDEN
with succession planting

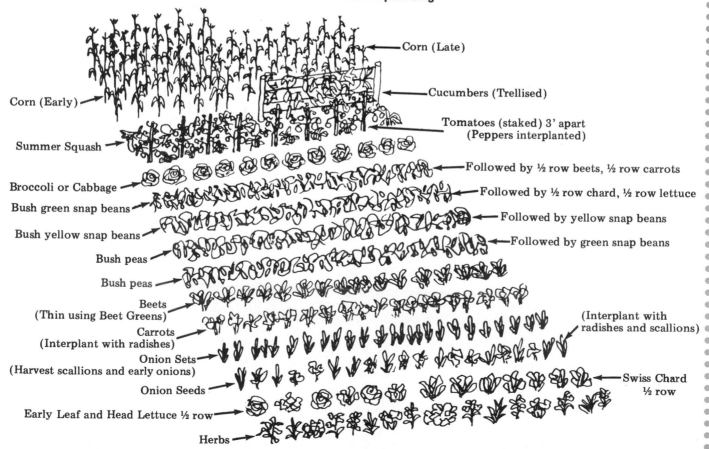

Corn (Late)

Corn (Early)

Cucumbers (Trellised)

Tomatoes (staked) 3' apart
(Peppers interplanted)

Summer Squash

Followed by ½ row beets, ½ row carrots

Broccoli or Cabbage

Followed by ½ row chard, ½ row lettuce

Bush green snap beans

Followed by yellow snap beans

Bush yellow snap beans

Followed by green snap beans

Bush peas

Bush peas

Beets
(Thin using Beet Greens)

Carrots
(Interplant with radishes)

(Interplant with radishes and scallions)

Onion Sets
(Harvest scallions and early onions)

Onion Seeds

Swiss Chard
½ row

Early Leaf and Head Lettuce ½ row

Herbs

Substitutions may be made for personal preference, for example; parsnips for carrots, rutabaga for late beets, eggplant for cabbage, cucumbers on trellis for tomatoes, bush squash for 2 rows of corn, or pole beans for corn.

LARGE GARDEN — INTENSIVE CULTURE: 120 BY 100 FEET

Providing a reasonably complete and continuous assortment of vegetables for fresh use throughout the season, for canning, and for storage. For additional plantings in late summer and fall, see page 5. Distance between rows may be adjusted to equipment used.

Planting	Row No. and width	←————————— 120 feet —————————→		
1st	1-4'	Asparagus	Rhubarb	Perennial onions
	2-4'	Onion seed planted with radishes		
	3-1½'	Onion sets	Spinach	
	4-3'	Early potatoes		
	5-3'	Early potatoes		
	6-3'	Early potatoes		
	7-3'	Early potatoes		
	8-3'	Leaf lettuce	Early turnips	Kohlrabi
	9-1½'	Peas		
	10-1½'	Peas		
	11-2'	Early cabbage seed		Head lettuce plants
2d	12-2'	Early cabbage plants		New Zealand spinach
	13-2'	Beets	Carrots	Parsley
	14-1½'	Parsnips planted with radishes		Swiss chard
	15-3'	Tomato seed		
3d	16-3'	Early sweet corn	Main-crop sweet corn	Main-crop sweet corn
	17-3'	Early sweet corn	Main-crop sweet corn	Main-crop sweet corn
	18-3'	Early sweet corn	Main-crop sweet corn	Main-crop sweet corn
	19-3'	Snap beans		
4th	20-1½'	Snap beans		
	21-1½'	Carrots		Beets
	22-2'	Peppers / Eggplant / Bush lima beans		Bush or pole lima beans
	23-3'	Tomato plants		
	24-5'	Muskmelons		
	25-5'	Squash	Cucumbers	
	26-8'	Watermelons		
	27-8'	Winter squash		
	28-8'	Sweet potatoes		
Special*	29-4'	Late cabbage seed		
	4'	(Border strip)		

(right margin, vertical:) ↕ 100 feet — Cooperative Extension Service of the University of Illinois

* The special planting of late cabbage is for fresh use in late fall, sauerkraut, or winter storage.

Planting Plan for a Garden 100 by 112 Feet

FIRST PLANTING GROUP	Early Spring Planting	Onion Sets, Onion Seed, Radishes, Lettuce, Peas, Spinach	17'
SECOND PLANTING GROUP	Mid-Spring Planting	Early Potatoes, Carrots, Beets, Parsnips, Chard, New Zealand Spinach, Transplants of Early Cabbage, Broccoli, Cauliflower	12'
THIRD PLANTING GROUP	Late Spring Planting	Tomatoes, Snap and Bush Beans, Cucumbers, Summer Squash, Winter Squash Succession of Sweet Corn—each variety blocked out in several short rows to insure good pollination	30'
FOURTH PLANTING GROUP	Early Summer Planting	Main Crop of Potatoes Late Cabbage, Broccoli, Brussels Sprouts Late Planting of Snap Beans	35'
FIFTH PLANTING GROUP	Mid-Summer Planting	Fall Crops of Carrots, Beets, Turnips, Rutabagas, Kohlrabi, Lettuce, Radishes, Spinach, Chard	20'

PLANNING CHART

GROUP A HARDY — Plant as soon as the ground can be worked in the spring. About 20-40 days before the last frost.

(Vegetables are grouped according to planting time.)

VEGETABLE	AMOUNT TO PLANT PER PERSON * — SEEDS OR PLANTS	LENGTH OF ROW IN FEET	SEEDS OR PLANTS FOR A 100 FOOT ROW	DISTANCE BETWEEN PLANTS IN THE ROW (inches)	DISTANCE BETWEEN ROWS (hand cultivation) **(inches)	DEPTH TO PLANT SEEDS (inches)	WIDTH OF ROW FOR WIDE ROW PLANTING ***	DAYS TO GERMINATION	DAYS TO FIRST HARVEST ****	PRIMARY VITAMIN SOURCE	CULTURE AND HARVESTING TIPS *****
ASPARAGUS	10 crowns	10-15 ft	65-75 crowns	12-18	36-60	plants 6-8			2 years	A, C	Start from 1 year old crowns. 3 years to harvest if started from seed. Harvest when 6-8 in. tall.
RHUBARB	2-3 roots	5-10 ft	35 roots	30-36	36-48	plants 6-8 seeds 1 in			1 year	C	Do not harvest the first year.
BROCCOLI	5-10 plants ¼ pkt	8-12 ft	65 plants	18-24	24-36	plants 4-6 seeds ¼ in		6-9	50-80 from transplant	A, B_2, C	Best started from transplants. 80-100 days from seed. Side heads will form after first head is cut.
BRUSSELS SPROUTS	5-10 plants ¼ pkt	8-12 ft	65 plants	18-24	24-36	plants 4-6 seeds ¼ in	12 in	6-9	65-75 from transplant	C	Transplants best. 100-110 days from seed.
CABBAGE	5-10 plants ¼ pkt	8-12 ft	65 plants	18-24	24-36	plants 4-6 seeds ¼ in		6-9	60-90 from transplant	(raw) C	Transplants best. 90-150 days from seeds. Can use thinnings for transplants.
CELERIAC	6 plants	3-5 ft	65 plants	6-8	18-36	¼ in		10-20	120	A	
CELERY	6 plants	3-5 ft	65 plants	6-8	18-36	¼ in		10-20	100-150	A	Start plants 8 weeks early indoors.
CHINESE CABBAGE	5-10 plants ¼ pkt	5-10 ft	1 pkt	12-18	24-36	½ in		6-9	70-90	A	
COLLARDS	3-5 plants ¼ pkt	4-6 ft	65 plants	18-24	24-36	plants 4-6 seeds ¼ in		6-9	65-85 from transplant	A, C	Primarily a fall crop in the south. Flavor improves with frost. Will stand cold weather and heat.
GARLIC	5 bulbs	3 ft	2 lbs 300 cloves	4	24-36	2 in	10 in		90		
KALE	¼ pkt	5-10 ft	¼ ounce	8-12	18-36	¼ in	12 in	6-9	50-65	iron A, B_2	Good fall and winter crop. Can be used as a cover crop.
KOHLRABI	¼ pkt	3-5 ft	¼ ounce	4-6	18-36	¼ in	10 in	6-9	50-70	C	Use when root ball is 2-3 in. in diameter.
MUSTARD	¼ pkt	3-5 ft	¼ ounce	3-4	18-36	¼ in	12 in	5-8	35-45	iron A, C, B_2	Popular southern fall crop.
ONIONS sets	1 lb	10-15 ft	8-10 lbs	3-4	18-36	1 in	12 in	7-12	25-35	calcium	For fresh use harvest when ¼ to 1 in. For storage when tops turn brown and fall over.
ONIONS seeds	¼ pkt	10-15 ft	½ ounce	3-4	18-36	¼ in	12 in		85-200	C	
ONIONS plants	1 bunch	10-15 ft	400 plants	3-4	18-36	1 in	12 in		25-35	C	
PEAS	¼ lb	15-25 ft	1 lb	1-3	18-36	1 in	12-36 in	7-10	50-80	A, B, C	Likes cool weather.
RADISH	½ pkt	5-10 ft	1 ounce	1	12-24	¼ in	10 in	3-5	25-35	B, C	Plant along with other root crops. Also use for bug control with warm weather vegetables.
RUTABAGA	¼ pkt	5-10 ft	½ ounce	6-8	18-36	½ in	10 in	6-10	80-90		
SPINACH	½ pkt	5-10 ft	1 ounce	2-4	18-36	¼ in	10 in	7-12	40-50	iron A, C, B_2	

Crop	Amount (small garden)	Row length	Amount (large garden)	Between plants	Between rows	Depth	Height	Days to maturity	Days to germinate	Food value	Remarks
STRAWBERRIES	15-25 plants	15-25 ft	75-100 plants	1-3 ft	18-36			1 year			Everbearing varieties will bear first year. But June bearing varieties are superior.
TURNIP	1/4 ounce	10-15 ft	1/2 ounce	3-6	18-36	1/4 in	10 in	40-60	5-10	(greens) A, C	Good fall and winter crop. Green tops can be cooked as greens. Some varieties only for greens.
GROUP B SEMI-HARDY — Plant a week or two after Group A. About 10-30 days before the last frost.											
BEET	1/2 pkt	5-10 ft	2 ounces	3-4	18-36	1/2 in	12 in	50-65	7-12	A, C, B$_2$	When thinning plants the tops can be cooked as greens.
CARROT	1/2 pkt	5-10 ft	1/2 ounce	2-3	12-24	1/4 in	12 in	55-80	12-18	(raw) A	Can be eaten at any size. Use largest when thinning.
CAULIFLOWER	3-5 plants / 1/2 pkt	5-10 ft	50-70 plants	18-24	18-36	1/4 in		65-80	6-9	A, B, C, B$_2$	Tie outer leaves above head when curds are 2-3 in. in diameter. Heads ready 4-12 days later.
ENDIVE	1/4 pkt	3-5 ft	1/4 ounce	12-18	18-36	1/4 in	12 in	80-90	10-14	A	Same culture as lettuce.
LETTUCE	1/2 pkt	5-10 ft	1/2 ounce	3-6	18-36	1/4 in	12 in	35-50	5-10	A, B, C, B$_2$	Head lettuce should be grown from transplants. Leaf lettuce excellent in wide row planting.
PARSLEY	1/4 pkt	3-5 ft	1/2 ounce	4-6	18-36	1/8 in		75-90	15-20	A, C	Seeds slow to germinate. Keep soil moist.
PARSNIP	1/4 pkt	3-5 ft	1 ounce	3-4	12-24	1/2 in	10 in	120-150	15-20	B, C	Good winter keeper, may be left in ground over winter and used in the spring.
POTATO	5-10 lbs	50-100 ft	10 lbs	12	30	4 in	12 x 12 ft under hay mulch	100-120	15-20	starch B, C	Plant cut sections of potato, containing one or more eyes. For storage harvest after vine is dead.
SALSIFY	1/2 pkt	5-10 ft	1 ounce	2-3	12-24	1/2 - 1 in	10 in	100-125	12-18		In moderate winters can stay in ground and dug as needed.
SWISS CHARD	1/4 pkt	5-10 ft	2 ounces	6-8	18-36	1/2 - 1 in	10 in	45-55	7-10	iron calcium A	
GROUP C TENDER — Plant on the average date of the last spring frost.											
DRY BEAN	1/2 lb	25-50 ft	1 lb	3-6	18-36	1 in	10-36 in	65-100	7-14		Let bean pods dry on vine before harvesting. — For dried beans.
SNAP BEAN bush	1/2 lb	25-50 ft	1 lb	3-6	18-36	1 in	10-36 in	50-60	5-10	A, B, C, B$_2$	Make succession plantings.
SNAP BEAN pole	1/4 lb	15-25 ft	1/2 lb	18-36	36-48	1 in		60-70	7-14		
SWEET CORN	1/2 lb	25-50 ft	1 pkt / 2-3 ounces	8-12	18-36	1 in		60-95	5-12	starch A, B	Make succession plantings in 2 week intervals or plant varieties with different maturity.
CUCUMBER	2-3 hills	10-15 ft	1 pkt	12 inches or 48 inches between hills	36-48	1/2 - 1 in		50-70	7-10	B, C, B$_2$	Leave 3-4 plants in each hill or plant in rows.
HORSERADISH	3-5 roots	8-12 ft	65 roots	12-18	36	2 in		45-55	15-20	A, B, C	Can be left in ground all winter and used as needed.
JERUSALEM ARTICHOKE	5-10 roots	10-15 ft	30-50 roots	12-18	24-36	3 in		180			
SPINACH (summer)	1/4 pkt	5-10 ft	1 ounce	8-12	18-36	1/2 in	12 in	75-80	5-10	iron A, C	Some varieties such as New Zealand, like hot weather and can be harvested all summer.
SUMMER SQUASH	2-3 hills	5-10 ft	1 ounce	36	36-48	1/2 - 1 in		50-70	7-10	A, B, B$_2$	Can be very early crop if started in peat pots and transplanted.

GARDEN PLANNING CHART CONTINUED

GROUP D VERY TENDER
Plant when the soil is warm. About 10-20 days after the last frost.

VEGETABLE	AMOUNT TO PLANT PER PERSON * (SEEDS OR PLANTS)	LENGTH OF ROW IN FEET	SEEDS OR PLANTS FOR A 100 FOOT ROW	DISTANCE BETWEEN PLANTS IN THE ROW (inches)	DISTANCE BETWEEN ROWS (hand cultivation) **(inches)	DEPTH TO PLANT SEEDS (inches)	WIDTH OF ROW FOR WIDE ROW PLANTING ***	DAYS TO GERMINATION	DAYS TO FIRST HARVEST ****	PRIMARY VITAMIN SOURCE	CULTURE AND HARVESTING TIPS *****
ARTICHOKE	2-3 plants	6-10 ft	25-30 plants	36-48	48-60				1 year		A perennial that grows best in warm climate along California coast. Can be grown in other areas as annual.
LIMA BEAN pole	¼ lb	10-15 ft	½ lb	18-36	24-36	1 in		7-14	80-95	A, B, C, B$_2$	Pole limas will bear continously if kept picked. Likes warm soil.
LIMA BEAN bush	¼ lb	10-15 ft	¾ lb	3-6	24-36	1 in	10 in	7-14	65-80		
SOY BEAN	¼ lb	10-15 ft	¾ lb	3-6	24-36	1 in	10 in	4-7	85-100	A	Choose variety to suit your climate.
CANTALOUPE - muskmelon	¼ pkt / 3-5 hills	15-25 ft	1 pkt	36 inches or in hills 5 ft apart	36-48	½ - 1 in		8-14	75-100	C	Leave 3-4 plants in each hill or plant in row. Can be transplanted in peat pots.
CROWDER PEAS, field, southern	1/8 lb	10-15 ft	½ lb	3-6	24-36	1 in	10-36 in	7-10	70-80	A, C	Popular southern pea. Shell when pod is semi-dry. Grow like snap beans. Likes hot weather.
EGGPLANT	2-3 plants	4-6 ft	1 pkt	24	36	½ in		10-14	80-90	A, B, C, B$_2$	Transplant well in peat pots.
GOURDS	2-3 hills / ¼ pkt	15-25 ft	1 pkt	48-60	36-48	½ - 1 in		14-18	130 days	A	Can be grown on fence or trellis.
OKRA	¼ pkt	4-6 ft	2 ounces	18-24	36	½ - 1 in		5-8	50-55	A, B	Enjoy hot weather. Long harvest season.
PEANUTS	30-40 nuts shelled	10-20 ft	300-400 peanuts shelled	3-6	24-36	1½ in		6-10	110-120		Needs long hot season. Can be planted in shell. Allow more space between seeds.
PEPPERS	2-3 plants / ¼ pkt	4-6 ft	1 pkt	24	36	½ in		10-14	60-100	C	Transplants well. For red peppers leave on plant until fully mature.
PUMPKIN	2-3 hills / ¼ pkt	12-18 ft	1 pkt	48-72	60-96	1 in		7-14	100-120	A	Give lots of growing room. For winter storage skin should be hard. Leave on 1 in. of stem.
SQUASH (winter)	2-3 hills / ¼ pkt	12-18 ft	1 pkt	36-48	60-96	1 in		7-10	85-120	A	Also needs lots of space for large vines. Same storage requirements as pumpkin.
SWEET POTATO	10-18 plants	20-24 ft	50-75 plants	18-24	36-48	3-4 in		6-10	150	A	Sprout potato in sand. Use these slips when 4-6 in. long for transplanting.
TOMATO	3-5 plants / ¼ pkt	10-15 ft	40-60 plants	24-36	36-48	¼ - ½ in		7-14	55-90	C	Start in peat pots or flats indoors. Transplants well.
WATERMELON	3-5 hills / ¼ pkt	25-40 ft	1 pkt	48 inches or in hills 6-8 ft apart	60-96	1 in		7-12	75-100	C	Leave 3-4 plants in hill. Can be transplanted in peat pots. Give lots of growing room.

* Amount to plant. Multiply this figure times number of members in family for approximate amount to plant. Double figure to allow for winter storage.
** Distance between rows. Allow enough room for cultivation with power equipment if available.
*** Wide-row planting. If space is blank in this column this vegetable is not suitable for wide-row planting.
**** Days to harvest. The wide range of harvest times for a given vegetable is due to variety differences and climate and cultural variations.
***** For complete cultural instructions look up each individual vegetable.

LAST EXPECTED FROST DATE IN THE SPRING

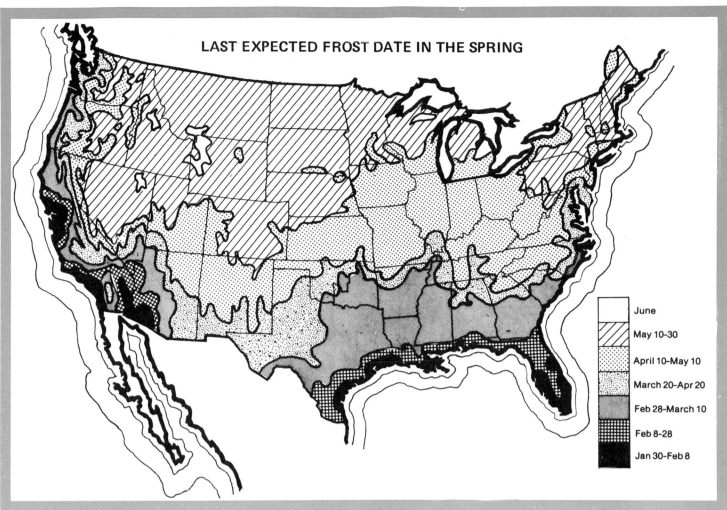

June	
May 10-30	
April 10-May 10	
March 20-Apr 20	
Feb 28-March 10	
Feb 8-28	
Jan 30-Feb 8	

FIRST EXPECTED FROST DATE IN THE FALL

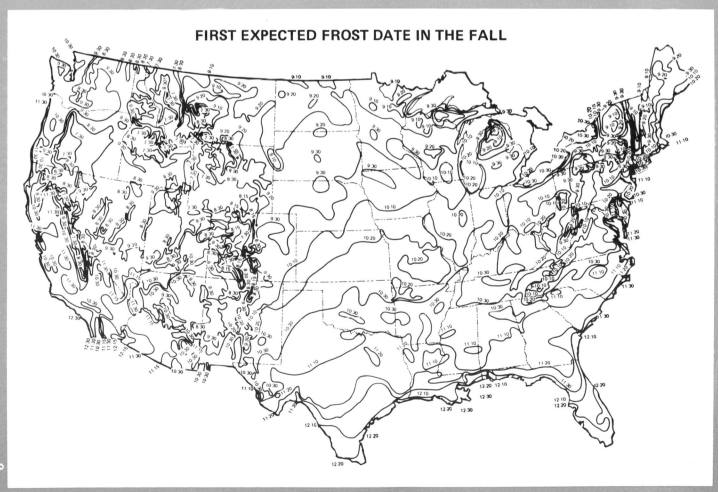

GARDENING VOCABULARY

The words given below are frequently used in gardening literature. They are explained to assist the reader in making more effective use of this publication.

ACID SOIL — Any soil with a pH below 7.

ALKALINE SOIL — Any soil with a pH above 7.

ANNUAL PLANT — A plant living one year or less. During this time, the plant grows, blooms, produces seeds, and dies (i.e. bean, sweet corn, cucumber, melon).

BARE-ROOTED PLANT — A plant to be set out which has no soil on roots.

BIENNIAL PLANT — A plant which requires 2 years or part of 2 years to complete its life cycle (i.e. beet, carrot, cabbage).

BLANCHING — Preventing sunlight from striking a plant part. As a result, the part is white in color.

BOLTING — The production of a seed stalk by vegetable plants such as spinach, lettuce, or radish. Bolting by these crops in the garden is undesirable. Bolting occurs when days are long and temperatures are warm.

BROADCASTING — Scattering a material such as fertilizer or seed evenly over a soil surface.

BULB — A plant structure made up of a short, fleshy stem, containing a growing point or flower bud. The stem is enclosed by thick, fleshy scales.

COMPACTED SOIL — Heavy soils that have been packed or worked too wet and are hard.

COMPANION CROPS — Crops which have different harvest dates but are grown in the same area. One crop is harvested and removed by the time the other crop requires the growing space.

COMPOST — Material resulting from the breakdown and decay of organic materials piled up in layers alternated with soil and fertilizer.

CONTAINER PLANT — A plant to be set out which has grown in a container (peat pot, etc.)

COOL SEASON PLANT — A plant which makes its best growth and produces the highest quality crop when grown at cool temperatures (45° to 60° F.).

COVER CROP — Usually a grass type crop planted in a garden area to protect the soil from being carried away during months when the area cannot be used as a garden. The cover crops also add valuable organic matter when turned under by plowing in the spring.

CROWN —The part of the plant where the stem and root join.

CULTIVAR —A term meaning cultivated variety now used in place of the word variety to indicate a specific type of horticultural plant. Cultivars may differ in growth habit, season of maturity, fruit color, fruit shape, etc. Example — Detroit Dark Red, Kathadin.

CULTIVATION — The loosening of a soil with either a hand or mechanical type implement chiefly for the purpose of controlling weeds.

CULTURAL PRACTICE — A specialized activity used in growing plants (i.e. pruning, cultivation, watering).

DUST — Chemical to be applied to plant in dry form.

EDIBLE PLANT PART — A plant part which can safely be eaten for food.

EMULSIFIABLE CONCENTRATE — Liquid chemical to be applied to plant in water by spraying.

FERTILIZER — A material which provides one or more nutrients in forms which can be used by plants in growing.

FOLIAGE — A name used to refer to the leaves of a plant.

FUNGICIDE — A chemical material used to retard or prevent the growth of fungi.

GERMINATION — The process of a seed sprouting and forming a young plant.

GROWING SEASON — The period of time from the last plant killing frost in the spring to the first plant killing frost in the fall.

GYNOECIOUS — Gynoecious cucumber plants produce mostly all female flowers. Such plants can produce heavy yields beginning early in the season.

HARDENING — A process of slowing plant growth by withholding water, lowering the temperature, or gradually shifting the plants from a more sheltered environment to a less sheltered environment. The process of hardening plants is used to increase chances for survival at transplanting time.

HARDPAN — A hard layer of soil a few inches under ground level as a result of constant shallowing plowing.

HARDY PLANT — A plant which can be planted before the last killing frost in the spring.

HEAVY SOIL — A soil usually difficult to work. Clay soils are considered to be heavy soils.

HERBACEOUS PLANT — A plant described as having a soft, non-woody stem. Generally, these plants live and grow for only one season.

HERBICIDE — A chemical material used to kill weeds.

HILL — A mound of soil in which several vegetable seeds are planted.

HORTICULTURE — The study of fruits, ornamentals and vegetables.

HYBRID — A plant resulting from crossing 2 plants of the same type which have different individual characteristics for a trait (i.e., tall or short for the height trait).

INOCULANT — A black powder-like material applied to seed coats of legume seed prior to planting in the garden so as to insure the presence of nitrifying bacteria in the soil.

INSECTICIDE — A chemical material used to kill insects.

IRRIGATION — Artificially applying water to the soil during periods when natural rainfall does not fall in enough volume to maintain a desirable level of soil moisture for plant growth.

LEGUME — A plant whose root system is invaded by nitrifying bacteria which convert nitrogen into forms which can be utilized by the plant in growing.

LIGHT SOIL — A soil easy to work. Sandy soils are considered to be light soils.

LIME — A material used to decrease soil acidity and supply amounts of calcium and magnesium required by growing plants.

LOAM SOIL — A soil made up of about equal parts of sand, silt, and clay-sized soil particles. This composition provides a good soil structure suitable for plant growth.

LONG SEASON CROP — A crop which requires a maximum of frost free days to produce a satisfactory crop.

MOSAIC — A disease of a number of different vegetables which makes distorted growth and is caused by one or more viruses.

MULCH — A material applied to the soil surface to conserve soil moisture, maintain a more even soil temperature, and/or aid in weed control.

NEMATICIDE — Chemical applied to soil to control nematodes.

ORGANIC MATTER — A soil component resulting from the decay of plant and animal materials.

PERENNIAL PLANT — A plant which normally lives more than two years.

pH SCALE — A scale used to report the degree of soil acidity or alkalinity.

PLANT NUTRIENT — One of the 16 chemical elements currently known as essential to plant growth.

PLANT SPACING — The distance in inches or feet between individual plants growing in a row.

PRUNING — The wise removal of plant parts to obtain a more desirable plant.

PUDDLED SOIL — A soil which has been worked while too wet with the result that it has a greatly reduced amount of pore space.

ROW SPACING — The distance in inches or feet between plant rows.

SEEDBED — The name given to a garden soil prepared to receive seed or plants as a result of plowing and disking, tilling or spading, and raking.

SEED GERMINATION — The beginning of growth of the young plant in a seed when heat, moisture, and air is provided.

SEEDLING — The young plant emerging from a germinating seed.

SHORT SEASON CROP — A crop which grows and produces its harvest within one or two months.

SIDE DRESSING — Applying fertilizers along the side of plants after they are established and growing.

SINGLE ROW — Plants grown in a straight line with the seed evenly spaced along the row in single file.

SOIL BORNE FUNGI — Small, non-green plants which live in the soil and are capable of causing plant disease.

SOIL CRUSTING — The formation of a thick hard layer of soil on the soil surface as a result of the impact of many rain drops during a heavy rainfall.

SOIL IMPROVEMENT — Making soils more productive by such practices as adding organic matter, fertilizers, and lime.

SPINDLY — Abnormally tall and thin.

STARTER SOLUTION — A liquid fertilizer applied to the base of transplanted plants to promote rapid establishment and growth.

SUCCESSION CROPS — Crops which are planted in a garden area after crops previously growing in the area are harvested and removed.

TENDER PLANT — A plant which is injured or killed by even a light frost.

THINNING — The removal of some plants from a row so that the remaining plants will have more room to grow and develop.

TOXIC MATERIAL — A poisonous material capable of severely damaging or killing a plant.

TRANSPLANT — A plant produced from seed germinated in a favorable environment for later planting in an area where the plant is to grow to maturity.

TUBER — A short end part of an underground stem which becomes thickened with the accumulation of food materials.

VIABLE SEED — A seed containing a small living plant which will begin to grow once conditions necessary for germination (sprouting) are provided.

VARIETY — See Cultivar.

WEED — A plant growing out of place.

WIDE ROW — A planting technique where certain crops, mainly greens, beans, peas and root vegetables, are grown in a row about 10-18 inches across. Seed is usually broadcast in this broad band.

SUGGESTED EXTRA READING

A good library is almost as essential to the successful gardener as a hoe or a rake. No gardener, no matter how experienced or successful, knows everything about gardening. New ideas, techniques, and theories are always being put forth, and the best way to keep up with them all is to keep your gardening library up to date. Besides, pouring over the pages of a new gardening book is a very satisfying way to spend one of those long, winter evenings when you're itching to get your hands in the soil again. There are, of course, lots of good books available; the ones listed below are all excellent choices.

The Basic Book of Organic Gardening, edited by Robert Rodale, 377 pp., paperback, $1.25.

An excellent reference book for beginners and experts alike, this compilation of articles from *Organic Gardening* magazine covers the fundamental theories and techniques of organic gardening. Also included are enough notes, novel suggestions, and creative gardening ideas to keep you happily reading and planning through the long winter months.

The Bug Book: Harmless Insect Controls by John and Helen Philbrick, 143 pp., spiral bound, $4.50.

Here's some good advice on combatting bugs without resorting to harmful pesticides. The authors explain a wide variety of proven, imaginative, insect-control techniques and provide sketches and descriptions to aid in insect identification.

Companion Plants and How to Use them by Helen Philbrick and Richard Gregg, 113 pp., hardback, $4.95.

This is THE book on the fascinating subject of companion planting. It will teach you how to create positive plant relationships in your garden and how to use common plants like marigolds and onions to ward off animal & insect pests.

Complete Book of Home Storage of Vegetables and Fruits by Evelyn Loveday, 160 pp., hardback, $5.50; quality paperback, $3.00.

If you haven't already started "putting up" your home-grown fruits and vegetables, now is the time to start. And this book tells all you need to know about freezing, canning, curing, drying, and salting. Also included are instructions for building a root cellar and storage mound. Plenty of good recipes too.

The Complete Book of Pickles and Relishes by Leonard Levinson, 336 pp., hardback, $5.95.

Everybody seems to have a favorite pickle recipe, and everybody's favorite pickle recipe seems to be in this book. Over 500 in all, including recipes for pickling vegetables, fruits, fish, and meats; for chutneys, mincemeats, sauerkrauts, and much more.

The Complete Guide to Growing Berries and Grapes by Louise Riotte, 142 pp., quality paperback, $3.50; hardback, $5.95.

Everything you always wanted to know about growing grapes, blackberries, raspberries, dewberries, currants, blueberries, elderberries, and strawberries — but didn't know who to ask. Every aspect of growing these juicy fruits is covered in this information-packed book.

Dwarf Fruit Trees for the Home Gardener by Lawrence Southwick, 118 pp., hardback, $5.95; quality paperback, $3.00.

A few dwarf fruit trees, a couple of years, and a little conscientious labor can turn an average suburban backyard into a lush mini-orchard. This well-illustrated book provides the know-how you need to do it — information on buying trees, planting, pruning, climate considerations, pest control, and more.

Gardening Indoors Under Lights by Frederick and Jacqueline Kranz, 241 pp., hardback, $7.95.

The indoor, artificial-light gardener will find this book as interesting as it is helpful. In addition to an explanation of the Kranz's balanced lighting technique and good solid information on lamps, soil, watering, and many other topics, the comprehensive text also provides insights into the history of this relatively new and fascinating science.

Growing Food and Flowers in Containers by Ted Flanagan, 128 pp., quality paperback, $3.95; hardback, $5.95.

What better way to banish the midwinter doldrums than to harvest a salad of greens and tomatoes from your own indoor container garden? Or maybe the beauty and fragrance of pots full of flowers are what you need to soothe your spirits after a day in the asphalt jungle. This is the book that will help you turn these fantasies into realities. All you need to know about growing fruit, berries, vegetables, herbs, and flowers in containers, indoors or out.

Herbs: Their Culture and Uses by Rosetta Clarkson, 226 pp., hardback, $5.95.

There are a multitude of herb books on the market these days, but this is undoubtedly the best and most complete of the lot. It includes complete cultural instructions; tips on drying; plans for formal and kitchen herb gardens; cooking advice and recipes; an illustrated glossary of 101 herbs; and much more.

The Home Gardener's Cookbook by Marjorie Blanchard, 192 pp., deluxe paperback, $4.50; hardback, $6.95.

This is not just another book of recipes. It also includes harvesting guidelines, information on varieties, and advice on planting and care. Mrs. Blanchard gives recipes for such mouth-watering treats as rhubarb cobbler and Greek stuffed peppers and provides plenty of tips on good, simple, vegetable cookery. All the information in this warm, readable book is conveniently arranged by months.

Improving Garden Soil with Green Manure by Richard Alther and Richard O. Raymond, 44 pp., deluxe paperback, $2.00.

The cost of chemical fertilizers is skyrocketing, and most gardeners are looking around for some cheaper substitutes. Green manuring, the growing and turning under of foliage crops solely for their soil-conditioning value, is a centuries-old technique that is again becoming popular. This book will tell you all you need to know — the effects of green manuring; how, when and what to plant; the tools you'll need; and much more. Also included are lots of photographs and a complete chart of green-manure information.

Let It Rot: The Gardener's Complete Guide to Composting by Stu Campbell, quality paperback, $3.95.

You probably throw away valuable organic matter every day. With this book, you can learn to recycle a surprising array of materials and turn them into soil-enriching compost. Includes illustrated instructions for building a compost pile with readily available materials, a discussion of the latest methods, the uses of compost, and more.

The Mulch Book; A Guide for the Family Food Gardener by Stu Campbell, 144 pp., quality paperback, $3.50.

Serious gardeners who want to know all the pros and cons of mulching, every technique, all the possible uses for mulch, and the hazards to be avoided will find answers to these questions and many more in this remarkably informative and readable book.

Non-Chemical Pest and Disease Control for the Home Orchard by Lisa Alther, 24 pp., paperback, $.90.

Many home orchardists find themselves trapped in an ecological dilemma; either spray their fruit trees with highly toxic, chemical sprays or resign themselves to wormy, diseased fruit and insect-plagued trees. There are, however, alternative solutions, most of which are explained in this small, but information-packed book.

Nuts for the Food Gardener by Louise Riotte, paperback, $4.50.

Nuts, an excellent source of protein, can be grown anywhere in the United States or Canada. And you don't have to wait forever. Peanuts ripen in one year; filberts and Chinese chestnuts bear in two to three years. Louise Riotte can tell you how to raise thirteen different kinds of nuts. For each type, she gives complete instructions on cultivation, care, pest control, and harvesting. Plenty of recipes too.

What Every Gardener Should Know About Earthworms by Dr. Henry Hopp, 39 pp., quality paperbook, $1.25.

Earthworm castings are just about the best fertilizer in the world — and it's free. These humble creatures can do a lot more good things for your garden, so you should encourage them to thrive and multiply. Dr. Hopp tells you just how to do it. Every gardener should own this essential book.

Available at your local bookstore, library, or from Garden Way Publishing Company, Dept. KH, Charlotte, Vermont 05445.

INDEX

Down-To-Earth VEGETABLE GARDENING KNOW-HOW, along with the books listed as "suggested reading" is available directly from Garden Way Publishing, Dept. KH, Charlotte, VT 05445, (include payment + 50¢ postage) or from your local bookstore.

Photographs on pages 66, 67, 68, 70, 72 and 73 were obtained from the United States Department of Agriculture.
The photograph on page 40 is by Peter Coleman.

All other photographs in the section on individual vegetables are from the W. Atlee Burpee Seed Company and the Joseph Harris Seed Company, whose help we sincerely appreciate.

Photographs on pages 5, 20, 22, 31, 35 and 45 were provided by Natalie Graham Obodeely. All other photographs are by Charles Cook.

Charts, maps, and articles on the pages listed below were taken from the sources cited.

Page 12: © 1973 by Rodale Press, Inc. from GETTING THE BUGS OUT OF ORGANIC GARDENING with permission of Rodale Press, Inc., Emmaus PA.

Pages 43-44: Excerpted from *The Whys and Hows of Liming* (published by the Cooperative Extension Service of the University of Vermont) with the author's permission.

Page 103: From THE COMPLETE BOOK OF HOME STORAGE OF VEGETABLES AND FRUITS by Evelyn V. Loveday. Published by Garden Way Publishing.

Page 153: From THE EX-URBANITE'S COMPLETE AND ILLUSTRATED EASY-DOES-IT FIRST-TIME FARMER'S GUIDE by Bill Kaysing. © 1971 by Bill Kaysing. Published by Straight Arrow Books. Reprinted by permission.